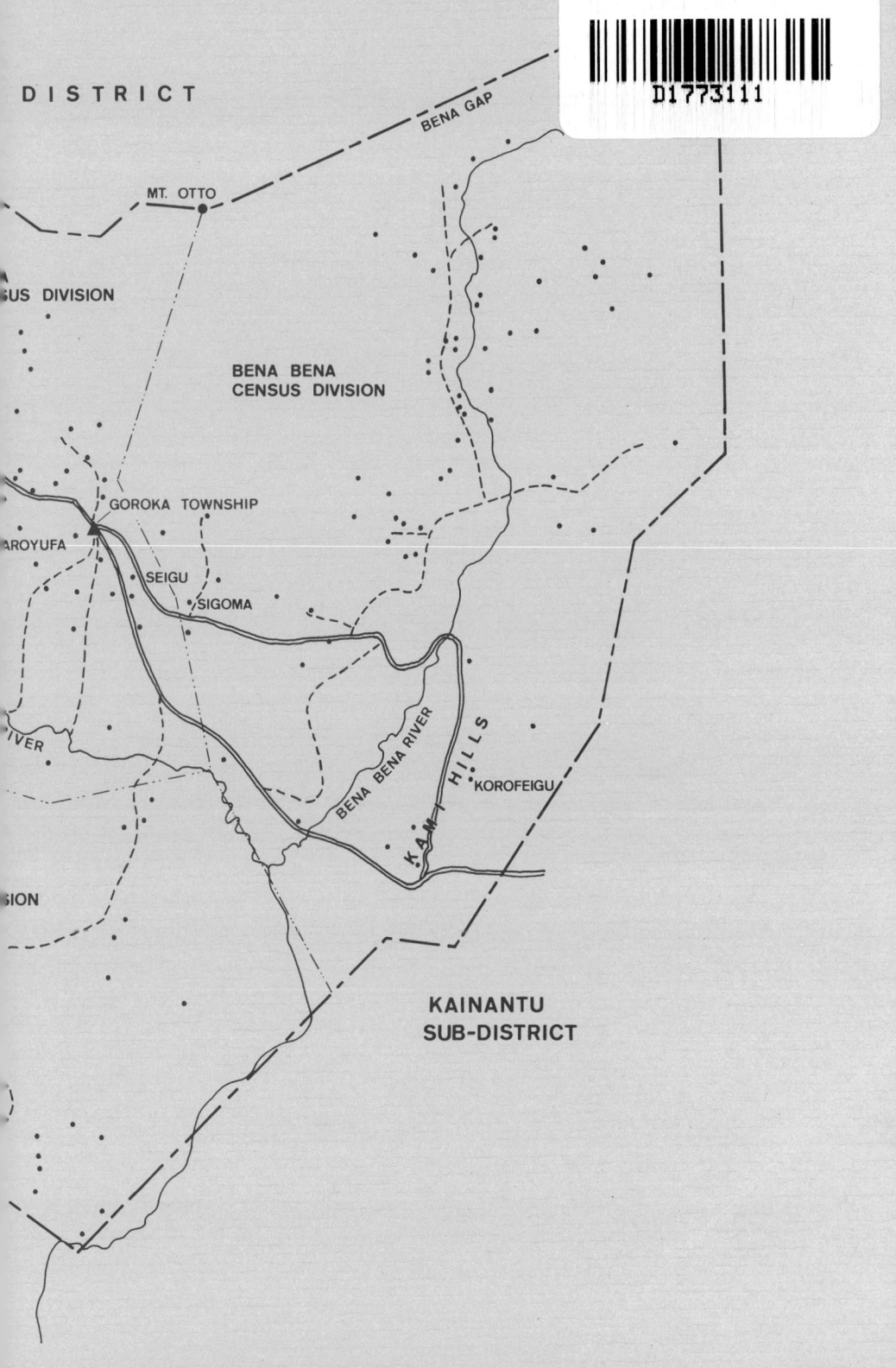

BIG-MEN AND BUSINESS

THE EAST-WEST CENTER—formally known as "The Center for Cultural and Technical Interchange Between East and West"—was established in Hawaii by the United States Congress in 1960. As a national educational institution in cooperation with the University of Hawaii, the Center has the mandated goal "to promote better relations and understanding between the United States and the nations of Asia and the Pacific through cooperative study, training, and research."

Each year about 2,000 men and women from the United States and some 40 countries and territories of Asia and the Pacific area work and study together with a multinational East-West Center staff in wide-ranging programs dealing with problems of mutual East-West concern. Participants are supported by federal scholarships and grants, supplemented in some fields by contributions from Asian/Pacific governments and private foundations.

Center programs are conducted by the East-West Communication Institute, the East-West Culture Learning Institute, the East-West Food Institute, the East-West Population Institute, and the East-West Technology and Development Institute. Open Grants are awarded to provide scope for educational and research innovation, including a program in humanities and the arts.

East-West Center Books are published by the University Press of Hawaii to further the Center's aims and programs.

Big-Men and Business
Entrepreneurship and Economic Growth in the New Guinea Highlands

Ben R. Finney

Foreword by Douglas L. Oliver

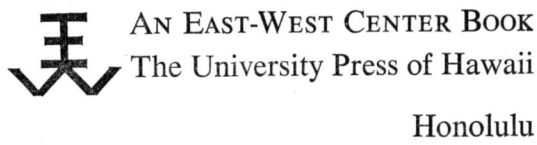

An East-West Center Book
The University Press of Hawaii
Honolulu

Copyright © 1973 by The University Press of Hawaii
All rights reserved
Library of Congress Catalog Card Number 72–93151
ISBN 0–8248–0262–4
Manufactured in the United States of America

Contents

	Foreword	vii
	Preface	ix
	Acknowledgments	xxi
1	A Stone Age Setting	1
2	Europeans Arrive	19
3	Money and Cash Crops	39
4	Gorokan Economic Growth	57
5	Business Leaders	83
6	Preadaption, Preconditions, and Cargo Cults	123
7	Problems and Prospects	146
	Notes	183
	Bibliography	191
	Index	201

Foreword

Dr. Finney's book is an important contribution to a very crucial debate: What are the factors that assist, or obstruct, economic development in "undeveloped" countries? By inserting the role of the local entrepreneur into the debate—a role which has been overlooked by most "development" economists—the author performs a valuable service, theoretically and practically. Focus on the local entrepreneur has lately begun to assume even greater importance as result of the higher priority that some economists and some intellectual leaders in undeveloped countries are now proposing to assign to small-scale rural economic development (in place of or complementary to the priority assigned large-scale and mainly foreign-controlled enterprise).

Specifically, the book is a study of the entry of a segment of New Guineans into the market economy introduced into the area by Europeans. The New Guineans in question, the people of the Goroka area in the Eastern Highlands, are notable for having made this entry quickly, successfully, and seemingly painlessly—in contrast to many other Pacific islanders. The author examines various possible explanations for this success, and focuses on the activities of the most successful entrepreneurs among the Gorokans in order to obtain his own data. His conclusion is that two factors were mainly responsible for the remarkable development by the Gorokans: the nature of the traditional culture (which "preadapted" the people to moneymaking), and the favorable natural and colonial environment of the area. He buttresses his argument by comparing the Gorokans with other New Guinean peoples who either have, or have not, made a success in the new market economy.

His underlying assumption is that all or most New Guinea peoples are "preadapted" by their cultures to market-economy activities, but his conclusion is that only those who enjoy favorable natural environments, and whose history of contact with Europeans has been supportive, have been successful.

Dr. Finney brings considerable regional experience and field research skill to this investigation. He has traveled and observed widely throughout the Pacific islands, and his comparative study of two Tahitian communities—one made up of cash-cropping rural "peasants" and the other of suburban wage laborers—has been widely acclaimed. More recently his current work at the Technology and Development Institute of the East-West Center of the University of Hawaii adds even more to his knowledge and insights about this hitherto neglected domain of "modernization."

DOUGLAS L. OLIVER

Preface

This book records an extraordinary case of rapid economic change: of how the Gorokans, a group of New Guinea Highlanders, became cash crop producers and small businessmen within a single generation. The Gorokans had been subsistence gardeners, living a Stone Age existence isolated from and unknown to the outside world until gold prospectors, patrol officers, and missionaries first penetrated the Highlands of New Guinea in the early 1930s. Now, less than forty years after their "discovery" and less than twenty years since their introduction to money and cash crops, the Gorokans are involved in a wide range of commercial activities they call, in Pidgin English, *bisnis*—the growing of coffee and other cash crops; the raising of beef cattle; and the operation of trade stores, passenger/freight trucks, restaurants, and other enterprises.[1] In particular, this study focuses on the leaders in this economic transition, the men known locally in Pidgin as *bikfela mun bilong bisnis*, a term which literally means "big-men of business," and how they have pioneered the growing of cash crops and the organization of commercial enterprises among their fellow Gorokans.

This analysis of entrepreneurship and economic change among the Gorokans is intended as a contribution to economic anthropology that will relate directly to problems of promoting economic growth in developing countries. Since the publication in 1922 of Malinowski's *Argonauts of the Western Pacific*, in which the complex *kula* exchange system that links the islands off the northeastern coast of New Guinea is described, studies of New Guinean societies have contributed greatly to the development of economic anthropology. Now studies of economic change in modern New Guinea are beginning to make an imprint on the thinking of anthropologists, economists, and other social scientists concerned with economic development. Starting with Belshaw's *In Search of Wealth* (1955a), which describes the efforts of the people from small islands off the southeastern tip of New Guinea to become copra producers and to operate their own trading cutters and small enterprises, a number of monographs examining economic change around New Guinea have appeared. These include: Salisbury's *From Stone to Steel* (1962), in which the economic and social impact of the introduction of steel tools among the Siane, a small group living on the edge of Goroka, is examined; Crocombe and Hogbin's *The Erap Mechanical Farming Project* (1963), which describes how a hill people of the Morobe District moved down onto the plains of the Markham Valley to start a mechanized farming venture; and two recent works, Epstein's *Capitalism, Primitive and Modern* (1968) and Salisbury's *Vunamami* (1970), both of which analyze how the Tolai of New Britain have become the most prosperous people in New Guinea through growing copra and cocoa and operating their own business concerns.

One common theme that emerges is how readily New Guineans accept economic innovations. They exhibit little of what is often termed traditional conservatism. The men portrayed in these studies appear almost to have been waiting for new economic opportunities, for once these have become available to them they have enthusiastically attempted to adapt to the new demands of cash cropping and commerce. Yet, while these groups have embraced new types of economic activity with alacrity, they have remained thoroughly traditional in many respects. Economic change among them has not involved a complete break with the past, with established ideas and patterns of social relationships. Indeed, traditional values and institutions have, so to speak, been one of the major resources tapped by these New Guineans in their efforts to grow cash crops and operate commercial enterprises.

This theme is explored further here by focusing on the role of entrepreneurship in Gorokan economic growth. The main argument is that Gorokan society was preadapted for economic change, that traditional values and institutions were positive assets rather than liabilities in the adoption of cash cropping and commerce. Although the Gorokans were basically subsistence gardeners, they had a flourishing local exchange system involving pigs, seashells, bird of paradise plumes, and other articles considered to be "valuables." This wealth exchange system was a central focus of Gorokan life; building up stores of valuables and then competitively exchanging them in intergroup ceremonies marking initiations, marriages, military alliances, and other vital events was a major concern of Gorokan groups and of ambitious individuals. Gorokan society was marked by a high degree of status mobility based on personal achievement. There was no fixed class structure, and, except for small units like the extended family or the lineage, age or seniority of birth were not prerequisites for leadership status. Gorokan leaders were, like most of their counterparts in other New Guinean societies, "big-men" who achieved their eminence through demonstrating their skill in warfare, ritual, or oratory, or, more importantly, through amassing and exchanging valuables. This combination of a cultural focus on wealth and its exchange, and an achieved-status system intimately linked with wealth accumulation and exchange, has proven, it will be argued, to be preadaptive for the rapid emergence of dynamic entrepreneurs and the adoption of new economic activities.

My interest in entrepreneurship and economic change dates from a research experience between 1961 and 1963 in French Polynesia. There I was primarily interested in analyzing social change in Tahitian society and found that recent economic changes—the increasing involvement of rural Tahitians in cash cropping and of Tahitians living near an urban center in wage labor—were the most important factors affecting social change (Finney 1965). I felt, however, that looking at social change primarily as a concomitant of economic change was not entirely satisfactory for several reasons. Among these was the fact that this point of view largely ignored the role of the entrepreneur in promoting change. Despite the presence of many European and Chinese businessmen and firms in French Polynesia, Tahitian entrepreneurs are also active in the local economy. They are prominent in large-scale plantation exploitation of cash crops, interisland trading, stevedoring, commercial fishing, trucking and transport, and construction and represent the dynamic economic element in a Tahitian society otherwise dominated by peasants and workers. Any description of Tahitian social change that focuses primarily on the latter and fails to systematically treat the entrepreneurs, therefore, ignores a crucial aspect of changing Tahitian society.

An opportunity to pursue my newly awakened interest in entrepreneurs came in 1966 when R. G. Crocombe, then field director of the New Guinea Research Unit of the Australian National University, invited me to undertake an anthropological investigation of some aspect of economic change in New Guinea. I selected the problem of entrepreneurship and started an intensive reading program of the literature on entrepreneurship and economic development in order to formulate a research strategy which would enable me to investigate the problem through fieldwork among New Guineans.

I found that economists on the one hand and anthropologists, psychologists, and sociologists on the other often seemed to be looking at entrepreneurship with diametrically opposed premises. This opposition can, as Kilby (1971:1–26) has recently pointed out, be neatly summarized in terms of theories concerning entrepreneurial supply and demand.

With the notable exceptions of the pioneering work of Schumpeter (1949) and that of a few contemporary economists like Hoselitz (1960) and Hagen (1962), most economic treatises on entrepreneurship that I consulted are based on the assumption that the supply of entrepreneurs or of entrepreneurial services is highly elastic and that a lack of entrepreneurship is attributable to failures in the economic environment. What the economists seem to be saying is to look at the demand for entrepreneurial services generated by the economic environment: if that environment is favorable, then a vigorous entrepreneurial response will follow; if it is unfavorable, then entrepreneurs or potential entrepreneurs will be inactive. In this view entrepreneurs are not the prime movers of the economy but, rather, are reduced to the status of rational calculators who make their moves in response to outside conditions over which they exert no control. Entrepreneurs, as independent agents of change, have therefore been removed from the economists' models, which, as Baumol (1968:66) points out, is like expunging the Prince of Denmark from a discussion of Hamlet.

In contrast, most other social scientists seem to say that factors affecting the supply, not the demand, of entrepreneurship are of utmost importance. Depending, it often seems, on the disciplinary affiliation of a writer, the message is to look at those psychological or social or cultural factors that either promote or inhibit the appearance of entrepreneurship. Most of these writers also tend either to ignore economic factors or to relegate them to secondary importance. Some, like McClelland (1961), even go so far as to state that the economic environment is not crucial, as sufficiently motivated entrepreneurs can overcome severe economic barriers.[2]

In formulating my research strategy I attempted to take into account both economic and noneconomic factors and to chart a course that touched on both the supply and the demand sides of the entrepreneurship question. I must confess, however, that as an anthropologist I started first to investigate theories of entrepreneurial supply. Belshaw's (1955b) advice to examine the cultural milieu of the entrepreneur seemed like a logical starting point, so, accordingly, I made a search through the entrepreneurship literature for promising theories on how cultural and social patterns might bear on the emergence of entrepreneurship. At the same time I examined the New Guinea literature to see which, if any, of these theories might be applicable to New Guinea.

The most promising approach that emerged from this reading was that which focused on the nature of the traditional status-mobility system of a society before it had been exposed to modern political and economic pressures. Here LeVine's (1966) work on Nigeria was most seminal. LeVine had taken the sociological dichotomy of ascribed *versus* achieved status (Linton 1936:115; Parsons and Shils 1959:80–88) and the psychological work of McClelland and his associates on the relationship between the basic human motive of need for Achievement and entrepreneurial growth and economic development (McClelland 1961) and combined the two to explain differential entrepreneurial and economic developments among the main tribal groups of Nigeria. LeVine showed, for example, that the Ibo, who had a traditional status-mobility system that stressed achievement, had significantly higher levels of need for Achievement than did the Hausa, who had a traditional status-mobility system that stressed ascription, and argued that this difference in status-mobility systems and the resultant motivational patterns provided the most satisfactory explanation as to why the Ibo produced more entrepreneurs than the Hausa and were more involved in the economic development of Nigeria than the Hausa. New Guinea seemed an ideal place to explore further the relationship between status-mobility systems and entrepreneurial development, for in most New Guinean societies status was traditionally achieved through personal accomplishment in warfare, wealth production and exchange, ritual, or some other field and not ascribed on the basis of birth, age, or any other criterion. Indeed, the great stress on personal accomplishments—on becoming a big-man by one's own actions—in most New Guinean societies suggested that if LeVine's study were to be universally applicable one should find in New Guinea a social situation extremely conducive to the emergence of entrepreneurs.

However, available literature on economic development in New Guinea, as well as conversations and correspondence with research workers personally acquainted with the area, seemed to indicate that examples of vigorous entrepreneurial growth were not common there. Only in two regions—the copra and cocoa growing areas of the Gazelle Peninsula on New Britain and the coffee growing areas of the Highlands—was there much indication of significant entrepreneurial activity within the New Guinean population. Since the developments in the Highlands were relatively unknown, while those on the Gazelle Peninsula had been thoroughly studied by T. S. Epstein and R. F. Salisbury, I decided to undertake my field research in the Highlands. After arriving in New Guinea in early 1967 and making a preliminary reconnaissance of the Highlands, I chose the Goroka area for intensive investigation. This choice was dictated primarily by the following facts: (1) coffee, the mainstay of the Highlands commercial economy, was first commercially exploited in Goroka; (2) Goroka, as the primary center of the coffee industry, was more highly developed than other Highlands areas; (3) the Gorokan people were sharing in this development and had thereby become the most prosperous people in the Highlands; and (4) published reports of anthropological research among several Gorokan groups provided basic material on traditional cultural and social patterns. This last consideration was almost as important as the first three, for the six months I had available for my fieldwork in 1967 were nowhere near the time that would have been required to

Preface

study both traditional cultural and social patterns and contemporary developments in entrepreneurship and economic change.

The shortness of the time meant that I could not hope to learn and effectively use a local language in my research. That would have been virtually impossible: Highlands languages are notoriously difficult to learn, and intensive work on learning a language would have left little or no time for my basic research; and, besides, five separate, though related, languages are spoken in Goroka. I therefore chose to learn Pidgin English and used it except when educated Gorokans preferred to converse in English. Although not being able to employ at least one of the local languages undoubtedly barred me from inquiring into many subtle questions, the use of Pidgin was not the handicap one might expect. Pidgin is often used by Gorokans with different natal languages to communicate among themselves, and Pidgin seems to be in many ways the primary language of commerce in Goroka. I have heard Gorokans who share a common language discuss commercial matters in Pidgin, and, even when local languages are spoken in such discussions, basic Pidgin terms like *bisnis* (commercial activity), *bungen mani* (pooling money), and *porofitmani* (gross receipts) can be heard.

I also departed from standard anthropological fieldwork techniques in that I did not base my research on a small local community. Anthropologists commonly reside in and study intensively a clan, a village, or some other small, discrete, local group. They then tend to generalize from the local group to the larger tribal, regional, or cultural whole. While this may produce little distortion in some situations—as, for example, in relatively static tribal societies—in an environment of rapid change it is likely to produce a markedly one-sided perspective. Since innovations generally originate from outside of any one local group, the analyst who works solely in the local group is liable to view change as something that has been imposed upon people. I wanted to avoid looking at change from this "bottom-up" perspective; instead, I wanted to look at change from the "top-down," and one way in which I sought to do so was to adopt a regional fieldwork strategy.

This decision was influenced by my previous research in French Polynesia, as well as an analysis of anthropological studies of change. Although in that study I had worked in two Tahitian communities, one made up of peasants and the other primarily of workers, I had found that this procedure did not allow me to gain a rounded picture of Tahitian society as a whole. In particular, I had found that my community-based research did not enable me to study directly the Tahitian entrepreneurs, who make up an important segment of Tahitian society. Only one entrepreneur of note resided in the communities I studied, and, although the activities of many other Tahitian entrepreneurs—interisland traders, employers, and urban businessmen—directly affected the lives of the people living in those communities, it was obvious that the perspective from the local community gave only limited information on them. A preliminary survey of Goroka revealed a similar situation: few villages boasted prominent entrepreneurs, and, in addition, Gorokan entrepreneurs, even though they were rurally based, seemed to be highly mobile and were constantly on the move between this village and that village, between the countryside and the town, between Goroka and other areas of New Guinea. As the best place to meet and talk with these entrepreneurs seemed to be where their business activities most frequently took them—the Goroka Township, the only urban center in Goroka—I decided to live there and to attempt to cover the whole region from my town residence. Living in town, I found that I was able to quickly identify and meet the most prominent Gorokan entrepreneurs, to follow their activities as they came to town for business or other reasons, and to talk with them frequently and on some occasions to interview them formally.

As a result of these repeated contacts with entrepreneurs, I was able to build up a large fund of data on each of them, including much material in the form of tape-recorded interviews. In addition, I was able to visit most of the entrepreneurs in their villages, to interview them further there, and to see how they conducted their commercial operations and interacted with their clansmen in their home milieu. This information on the entrepreneurs derived from direct observations and interviews was supplemented with information on them derived from interviews with other residents of Goroka—Europeans, Gorokans, and other New Guineans. To enable me to place all these bits of information on the Gorokan entrepreneurs in the context of overall economic developments in Goroka, I also gathered statistical data on the growth of Gorokan cash cropping and commercial enterprises from records in the local

Preface xvii

offices of the Department of Agriculture, Stock and Fisheries, the Department of District Administration, the Department of Lands, and the Business Advisory Service of the Government of Papua New Guinea. These data, in turn, were supplemented by general surveys of Gorokan coffee gardens, trade stores, trucks, and market gardening activities I made in selected areas of the Goroka countryside. These three types of data—that on the entrepreneurs, that on general growth trends, and that on specific economic activities—formed the basis for my 1967 study. At the request of the New Guinea Research Unit, a preliminary monograph utilizing some of these data was prepared in early 1968 (Finney 1969). In that monograph I maintained that the rapid emergence of entrepreneurship among the Gorokans could not be explained solely by reference to their social system. It seemed obvious that Gorokan entrepreneurship had flourished in an extremely favorable economic environment—one shared by few other New Guinean groups—and that without that environment the Gorokans would have remained economically stagnant like so many other New Guinean groups. In other words, I found that any explanation of the emergence of Gorokan entrepreneurship based solely on social, cultural, or psychological factors would be incomplete in that it could only look at the supply side of the question when clearly factors in the economic environment (factors over which the Gorokans had little or no control) that, in effect, determined the demand for entrepreneurship were also crucial.

In late 1968, upon my appointment to the Department of Pacific History at the Institute of Advanced Studies of the Australian National University, I was able to extend my research and to spend another three months in New Guinea gathering data on Goroka. In addition to updating my 1967 material with more interviews, statistical data, and case studies, I took the opportunity to systematically examine the factors in the economic environment which had been so favorable to Gorokan economic growth. Here Fisk's (1962, 1964) theoretical work on the importance of the way in which a people living in a subsistence economy become linked to the cash economy was most stimulating, and I set out to document how the Gorokans had done so and how this linkage made Gorokan entrepreneurial development and economic growth possible. I wanted to find out exactly how money and cash crops were introduced into Goroka, how roads and air transport gave Gorokans access to outside markets, and how government programs facilitated Gorokan entry into the cash economy. Since these events and processes had taken place primarily in the period from the late 1940s through to the early 1960s, I had the rare opportunity of discussing them with eyewitnesses as well as leading actors in the drama of change. I interviewed many Gorokans whose recollections of how they became linked with the cash economy were vivid, and I tracked down—in Australia and various locales around New Guinea, as well as in Goroka—and interviewed those Europeans who, as administration officers, agricultural workers, and private businessmen, were instrumental in introducing civil order, cash crops, roads, and other innovations necessary to effect that linkage. I also consulted all records made available to me in the archives of Papua New Guinea in Port Moresby, as well as in Gorokan branches and the Port Moresby headquarters of the Department of District Administration and the Department of Agriculture, Stock and Fisheries that related to the political and economic history of Goroka since contact. Here it should be emphasized that although these materials—patrol reports, district reports, agriculture extension diaries, and similar documents—contained much valuable information on recent Gorokan history, taken by themselves they would not have been sufficient to provide a meaningful picture of developments in Goroka over the past three decades. Only with the aid of a personal knowledge of the area, derived from fieldwork there, and oral data provided me by knowledgeable Gorokans and Europeans, was I able to utilize these tersely worded and often sketchy documents effectively to reconstruct the events in Gorokan history crucial to my analysis.[3]

A word needs to be said about psychological measures and entrepreneurship. In my research I focused on the relationship between Gorokan social and cultural patterns and the Gorokan record of entrepreneurial development and economic growth, and did not administer, as LeVine did among the Ibo and other groups in Nigeria, any psychological tests to determine motivational patterns.[4] However, my wife, R. S. Finney, did undertake an examination of psychological motivation in relation to entrepreneurship in Goroka and five other regions of New Guinea, which is cited in chapter 5.

Preface

One problem which the ethnographic data from New Guinea raises relates to the need for Power, a psychological motive which researchers do not ordinarily associate with entrepreneurship. LeVine links achieved status-mobility systems, need for Achievement, and entrepreneurial development, yet, in ethnographic terms at least, it would appear that power—that is, political leadership, status, or prestige, not the particular achievements which are accomplished to gain power—is the ultimate goal of ambitious persons in societies like the Ibo and those in New Guinea described in this book which place such stress on achieved status. Hence, it would seem that although persons from such societies might score relatively high on need for Achievement in psychological tests, they would probably also score high on need for Power. Indeed, the ethnographic evidence from New Guinea, as well as that on the Ibo (Uchendu 1965), suggests that power motivation, along with achievement motivation, may be crucial to the emergence of entrepreneurs in societies marked by a high degree of achieved status-mobility.

MARCH 1972 BEN R. FINNEY
Honolulu

Acknowledgments

The field research on which this study is based was made possible by grants from the Australian-American Foundation and the New Guinea Research Unit, Australian National University (1967), and the Research School of Pacific Studies, Australian National University (1968). Analysis of data and preparation of this report were done while I was attached to the Department of Pacific History, Australian National University (1968–1970), the Department of Anthropology, University of Hawaii (1970–1972), and the Technology and Development Institute, East-West Center, Honolulu (1971–72).

I owe special thanks to R. G. Crocombe, who, as field director of the New Guinea Research Unit, Australian National University, was primarily responsible for my going to New Guinea to study entrepreneurship; to the staff of the New Guinea Research Unit for their efforts at facilitating my stay in New Guinea; to J. W. Davidson and H. E. Maude, professor and professorial fellow, respectively, of the Department of Pacific History, Australian National University, for allowing an anthropologist to find a home in their department in order to analyze historical aspects of economic change in New Guinea; and to Hahn-Been Lee and R. M. Pearce, director and assistant director, respectively, of the Technology and Development Institute, East-West Center, for their invitation to join their institute during the final preparation of the report. I would like also to thank A. Dewey, A. L. Epstein, T. S. Epstein, R. S. Finney, E. K. Fisk, Kee-Chun Han, B. F. Hoselitz,

L. Langness, N. Meller, D. Penney, P. Philipp, M. Reay, A. Strathern, M. Strathern, M. Ward, and other colleagues in New Guinea, Australia, and Hawaii for their comments and criticisms of this study in its various stages.

For help in preparing the final manuscript I am indebted to I. McKenzie, F. Hellinger, S. Chong, and L. Tagawa.

Turning to Goroka, I wish to register my special debt to the Gorokan business leaders mentioned in Chapter 5 for their help and cooperation in the analysis of their careers, as well as to G. Gerepaima, B. Heiro, B. Kapo, A. Miakwe, U. Mikave, A. Sapumei, and the many other Gorokans who aided me. I also thank the following past and present members of the Australian administration and business community in Goroka for their assistance in gathering data: J. Black, B. Bond, R. Carne, W. Conroy, R. Cottle, D. Duggan, S. Fox, N. Grant, G. Greathead, F. Kaad, J. Leahy, R. McKillop, O. Mathieson, N. Mullins, M. Orken, J. Sinclair and J. Taylor.

Photographs 1, 2, 3, and 7 are reproduced here by permission of the Department of Information and Extension Services, Government of Papua New Guinea, Port Moresby; photographs 4 and 5, by permission of the Department of External Territories, Commonwealth of Australia, Canberra.

1

A Stone Age Setting

The Goroka Sub-District, the setting for this narrative, is one of the administrative units of the Eastern Highlands District in the Australian-administered Territory of Papua and New Guinea.[1] It includes 680 square miles of valley and mountain lands, ranging from about 4,500 feet to over 11,000 feet in elevation. The Goroka Valley, one of a series of valleys which occur between the mountain ranges along the central cordillera of New Guinea, forms the main section of the sub-district. The valley is wedge-shaped, pinched in the northeast where the commanding Bismarck Mountains, dominated by 11,600-foot Mount Otto, and the Asaro Range, less commanding, but studded with peaks reaching up to 8,000 and 9,000 feet, come together, and opening out toward the southeast to a rolling plains landscape almost twenty miles wide. The low Kami Hills rise out of these plains thirty-five miles from the northeastern tip of the valley and cut the Goroka Valley off from other low-lying areas to the east. Two rivers drain the valley, the Asaro and the Bena Bena. Both flow south from the foothills of the Bismarcks, then join at the southeastern edge of the valley, and flow out through a gorge separating the Kami Hills and the Asaro Range to form part of the headwaters of the Purari River, which eventually empties into the Papuan Gulf. Appended to the Goroka Valley to complete the sub-district is the small and mountainous Watabung region, just over the Asaro Range.

Although Goroka lies only 6 degrees below the equator, because of its elevation the climate is relatively pleasant compared to the hot and humid lowlands of New Guinea. Along the heavily populated valley floor and on the lower elevations of the mountain slopes daytime temperatures in the eighties are common but are bearable because of the relatively low humidity. Nights are cool—frequently in the fifties even at the lowest elevations—and frosts occur above 8,000 feet or so. There are two distinct seasons—the wet season, during the Southern Hemisphere summer months of November through March, when about three-quarters of the annual rainfall occurs, and the dry season of the winter months. Rainfall varies with local topography. The lower elevations along the southeastern border of the valley get only 50 to 60 inches a year and are subject to prolonged droughts, while in the upper reaches of the valley, particularly at the narrow northeastern end, annual rainfall is in the 100-inch range, and seasonality is less marked. Throughout the year morning mists along the valley floor are common, and a heavy cloud cover usually surrounds the ranges each afternoon. Particularly in the wet season these cloud formations result in thunderstorms, lightning, heavy showers, and sometimes hail (Howlett 1962:7–17).

Well before the coming of Europeans and the introduction of cash crops, man had evidently altered the vegetation of Goroka. The climate of Goroka and much of the Highlands is potentially a forest climate; rainfall and temperature patterns provide a habitat in which forest would be the natural climax vegetation for all but the tops of the highest mountains and the low-lying swampy areas. Yet, when the first Europeans arrived, they found extensive grasslands covering the valley floor and the lower slopes of the ranges. The lowland forests had apparently been gradually removed by successive generations of settlers, who had cleared the land for cultivation by ringbarking and burning. The resultant grasslands were probably then stabilized by continual fallowing and reuse of the land, plus use of fire to burn off brush for hunting drives (Robbins 1963). These grasslands appear to be most permanently established in the dry southeast end of the valley, that area of Goroka which, because of low rainfall and relatively poor soil, is least conducive to regeneration of forest cover. Above the practical limit of cultivation, which usually varies a few hundred feet either way of 7,500 feet, the forest cover remains. Between 7,500 feet and 9,000 feet the ranges are covered by a dense rain forest dominated by evergreens. Above 9,000 feet the cloud forest of stunted trees covered by mosses and

A Stone Age Setting

lichens begins, and above 10,500 feet, on Mount Otto alone, alpine shrub and grasslands appear (Howlett 1962:21–26).

THE COMING OF MAN

Archaeological research in the Highlands started barely a decade ago with Susan Bulmer's pioneering excavations of rock shelters (Bulmer and Bulmer 1964), and it is still too early to reconstruct Highlands prehistory with any confidence. Nonetheless, enough evidence has accumulated to suggest a tentative outline of the main benchmarks of human occupation of the area. If anything, this outline should serve to dispel any view of Highlands societies as static entities unchanged for thousands of years and to promote the notion that they have been subject to constant change. The recent transformation of Highlands societies stimulated by the late arrival of Europeans in New Guinea has come at the end of a long history of exploration, occupation, and development of the region by New Guineans.

The first evidence for human occupation in the Highlands comes from excavations made in rock shelters, including one at Kafiafana in the Goroka Valley. Radiocarbon dates of organic materials taken from these shelters indicate that man has been in the Highlands for at least 11,000 years. The first Highlanders were probably small groups of hunters and gatherers who moved into the area from the earlier-settled coastal and foothill regions of New Guinea. They probably lived in the warmer valleys, seeking shelter in caves and under rock overhangs, hunting birds and small mammals, and also gathering various edible nuts, fruits, and tubers. They used pebble and flaked tools (and later ground stone tools), presumably made wooden artifacts like the bow and arrow, and had trade links from the coast, as is evidenced by seashells found at the lower levels of excavated sites. At the Kafiafana rock shelter, for example, small cowries (*Cypraea moneta*) were found at a level dated at about 7000 B.C. (White 1967).

Over time, these first hunting groups undoubtedly explored their new habitat, killing off some of the larger fauna as their numbers grew, and extended their hunting activities throughout the valleys and up the mountain slopes. The first signs of what may have been a period of major economic change occur in archaeological diggings at around 4000 B.C., when the first pig bones appear in the sites.

These bones could, however, be from feral pigs, as there is no direct evidence to suggest that Highlanders were then agriculturists and could raise domesticated pigs as they do today. About 3000 B.C. the rock shelter sites were abandoned, an event that may indicate that agriculture had been introduced and that Highlanders were shifting their living sites to open, cultivated areas. However, the first firm evidence for agriculture does not come until about 500 B.C., from an open site in the Wahgi Valley, west of Goroka. There a system of water-control ditches has been uncovered, along with fence posts, digging sticks, and a wooden spade, all of which indicate the existence of a well-developed agricultural complex, although evidence as to what crops were involved is lacking (Brookfield and White 1968).

The most recent changes in the Highlands, for which there is not yet any firm archaeological evidence, probably occurred between two hundred and three hundred years ago, when the sweet potato was introduced. The sweet potato, a South American plant that was probably taken to Indonesia by the Portuguese and then to New Guinea by Indonesian bird of paradise hunters and traders, proved to be an ideal crop for the Highlands. Its caloric yield per acre was higher than those of taro, yams, and other foods that must have been the first staples, and its relative hardiness against frost allowed cultivation to be pushed higher up the mountain slopes than was possible with the previous crops. Watson (1965) considers that the introduction of the sweet potato led to a subsistence revolution: population greatly increased, the process of converting forest to grasslands was accelerated, and the elaborate subsistence systems based on the intensive cultivation of sweet potatoes and the breeding of pigs which so impressed the first European explorers were developed.

THE GOROKANS

The Gorokans now number about 60,000, perhaps 10,000 more than at the time of first contact. They are a short, stocky mountain people. A sample of more than a thousand Gorokans studied in the late 1950s revealed that men averaged just over five feet in height and about 120 pounds in weight, while women were on the average three inches shorter and fifteen pounds lighter (Kariks et al. 1960). Gorokans are dark-skinned, ranging in color from light brown to black. Their hair is normally black and is crisply curled in its natural state, although traditionally it was worn in long, narrow plaits, reaching the shoulders or below. Men have abundant facial and body hair, although few grow full beards. The rugged, muscular physique of mature men is matched in many of them by prominent facial features, although there is much variation and some men have markedly delicate features.

Despite the coolness of the nights and misty mornings, traditional Gorokan dress was scanty. Modesty required a pubic covering. Most men wore bark cloth G-strings, often combined with a back covering of netting slung from the shoulders to the knees. Others, influenced by neighboring Chimbu groups from the west, wore wide belts from which were suspended bark cloth or netting coverings in front and bundles of leaves in back. Women wore string aprons—wide ones in front and narrow ones in back—and net carrying bags suspended from their heads that reached down to their buttocks. Women completed their costume with shells and other ornaments worn around the neck or the head, but male finery was much more impressive. Particularly for important ceremonial occasions, men wore elaborate headdresses featuring bird of paradise plumes and other feathers, headbands made of small shells, and breastplates of mother-of-pearl shell or strands of large cowries—both important symbols of wealth—slung from their necks. Plaited armbands and belts, shell ear pendants, and bone or shell ornaments piercing their septums completed their dress. The New Guinean artistic verve so evident in the wood sculptures of Sepik and other coastal peoples was clearly expressed by the Gorokans, like other Highlanders, in their elaborate costumes.

New Guinea is noted for its linguistic diversity; estimates of the number of languages spoken there usually run into the many hundreds. The Highlands follow this pattern of diversity, although language communities there tend to be somewhat larger and more closely related than elsewhere in New Guinea. For Goroka, Wurm (1964) identifies five separate languages: Asaro, Gahuku, and Bena Bena of the Bena Bena subfamily and Siane and Yaviyufa of the Siane subfamily. These he considers to be part of the East-Central family of the East New Guinea phylum, a grouping that includes all but a few of the languages spoken in the Highlands of Australian New Guinea. The Gorokan languages, like the others in the phylum, are classed as non-Austronesian or Papuan languages, in distinction from the Austronesian languages spoken on some offshore islands and by some coastal communities. The non-Austronesian languages probably represent modern developments descended from the first New Guinea languages, while the Austronesian languages—being part of a great oceanic language family that stretches from Madagascar to Polynesia—probably stem from languages spoken by seafaring intruders who arrived relatively late in New Guinea's history.

The Gorokan languages, particularly those of a single subfamily, seem to be relatively close to the boundary between being separate languages and being dialects. Even the most stay-at-home Gorokan can usually understand something of a neighboring language, even if he cannot actually speak it. Gorokans who live near linguistic boundaries are often multilingual, as are those who do a lot of traveling around the area. Now, as I have indicated, Pidgin has been widely adopted as a lingua franca and is commonly heard in conversations when people from different groups gather.

Goroka has five census divisions, which partially follow linguistic boundaries. Asaro is the main language of the Upper Asaro census division, Gahuku is spoken in the Lowa (short for Lower Asaro) census division, and Bena Bena is the language of the Bena Bena census division. Yaviyufa is spoken in the Unggai census division, and Siane is the main language of Watabung,[2] although most Siane speakers live outside this census division and outside the sub-district, altogether.

Between linguistic communities (and census divisions) there are some cultural differences; variations in ritual, dress, and other customs are apparent. However, the similarities among Gorokan groups are much more impressive. Read (1954:20, 34–35) regards the whole of the Goroka Valley as a single culture area and considers that the Siane are probably closely related. In this study what cultural variation exists is largely ignored, particularly because the people of Goroka are conscious of their close linguistic, cultural, and social ties, which have been reinforced by their being grouped together in a single administrative unit by the Australians. Although they seldom refer to themselves as Gorokans (*man bilong Goroka* in Pidgin), in this study it is convenient to refer to them all by this label.

Social and Political Groups

In traditional Gorokan society the clan was the basic social unit. Typically, members of the same clan lived together in one village, forming a community of two hundred men, women, and children, on the average. Villages were usually located on ridges and were stockaded for protection against attack. Other stockaded villages were usually located farther up a ridge or lower down it and on parallel ridges. Outside the village stockade were the clan's lands, either being cultivated, lying fallow, or temporarily being left to grazing pigs. Pig houses were scattered throughout the clan's land as shelter for pigs and for persons working on the gardens. Although people sometimes spent the night in these houses, usually they slept in their villages, particularly if there was fear of attack from hostile groups. Within the stockade there was usually a single or double row of women's houses—low, round huts—and one or several men's houses—larger, elliptical structures. As men feared contamination from too close and prolonged contact with women, they preferred to sleep as a group in their men's house, leaving their wives to sleep alone with their children (and often the pigs), each in her own house.

Clansmen formed a tightly knit group, living in close daily association, sharing similar interests, and working together for common goals. The injury or death of one member at the hands of an outsider brought retaliation by the victim's clan against the outsider's clan. Each clan was normally exogamous, and clansmen had to pool their resources to make payments to other groups to bring in brides. The ability of clansmen to pay a respectable brideprice and to contribute handsomely to wealth exchanges with other clans on various occasions was a great source of clan pride. In addition to these crucial wealth-exchange situations, a clan's solidarity also was evident on more mundane occasions. Clansmen combined to form working parties to build and maintain stockades and men's houses and stood ready to aid each other in such arduous tasks as clearing land for new gardens.

In theory, the clan was a patrilineal unit composed of patrilineages—often grouped into subclans, all linked by descent from a common ancestor. In practice, however, deviation from the patrilineal ideal was common, and men were recruited into the clan by other means than birth (compare Langness 1964).[3] A man sometimes settled, for example, in his wife's village rather than his own and identified with her natal clan rather than his. Or in times of war refugee groups from defeated clans might seek to settle in a friendly village and, in effect, join the local clan. However loosely structured the resultant groups might appear in terms of anthropological models of patrilineal descent groups, from the point of view of the individuals seeking the resources and protection of the host group, or from the point of view of a small, undermanned clan needing manpower to cultivate its land and defend its boundaries, nonpatrilineal recruitment made practical sense to the Gorokans.

Clans often joined together to form a social unit called a phratry, or a subtribe, and marriage prohibitions might be extended throughout the unit, making it exogamous. The most dramatic occasions when members of a subtribe acted together were in times of war, when they united to fight a common enemy, and when they held joint religious ceremonies and festivals. Of the latter the pig festival was the most notable, for it was the occasion when the clansmen of a subtribe joined in celebrating the alliance of clans with the ostentatious exchange, slaughter, and consumption of their most highly valued pigs.

The largest social unit in precontact Goroka was the tribe, a group composed of anywhere from a pair to almost a score of clans. Tribes varied in size from a few hundred members to as high as fifteen hundred or so, with a mean of perhaps around a thousand. Although kinship terms might be used by tribesmen to emphasize their ties, the tribe was not a genealogically structured unit. The tribe was, above all, a unit of political expediency, a grouping of clans willing to fight together and defend their territory from other tribal clusters of clans surrounding them.

Gorokans distinguished two types of fighting, called in Gahuku, for example, *hina* (feuding) and *rova* (warfare) (Read 1954:37–42). Disputes over land, pigs, women, or sorcery, the classic overt precipitants of conflict in New Guinea, that broke out between members of the same tribe led to hina. Although hina fighting often involved confrontations of heavily armed warriors and sometimes resulted in death or serious injury, it was a limited, controlled type of fighting, terminated either when the aggrieved group felt it

A Stone Age Setting

had done sufficient damage to pay back the other group or upon payment of blood money in the form of traditional valuables. Rova, in contrast, was more a matter of unlimited warfare of tribe against tribe, and was never completely terminated. Every tribe was a potential, if not an actual, enemy of every other tribe, and when warring groups broke off fighting, only a temporary truce came into effect, and hostilities were always likely to be renewed. The object of intertribal fighting was the complete destruction of the enemy and the taking over of his lands. Although this was probably seldom achieved completely, numerous tales are still current among Gorokans of large massacres of men, women, and children and of routs of tribes, or sections of tribes, which were then forced to seek refuge with friendly groups.

In Goroka, then, there was no state, no government, as such. Cultural-linguistic groups were in no way politically united. There were only warring tribes or potentially hostile tribes and their constituent subtribes and clans. This social and political atomism was typical of New Guinea and has only begun to change through the imposition of a governmental system of districts, sub-districts, and local government councils.

Subsistence Patterns

Almost without exception, the first explorers who penetrated the Highlands valleys reacted with astonished admiration to the agricultural accomplishments of the people (Brookfield 1962:243). Instead of the scattered gardens littered with half-burned logs found in much of lowland New Guinea, they found extensive tracts of cleared and intensively cultivated land. For example, Michael Leahy, who led the first party into the Goroka Valley, remarked:

> The gardens of the people inhabiting the headwaters and numerous tributaries of the Purari are probably the most scientifically worked of any native cultivations in New Guinea. The ground is first turned over by means of pointed sticks, then allowed to fallow for some time, then it is dug up again with pointed sticks, every weed or grass root being taken out and the soil rubbed into a fine mulch between the hands. It is then arranged in long, straight rows, a shallow drainage channel cut between the beds and their sweet potatoes, yams, beans, etc., planted. Looked at from a distance the general layout is symmetrically perfect. (1936:230)

This description refers primarily to the valley peoples of Goroka and the Wahgi Valley farther west; cultivation on the lower slopes of the Bismarck and Asaro ranges involved slightly different procedures, such as the clearing of primary or secondary forest with axe and fire, but the resulting gardens, located on steep slopes, were no less impressive.

The sweet potato was the main subsistence crop of the Gorokans, forming about 90 percent of their diet (Howlett 1962:79). Sugarcane, bananas, yam, taro, maize (apparently introduced before 1930), and a range of other root crops, legumes, and green vegetables were grown as secondary crops. In addition, the oil pandanus was cultivated for its oil, which was used as a food, a dye, and for smearing on the body, and the fruit of the mountain-loving nut pandanus was highly prized as a luxury food. Animal protein intake was low, mainly coming from pigs fed with sweet potatoes and allowed to graze on fallow land. Game was a scarce addition to the diet. In the valley lowlands children caught some birds and rats, and on the mountain slopes an occasional game bird, tree kangaroo, possum, or other small marsupial was taken by a hunting party of men.

The extensive cultivation of the sweet potato, a crop which matures in as few as four months in favorable areas, supplemented by other gardening activities, as well as the raising of pigs, allowed a considerable population to develop in Goroka, as in other favorably endowed Highlands areas. The precontact density of about seventy-five persons per square mile for the entire Goroka area is not, however, particularly high, for the sub-district contains much uncultivable mountain land. In the Goroka Valley proper, population densities varied from between around one hundred persons to the square mile at the eastern edge to about three hundred in the center and at the western end (Brookfield 1962:244–245). The difference in population density between the two areas probably correlates with the contrast between the relatively poor soils and low rainfall (as well as frequent drought conditions that interrupted the growing season) of the east and the richer soils and higher and more evenly distributed rainfall in the center and the west of the valley.

Around the villages were the lands of the clan: fenced gardens interspersed with casuarinas planted for firewood, shade, or soil conservation; adjacent fallow stretches covered by grass or shrubs

A Stone Age Setting

but showing signs of former cultivation; and forested lands, either uncultivable or awaiting cultivation, in gullies or on the mountain slopes. These were all clan lands, but they were not necessarily communally owned or exploited. The constituent subclans, lineages, or both, had their own parcels of land, usually marked by borders planted with tall, long-leafed, cordyline plants. Within these group boundaries members of the proprietary subclan or lineage had the right to claim individual plots of land for exploitation. Ordinarily, rights to this land were inherited through the male line. Given, however, the loosely structured character of Gorokan groups, there was probably considerable flexibility in matters of inheritance and allocation of land to men recruited into the clan through marriage or as a result of their being driven from their own lands in warfare.

Men were charged with subsistence tasks requiring the axe; women did the rest. Thus, men used their axes to clear land, build fences, and cut support poles for sugarcane and yams (which then became "male crops") and to chop down banana trees for replanting (Salisbury 1962:49). Women, using digging sticks as their main tool, did the more routine and prolonged tasks of planting, weeding, and harvesting. As women also did the cooking and cared for the children, they were kept relatively hard at work all day. Although men had to build and maintain the village stockade and houses in addition to keeping up with their gardening duties, it is easy to gain the impression—particularly in reading postpacification accounts—that men led a highly leisured existence in comparison to their wives. However, before the Australian administration stopped warfare, men probably had to spend a great deal of their time on guard duty watching out for sneak attacks (compare Langness 1967:164), and, if the tales of old Gorokan warriors are to be believed, some men spent considerable time fighting, particularly in the dry season, when open warfare was endemic.

WEALTH AND PRESTIGE

The preceding outline of subsistence patterns gives little indication of the Gorokan's "ebullient materialism," to borrow a phrase Stanner (1962:viii) applies to Siane economic behavior. Gorokans have traditionally been passionately interested in wealth and in prestige associated with wealth. Read succinctly describes this wealth-prestige orientation and how it is publicly expressed among the Gahuku, who are, he writes:

> . . . materialists concerned to the point of exhaustion with the acquisition of wealth and its distribution in a never-ending series of competitive exchanges. They lose interest quickly in ideas and measure the good life in terms of worldly success, bestowing prestige on those who have acquitted themselves conspicuously in the pursuit of its riches. Wealth signifies both power and strength, testifies to the achievements of individuals, of the clan, and of the tribe; reputations are placed on the ballot of public opinion each time the great festivals are held, when the slaughtered pigs, the array of plumes, the necklaces of shell and the breastplates of mother-of-pearl hopefully win both envy and respect. (1965:60)

This aspect of Gorokan life is essentially separate from mundane subsistence activities and involves the ceremonial exchange of valuables.[4] Pigs, various seashells, ornamental stone axes, necklaces of dog's teeth, bird of paradise plumes, headdresses of cassowary feathers and bundles of salt were all regarded traditionally as valuables by Gorokans and used by them in ceremonial exchanges. Pigs and shells appear to have been the main items of wealth. Pigs, of course, could be raised locally, but shells had to be obtained through ceremonial exchange or trade with neighboring groups. Both the Papuan Gulf and the north coast of New Guinea appear to have been source areas for shells, which were traded up to the Gorokans through chains of transactions involving coastal, foothill, and Highlands groups. The small cowrie (*Cypraea moneta*) and the tiny nassa (*Nassa* sp.) shells favored for making necklaces and headbands may have reached Goroka from both coasts. The Asaro Range, however, was a major dividing line for the flow of mother-of-pearl shell (*Pinctada maxima*) from the Papuan Gulf and the large, white egg cowrie (*Ovula ovum*) from the north coast. Jim Taylor, the first patrol officer to enter and traverse the Goroka Valley, has told me that until Europeans began importing mother-of-pearl shell it was extremely scarce in the Goroka Valley and was only found in abundance west of the Asaro Range. The egg cowrie was the primary traditional shell valuable of the Goroka Valley peoples and was most common among those living at the eastern end closest to the trade routes that came up the Markham Valley and through the Kami Hills, or across the Bismarcks from the Ramu Valley (compare Read 1954:9).

A Stone Age Setting

Among some groups in New Guinea, notably the Tolai of New Britain and the Kapauku of the West Irian Highlands, it has been shown that shells were used as general currency for buying and selling a wide range of goods and services, as well as for valuables in ceremonial exchange (Epstein 1968:19–23; Pospisil 1963:300–305). In Goroka shells were undoubtedly used from time to time to buy pigs and other articles, but there is no firm evidence of their systematic use as a general currency in precontact times. The main function of shells and other valuables was as symbols of wealth—and therefore prestige and power—to be displayed and exchanged on ceremonial occasions.

The exchange of valuables took place primarily at life crisis ceremonies—the most notable being marriages and the initiation of youths—and at pig festivals, for which Gorokans and other Highlanders were renowned. These exchanges were intergroup events, drawing together pairs of clans or subtribes in dramatic demonstrations of the social ties binding them. Marriages brought together clans which, while they might have had a record of hostility in times of war, often also had long-standing histories of intermarriage. The pig festivals were the largest and most spectacular of all the occasions for exchanging wealth, and ideally they were coordinated with initiation rituals. As pig festivals served primarily to affirm ties between clans or subtribes that had previously fought as allies, they were fitting occasions for introducing the newly initiated youths—the future warriors—to society. Although pig festivals and other occasions for exchange were events in which the financial achievements of big-men came to the fore, they were also of paramount concern to the entire social group as the following summary of the Gahuku pig festival as described by Read (1952a) illustrates.

The common goal of members of a subtribe sponsoring a pig festival was to acquit themselves well in the exchange of valuables with their allies. To this end, well before the appointed time of the festival, the men of each clan began to build up their pig herds by fattening them from their gardens, by farming some pigs out to friends and relatives with abundant supplies of sweet potato, by temporarily moving their herds to areas reported to be favorable for pig growth, and by using mother-of-pearl shell and other valuables to augment their herds through traditional channels of trade. As the time for the festival approached, the prospective guests of the other subtribe were invited for a small feast. On this occasion bundles of sticks were handed to the visitors as a formal invitation to the festival; each stick represented a pig to be given them, and the largest ones, decorated with cassowary feathers, represented the biggest and best quality pigs. Both donor and recipient were singled out, the latter being designated to receive his pig in honor of a deceased kinsman who had fallen in battle when both groups were fighting a common enemy.

The weeks following this preliminary ceremony were devoted to the intensive care of pigs and other preparations. Young people traveled as far away as the Ramu Valley over the Bismarcks in search of bird of paradise plumes, vegetable dyes, and bark cloth, and both men and women prepared shell valuables and personal adornments. Finally, on the eve of the main ceremony the guests arrived, bearing countergifts of egg cowries, bark cloth, and other valuables to present to the donors of the pigs. The following day the pig-killing took place. The largest pigs, decorated with cowries, plumes, and shell necklaces, were killed by the guests designated to receive them in honor of their group and its deceased heroes, and the pigs were prepared for the ovens. The festival was concluded on the following day with dancing and the final distribution of pig meat and other valuables; crowds of up to a thousand or more participants, as well as spectators from other clans who had come to watch the excitement, were common. The events on this final day represented the culmination of months of preparation by members of the host subtribe. If the number,[5] size, and quality of the pigs presented, as well as the mass of other donated valuables, was impressive, and if they were well received by the visiting group, a pig festival brought the host group great renown among its neighbors and gave its members a feeling of great pride.

LEADERSHIP AND STATUS MOBILITY

One common element that cuts across the seeming diversity of New Guinean societies and extends eastward to the other Melanesian societies in the Solomon Islands and the New Hebrides is an open system of status mobility. Unlike Polynesian societies and the societies of Fiji and New Caledonia, on the extreme eastern edge of Melanesia, where hereditary rank and genealogical position have been prime determinants of status, most New Guinean societies lack a fixed class structure, and their leaders achieve eminence through personal accomplishment.

A leader in New Guinea is commonly known as a *bikfela man* (big-man), a Pidgin term denoting the scale of a man's reputation. In traditional society a man became known as a big-man because of his deeds. Being a skillful warrior, a forceful orator, an expert in ritual, or a wealthy man and financier of wealth exchanges were the main accomplishments that brought an ambitious New Guinean renown and a political following. The system was open and fluid. There was no formal office of big-man to succeed to; men became known as leaders because of their skills and their ability to use these to create ranks of followers. At any one time several big-men might be competing for status in a clan or tribal group, each perhaps representing a different faction or a different level of competence. An especially strong and forceful man might achieve dominance over the others, but his influence, like that of lesser big-men, was always transitory. Ultimately, it depended on his physical and intellectual powers, and as a man aged and could no longer demonstrate his powers on the field of battle or in wealth production and exchange, his reputation waned and he was superseded by younger and more vigorous men, anxious to assert themselves as big-men.[6]

There were exceptions in New Guinea to this extreme pattern of status mobility, the most famous being from the Trobriand Islands, where local leaders ordinarily came from the senior members of the highest ranking descent group in each locality. However, even in the Trobriands a junior man might compete with and win out over a genealogically more qualified man for the role of acknowledged leader (Powell 1960:118). And elsewhere in New Guinea where hereditary rank enters the picture, it seems that in most cases some status mobility is still expressed, either through competition between those in the ranking class, as in the Trobriands, or in struggles for leadership in which an achieving commoner could, in a big-man style, best a hereditary leader (Meggitt 1967a:23).

In Goroka, as elsewhere in the Highlands, the big-man system was strongly entrenched. Only at the lineage level was ascribed status important; ordinarily the senior male was the lineage leader. Above the lineage level, leadership was achieved (Langness 1963: 158; Newman 1965:43–44; Salisbury 1962:28; Read 1959).

Among the Gahuku, for example, the man who demonstrated his strength in fighting, oratory, and wealth accumulation and exchange was the ideal candidate for becoming a "man with a name," or big-man, as a leader was known in the vernacular.[7]

Read (1959:428) cites warfare as being the archetype of "strength-demonstrating" pursuits among the Gahuku. Elsewhere in the Highlands the prime role of prowess in warfare in achieving status is stressed by a few writers, but in most descriptions, including those from Goroka, wealth accumulation and exchange receives more attention as the basic means for becoming a big-man. This apparent discrepancy may reflect two related factors: first, that most descriptions of leadership date from postpacification times when open warfare had already been suppressed by the administration, and, second, that a noted warrior was often also a wealthy man who used his wealth to revalidate or even upgrade his status in peacetime pig exchanges. After pacification, then, men who had won their spurs in battle would be seen as conspicuously active in wealth exchanges, and ambitious younger men, who might previously have expressed their achievement drive in warfare, would be seen throwing all their energy to the more peaceful activities of wealth accumulation and exchange (compare Berndt 1952–1953:147). Whatever the case, of the two main paths to achieved status, the economic road is most relevant to this study, and it is the one that requires some examination in the Gorokan context.

To begin a career based on wealth and its circulation, a young Gorokan had first to amass a fund of pigs. Although the ethnographic record for Goroka is not entirely clear on this score, the process probably involved a combination of "home production" and "finance," as elsewhere in the Highlands (Strathern 1969). Home production of pigs normally came first. For this a man needed at least one sow (received as a gift or borrowed), land for growing sweet potatoes (the main pig fodder), and female labor for tending both gardens and pigs. The labor could be supplied at first by a man's mother or sister, but eventually he had to acquire a wife, or perhaps several wives, to guarantee himself a constant labor force. Building up a pig herd from a single sow took time, particularly if disease struck, and a portion of the pigs produced had to be allocated to paying off obligations assumed in starting his career. The lender of the original sow had to be paid a piglet from the first litter, and eventually a sow, as well. Furthermore, after marriage the young man found himself in a web of debt to those who had contributed to his brideprice, which tended to drain his pig wealth, either through direct repayments or through donations to the bridewealth funds of young relatives of those who had helped him pay for a wife.

Once, however, a man had shown himself to be a successful pig breeder and had demonstrated that he could repay his debts and manage his obligations, he was in a position to expand his wealth holdings by "financial" means. Pigs could be advantageously traded to people or groups needing pigs for festivals, in return for shells and other valuables. Or they could be loaned out to younger men anxious to start their first pig herds, and they could also be farmed out to relatives who would tend them in return for a portion of any litters produced. (These arrangements also served as a protection against the loss of a man's entire pig herd, which could be wiped out by disease if it were concentrated in one place and that area was hit by a local epidemic.) By both loaning pigs and farming them out the owners stood to gain "interest" in the form of piglets, which, especially if the original loans were not immediately repaid, as was common, could augment his pig herd considerably over the years (compare Salisbury 1962:92–93).

A man who had started to trade pigs for other valuables and to loan his pigs to others had already gone beyond the point of merely accumulating wealth; he had begun to weave a network of ties which, if shrewdly exploited, could serve to create a political following composed of trade partners and those indebted to him. His following and reputation could then be greatly increased through prominent participation in pig festivals, bridewealth exchanges, and other occasions for wealth exchange. His role in these was twofold. First, as a man of standing and of proven financial ability, he took a leading role in organizing the pooling of his clansmen's valuables for presentation to the other group and then in distributing the counterpresentation among his clansmen. Second, as a wealthy man interested in using his wealth as a means for achieving more status, he made major contributions of pigs, shells, and other valuables to his clan or subtribe's exchange fund.

In the arena of ceremonial exchange a big-man therefore had an opportunity to further his own career. But at the same time he was also serving his group's interest by augmenting its wealth presentations, and hence its prestige. In the Gorokan system, then, individual and group ambitions were complementary. Read (1952a:19), for example, describes how in the Gahuku pig festivals the subtribe needed the contributions which only its wealthy big-men could supply to uphold its honor, while, at the same time, the big-men needed a socially sanctioned context for the use of their wealth to enhance their personal prestige. The pig festival therefore maintained "its corporate character while simultaneously according social recognition to important individuals."

Related to this balance between individual and group interests in wealth exchanges is a basic principle of Gorokan social behavior, which stands in opposition to the value placed on "strength." Read (1959) terms this principle *equivalence* and explains it in terms of the desire for a degree of parity in relations between groups and between individuals. A subtribe, for example, should not strive to completely outdo another in wealth presentations at a pig festival; its contributions may be considerable, but not so great that the other group cannot immediately or eventually match them with counter-presentations. In individual behavior this means that a man should not try to completely dominate others—as, for example, in giving overly large gifts or in demanding too stringent repayment terms of a debtor. The main sanction against an individual's showing too much strength and flagrantly violating the principle of equivalence is apparently the withdrawal of public support so that he no longer commands the respect of his fellow clansmen and cannot call upon them for support, economic or otherwise. Attempts to harm or kill the overly strong individual by physical assault or by means of sorcery are apparently ultimate sanctions, sometimes applied in extreme cases. The Gorokan status-mobility system thus includes some checks against rampant individualism; the rising big-man has to pay heed to the feelings and needs of others and to stop short of blatantly exploiting his fellow clansmen.

2

Europeans Arrive

Living in the valleys and on the mountain slopes of the central cordillera, which extends almost the entire 1,500-mile length of New Guinea, are a million people. They represent the last major group of mankind to have been discovered by the outside world; firm knowledge of their existence only dates from the 1930s. This late discovery of the Highlanders can largely be explained by the preoccupation of the colonial administrations—Australian, Dutch, and German—with exploring and pacifying the coastal and foothill regions and the tremendous difficulties presented by the terrain, the climate, and the sometimes hostile populations to mounting overland expeditions into the interior before the coming of the air age to New Guinea. Prior to the 1930s a few overland expeditions were successful in reaching or crossing the central cordillera; between 1905 and 1910 there was an international race by explorers of various nations to reach the snow-covered peaks on the Dutch side (Brookfield 1961:436), and in the 1920s two parties, one Dutch and the other Australian, crossed segments of the Highlands (Watson 1964:1). But none of these expeditions explored the Highlands thoroughly enough to realize the extent and density of the valley populations there. Detzner, a German surveyor who eluded Australian capture during World War I by hiding in the interior, claimed to have entered populated grassland valleys during an attempt to reach the Dutch border and cross over into neutral territory (Detzner 1921), but his claim was suspect, and rightly so, for he later recanted his tales of Highlands exploration (Biskup

1968). During the 1920s there was, in fact, a considerable body of opinion which held that New Guinea's interior was entirely mountainous and, if populated at all, was only thinly so, like many of the foothill areas.

PROSPECTORS AND PATROL OFFICERS

Souls and gold were the main incentives for the exploration of the Highlands of Australian New Guinea. In the late 1920s Lutheran missionaries, who were by then established in the Markham Valley approaches to the Highlands, entered the edge of the Highlands at a point just east of Goroka (McRae 1969). Although they left a few New Guinean evangelists settled in the area, they kept the news of their discoveries to themselves, so that for the world at large the Highlands remained undiscovered until gold prospectors entered the area a few years later. During the 1920s rich alluvial gold finds were made at Bulolo Creek and its tributaries in the mountains that rise abruptly near the coast at the northeastern end of the territory. News of these rich finds brought boatloads of prospectors from Australia, but most arrived too late to get in on the rich finds, and many left New Guinea. Some stayed on, however, to seek their fortunes by pushing farther and farther into New Guinea's mountains in search of new finds. Included among these were two young Australians, Michael (Mick) Leahy and Michael Dwyer. In 1930 they ascended the Markham Valley, crossed over into the watershed of the Ramu River, and then entered the eastern edge of the Highlands. From a distance they sighted the grasslands of the Goroka Valley, but instead of pushing on toward them, they turned south on a trek that eventually took them, via the Purari River, to the Papuan Gulf. Later that year Leahy and Dwyer returned to the Highlands, entered the eastern edge of Goroka Valley, and briefly tested the Bena Bena River and other streams there for gold-bearing sands and gravels such as had been found earlier at Bulolo.

Their report of the populous villages dotting the ridges of the Goroka Valley was the first real indication that the interior of New Guinea might be heavily populated. Their discovery was not, however, immediately followed up with official patrols by the understaffed and underfinanced mandated territory administration. Commercial motives directed when Goroka was to be revisited. In 1932, as gold prices rose with the deepening of the Depression, gold-mining companies became anxious to check out any possible new source of gold. On the strength of Leahy and Dwyer's report of gold traces along the banks of Gorokan rivers and streams, the New Guinea Goldfields Company, which already was working Bulolo Creek with gold dredges, commissioned Leahy to return to Goroka to test the area further and to build an airfield to fly in equipment and company personnel. That the stakes were high is indicated by what Leahy was finally offered if the Goroka deposits proved economical —£10,000 for each dredge installed plus 2.5 percent on any future finds.[1]

Mick Leahy, accompanied by his brother Dan and a work force of New Guineans from the coast, returned to Goroka in late 1932 and immediately selected an airfield site on a terrace just west of the Bena Bena River. They were soon visited by Jim Taylor, who walked in from the newly established patrol post in the Ramu Valley, where he was assistant district officer. Taylor stayed only a few days but left some of his policemen and laborers to help level the airfield. On Christmas day 1932 the field was ready, and Taylor flew in for another brief visit. Taylor soon returned again, only this time to stay to set up the Bena Bena patrol post. With an operational airfield to bring in supplies, equipment, and personnel and the protection of a patrol officer and his policemen, Leahy was ready to begin intensive prospecting around Goroka and, using the airfield as a forward base, to explore the unknown country farther west.

Of the work that followed, the explorations, not the prospecting, hit the real paydirt. The Bena Bena River and the other Goroka rivers and streams were exhaustively tested, but they, like the rivers and streams encountered farther west, showed only slight traces of alluvial gold—too low in concentration to justify full-scale commercial dredging. In contrast to this disappointment, the explorations were markedly successful in opening up new and heavily populated country to the west. The Leahys, Taylor, and their police escort and carriers left the Bena Bena base camp early in 1933. They crossed the lower Asaro River, went through what is now the Unggai census division, climbed the Asaro Range, and entered Siane country. From there they moved on through the mountainous, but densely populated, Chimbu country to the flat Wahgi Valley. There they built another airfield to receive supplies and to use as a base camp for explorations to Mount Hagen and farther west, which opened up more and more heavily populated upland regions. The significance of these discoveries was pointed out by Taylor in a résumé of his patrol report, which was sent to the League of Nations:

> Many thousands of natives whose existance was previously unknown, had been visited. A new mountain range and several valleys had been discovered . . . also it is definitely established that the main range, which was hitherto believed to be a backbone of high, forest-clad uninhabited mountains, is in these parts at any rate, a cartographic myth, and in its place we have a fine grass upland region, which may prove to be the best and most important part of New Guinea of the future.[2] (1935:117)

These first European intrusions into the Highlands were not absolutely peaceful, but they were not as bloody as one might imagine, given the pattern of warfare in the Highlands and the necessity of the prospecting parties and patrols to contact so many separate and potentially hostile groups. Bloodshed during these encounters was kept down by a combination of circumstances. When Europeans first entered an uncontrolled area, they were often considered to be spirits and were treated with awe. Also, they were sources of much-desired trade goods, which the people could, as Taylor and Leahy went to great lengths to make clear, obtain peaceably by furnishing food or labor. And, when groups did turn hostile—as frequently happened when a patrol returned through a previously visited area after the people had recovered from their initial fright or when a group became dissatisfied with obtaining goods through peaceful trade—patrol officers and prospectors usually tried to avoid bloodshed. Nevertheless, when prospecting parties and patrols were seriously challenged or actually fired upon by Highlands bowmen, there was little they could do but fire back in self-defense. A number of Highlanders were killed in these encounters, although the fights in and around Goroka resulted in few casualties, except for one battle between patrol officers investigating the killing of a miner and villagers living a few miles northeast of Goroka. This encounter, which was called in the Australian report to the League of Nations "one of the most desperate affrays in the history of New Guinea," resulted in the death of nineteen Highlanders (Commonwealth of Australia 1935:28).

Europeans Arrive

In Goroka seven local men were reported killed in armed encounters. Taylor, while returning from the Wahgi Valley to the Bena Bena base camp was challenged by a group of Siane warriors and was forced to shoot one of them. Commenting on this incident Taylor wrote:

> One of the leading men of the tribe drew his bow on Spinks [a surveyor]. I called to him and warned him to desist. He then relaxed for a few minutes, but someone shouted something, to him from behind (that is one of his own people), and he immediately refitted his arrow and prepared to shoot Spinks. I then fired a shot and he fell. The remainder of the local people then withdrew a short distance, and by firing over their heads we were able to pass on without further trouble. (1933)

Leahy and his party accounted for the other deaths, all of which occurred during a dispute over a stolen axe at Korofeigu, along the Bena Bena River. According to Leahy (1933: November 19, December 16), a group of Bena Bena men stole an axe from the prospectors' camp and, after gaining confidence from the theft, started showering arrows on the mining party, who returned the fire, killing six of the attackers.[3]

Leahy, who was later criticized for causing unnecessary deaths during his various explorations and prospecting ventures throughout the Highlands, was apparently able to control the situation sufficiently in Goroka to avoid all but this one serious clash.[4] That Leahy was proud of this accomplishment is apparent from a diary entry made the day the last aircraft carrying New Guinea Goldfields Company personnel flew out of Bena Bena. His comments that day, which effectively marked the end of his hopes of striking it rich in Goroka, were:

> . . . so ends the chances of Bena Bena ever seeing a dredge ploughing up the gravel. However it [the prospecting] has done a lot towards leaving the locals see that the white man does not get hostile just to show his superiority over their weapons and that they would much prefer to sit down near them and trade useful articles for native food. (1933:October 21)

ADMINISTRATIVE CONTROL AND THE WAR

Older Gorokans speak of the time "before Jim Taylor" and of the time "after Jim Taylor," using his appearance on patrols through

Goroka during 1932 and 1933 to mark the divide between the pre- and postcontact worlds. However epochal Taylor's first patrols were, they did not mark the beginning of full and continuous administrative control in Goroka. Extending control was a slow process, haltingly pursued in the 1930s, partially interrupted by the war in the early 1940s, and not completed until the late 1940s or, in some remote corners of Goroka, perhaps not until the early 1950s. Documentation of events in Goroka during the 1930s is difficult; most of the patrol reports and other records were lost during the war. It seems clear, however, that the Bena Bena patrol post was abandoned when the New Guinea Goldfields Company pulled out of the area and that it was used thereafter only as a temporary base camp for patrols moving through Goroka (Commonwealth of Australia 1938:28). The first permanent patrol post in Goroka apparently was established around 1939 on a small plateau nearer the center of the valley than the old Bena Bena site. This new center was at first called the Bena Bena station but later became known as the Goroka (frequently spelled *Garoka* in the 1940s) station, after a small area adjacent to the plateau called that by the local Gahuku people. The name *Goroka* was later applied to the township that developed south of the station after the war, as well as to the whole valley and sub-district.

Between 1933 and 1939 the Goroka region was largely bypassed by the administration. The principal administration stations from the Eastern Highlands during this period were at Kainantu, some twenty air miles over the Kami Hills to the east, and at Chimbu, well to the west. Patrols into Goroka were usually mounted from Kainantu or Chimbu. The only patrol report available for this period is of a patrol into Goroka made by J. R. Black in 1934. In it Black (1934–1935) expresses his regret that the Bena Bena post had been closed, as intertribal warfare had broken out immediately after its abandonment. Sporadic fighting continued in the valley for some years, and administration control was minimal until the Goroka station was established in the late 1930s. T. G. Aitchison, who was in charge of the Kainantu station during the mid-1930s, has commented that with only one patrol officer and one cadet as administration staff "to establish law and order from the Markham Valley to the Goroka/Chimbu Divide, it was impracticable to stop all inter-group fighting." He found it easy enough to interrupt a battle but noted that the groups "would resume their fight after the patrol passed through" (Aitchison 1964:6).

However slight administration control in Goroka was from a military point of view, one subtle effort to extend government influence should not be overlooked. As patrols moved through Goroka and surrounding areas, young boys would tag along as the patrols passed from village to village. Motivated by the lure of adventure, the chance to see new goods close up, if not actually to obtain them, and the possibility of learning some of the secrets of the powerful intruders, these boys followed the patrols everywhere and tried to make themselves useful by performing small tasks for the patrol officers and their police escort. From the latter they soon began to pick up Pidgin, and the patrol officers—seeing a chance to create a corps of Pidgin-speakers who could mediate between the patrols and villagers—decided to formalize the process by picking the most able boys and enrolling them in bush Pidgin schools taught by the policemen. For example, at the Finentegu base camp Patrol Officer Black set up a school that included at times as many as sixty pupils, many of whom were probably from Goroka. Commenting on this effort, Black (1934–1935) wrote: "this has proved the best way of influencing the area quickly and satisfactorily. A representative of every village in the area is aimed at." Whatever the benefits to the administration, these schools and the more informal contacts ambitious youths had with patrols were crucial elements in the education of some of the first Gorokan entrepreneurs.

Lutheran, Seventh Day Adventist, and Catholic mission stations were established in Goroka within a few years after Leahy and Taylor's initial explorations of the area, and prospectors continued to work there despite Leahy's failure to find payable amounts of gold. However, this free movement of nonadministration Europeans into Goroka and other Highlands areas was stopped in the mid-1930s. When Leahy read a paper on his explorations at the Royal Geographical Society in London (Leahy 1936), he reportedly admitted that he and his men had been forced to shoot forty New Guineans in various armed encounters in and around the Highlands from 1930 to 1934. Although a later inquiry judged that Leahy's actions had been justified in order to save lives in his party (McNicholl 1968:6–7), his actions and the Australian government's policy of allowing prospectors to work in uncontrolled areas were severely criticized before the Permanent Mandates Commission in Geneva. Deaths in European-Highlander encounters were not confined to Highlanders. Although Leahy and his coworkers escaped serious injury, one miner was killed just east of Goroka, and a Catholic priest and a Catholic lay brother were killed in Chimbu, just to the west of Goroka. These killings, plus the criticisms stemming from Leahy's actions, convinced the administration that the Highlands should be closed to nonofficial personnel until full administrative control could be established. This decision, and then the advent of the war a few years later, effectively prevented any European commercial exploitation of the area until the late 1940s, when the Highlands were opened up once again to private interests.

When the Japanese invaded New Guinea in early 1942, they quickly took the major offshore islands and established themselves all along the north coast of New Guinea proper. Although Australian troops turned back their advance on Port Moresby, the Japanese remained entrenched on the north coast for the next two years and from there threatened the Highlands and other inland regions. According to Dexter (1961:231), the Japanese planned to strike through the Ramu Valley, across the Bismarcks, and then into the Goroka Valley.

Allied commanders anticipated the Japanese plans to move into the Highlands, and in January 1943 Australian troops were flown into the old Bena Bena airfield, built ten years earlier by Leahy, with orders "to secure the Bena Bena drome against enemy attack; to deny the enemy freedom of movement in the Bena Bena [Goroka] Valley; to harass and delay any enemy movement in the area between Bena Bena and Ramu" (Dexter 1961:234–235). This Bena Force, as it came to be known, immediately began to rebuild the Bena Bena field, link it by road with administration headquarters in Goroka, and improve the small airstrips at administration headquarters and at the nearby Lutheran mission. Japanese reconnaisance aircraft spotted this activity, and in May and June the installations were bombed repeatedly.

Because existing airfields were inadequate to cope with what looked like a major enemy drive developing toward Goroka, in late June 1943 Australian army engineers, assisted by over a thousand local laborers, built a 6,000-foot airstrip designed to take fighters and bombers on a flat plain just south of the Goroka station. Eventually the Allied force—consisting of Australians, New Guineans (members of the Royal Papuan Constabulary), and Americans—assigned to the main field and outlying installations in Goroka totaled almost twelve hundred men (Dexter 1961:599). Although the Goroka field apparently never was used as a major base for air strikes against the Japanese, it and the troops stationed in Goroka served to deter the Japanese advance on the Highlands. Japanese patrols had actually penetrated as far as the Ramu Valley, where they were contacted in short but bloody clashes with Australian troops operating out of Goroka, but by late 1943 acute pressure in the Highlands had been relieved. Thereafter Goroka served mainly as a transit point for aircraft and airborne troops shuttling to and from the Allied offensives along the north coast and the foothills region.

Relations between Allied forces and Gorokans were mediated by the Australian New Guinea Administrative Unit (ANGAU), which took over civil administration of New Guinea after the outbreak of the war. With the aid of ANGAU personnel stationed at Goroka, the military authorities were able to organize local workers for building airfields and other tasks, and for growing vegetables. Most of the heavy construction work was done by men recruited from the Chimbu region, who came in on three-month contracts and then were paid off in shell and sent home. The Chimbus were preferred to the Gorokans as laborers because of their reputation for being hard-working and because much of the local population was busy growing food for these imported workers, for local Allied personnel, and also for troops stationed at Nadzab, the main Allied air base in New Guinea, located in the lower Markham Valley (Dexter 1961:240; Bowman 1946:437–438). Shell and salt apparently were the main trade goods used to pay for the vegetables, and these items were carried by Allied patrols throughout the area to barter for food as they traveled (Dexter 1961:438).

The Gorokans did suffer some casualties during the war. Japanese bombers hit gardens and villages adjacent to airstrips, and four Gorokan fatalities from these raids are mentioned in the official Australian army history of the campaign (Dexter 1961:239,242). Although there may have been more, unreported Gorokan bombing victims, wartime diseases struck the Gorokans much harder than did the Japanese raiders. When soldiers carried dysentery up from the coast, the Highlanders, lacking immunity, died in the thousands, according to Gunther (1965:405). No mortality figures are available for Goroka, but present-day informants remember many deaths, and Salisbury (1962:123) reports that fatalities among the Siane were high. Fortunately, however, the disease did not get entirely out of hand; hundreds of thousands of sulfaguanadine tablets were flown in and doled out to Gorokans in villages and in the field hospitals set up throughout the area during 1944 and 1945. Judging from local recollections and a few surviving patrol reports, one of ANGAU's main tasks during this period was fighting the epidemic; the Gorokans particularly remember ANGAU officers for their strict campaigns to have all villages construct latrines and carry out other sanitary measures to prevent the spread or recurrence of the disease.

Civil administration was restored throughout New Guinea by 1946. In Goroka civilian personnel replaced ANGAU officers and reestablished administration headquarters at the prewar site just north of the main Goroka airfield. By 1947, when Jim Taylor returned to Goroka to take over the station as district officer for the entire Highlands area, the Goroka region was—in comparison to many outlying areas, some of which had yet to be visited by patrols—fairly well under administrative control. Except for a few remote areas on the upper slopes of the Asaro and Bismarck ranges at the northeast end of the valley,[5] and perhaps some portions of the Watabung area, regular intertribal warfare had been stopped and patrols could move about the region freely. Missionary groups already established in Goroka were allowed to expand at this time, and new sects were allowed in. However, Goroka and the other Highlands areas were still closed to European commercial interests, as in the immediate prewar days.

GOROKANS UNDER EUROPEAN CONTROL

By 1947 Gorokans had been in intermittent contact with Europeans for a decade and a half. Their isolation had been broken by prospectors, with patrol officers, missionaries, and considerable numbers of Allied troops following in their wake. However, the initial fifteen years of contact were not as traumatic as might be expected; the Gorokans survived this crucial period better than had many of their fellow New Guineans on the coast who had been contacted in earlier decades. In comparison to the latter and to many other peoples around the world who suffered severe political, social, or demographic consequences from contact with Europeans, the Gorokans got off lightly. It was probably most fortunate that they remained isolated from Europeans as long as they did. By the 1930s administrative practices had evolved to a point where heavy-handed attempts to radically alter local societies were largely past. In addition, the administration was learning to keep prospectors, labor recruiters, and other nongovernmental Europeans in check and also to moderate the efforts of overzealous missionaries. And, from the point of view of sheer survival, the late date of contact was most crucial: had sulfa drugs, an innovation of the 1930s, not been available, the wartime dysentery epidemic could have greatly reduced the Gorokan population, just as other epidemics had done among coastal peoples of the Pacific throughout the eighteenth and early nineteenth centuries.

Gorokan society in 1947 was not, therefore, a shattered one. Deaths in contact confrontations had been minimal; and, although the dysentery epidemic had been severe, most tribal groups seem to have retained their numerical strengths of precontact days. To be sure, prospectors had enjoyed a free hand in Goroka during the early 1930s, but from the late 1930s on, commercial interests had not been allowed to disturb the local population. Immediately after the war, owners of coastal plantations were clamoring for laborers and made repeated requests to be allowed to hire men from Goroka and other Highlands areas. Their requests, however, were denied, mainly because of the fear that Highlanders would contract malaria, tuberculosis, or some other disease from which they had no immunity. Missionaries for over a decade had been actively preaching new faiths that required, among other things, the abandonment of men's houses and male dominance, initiation ceremonies, polygamy, the eating of pork (by Seventh Day Adventists), and other basic elements of Gorokan life. But, as of 1947, at least, their influence had been mainly restricted to areas immediately contiguous to mission stations, and the numbers who embraced Christianity and abandoned traditional ways were still very few (compare Read 1952b). Acceptance of administration control had meant, of course, the formal abandonment of warfare and feuding in intergroup conflicts, but the internal structure of tribes, subtribes, and clans was little tampered with. It was not administration policy to force radical change in this area, and, as might be expected with an understaffed administration, the few patrol officers operating in Goroka were only too glad to allow local groups to regulate their own internal affairs, and even their intergroup relations, as long as violence was avoided.

It would be reasonable to expect that pacification would have left a people like the Gorokans, who were so dedicated to fighting and the glories of war, in an extremely depressed state. However, the impact of pacification seems to have varied from group to group and overall to have been more uplifting than depressing to local spirit. Militarily powerful groups, such as those around Korofeigu in the southeast Bena Bena grasslands who dominated the entire lower Goroka Valley at the time of contact, bitterly resented pacification, as they were forced to relinquish their ascendancy and to remain within their normal boundaries. On the other hand, weaker groups welcomed pacification, as it meant they were safe from attack by their more powerful enemies. As for the overall reaction to pacification, Jim Taylor's comments may be particularly apt (despite whatever bias he may have as the prime "pacifier" of Goroka), as they seem to fit in with the views of many of my Gorokan informants. Though some of the latter, particularly elderly ex-warriors, recall the precontact *taim bilong pait* (warfare period) with nostalgia, they also speak appreciatively of the benefits of peace. Here Taylor is emphatic: peace, he says, brought the Gorokans into a golden age. Taylor speaks of the exuberance of the Gorokans in the immediate postpacification days, when the people realized that they were free of the constant fear of attack, and particularly of how the Gorokans celebrated their freedom by traveling about the countryside as would have been difficult before. Prior to pacification, a man's normal radius of action would have been his tribal territory —about five to ten miles in most cases. With peace he was free to roam beyond his tribal confines—though at first he might keep mainly to administration roads, as they were neutral ground—and to visit sites and people previously inaccessible because of active or potential intertribal hostilities.

Peace allowed Gorokans to relax their guard and even to change their living sites. Heavy protective stockades around villages no longer were necessary, and in some cases Gorokans shifted their villages from the protection of ridge sites to the exposed and previously unsafe valley floor, to be near good land and administration roads. In addition, the process of forming new villages seems to have accelerated at this time, for subclans could break off from the main village-clan unit to form small, independent villages, which would have been indefensible in prepacification days (compare Langness 1967:164). In a sense, peace also saved the Gorokans a good deal of time and energy that formerly went into building stockades and standing guard duty, as well as actually preparing for and fighting wars. However, not all this freed time and energy went into roaming the countryside or other leisure activities. Much of it went, it seems, into intensified activity in traditional wealth exchanges. This development is, in fact, the most significant economic change that occurred among the Gorokans during this hiatus between their first contacts with the outside world and their actual entry into the market economy.

The Premarket Boom

The opening of the Highlands was greatly facilitated by the use of trade goods to pay for local food and labor needed by exploratory patrols and for government stations. Without the use of trade goods, patrols could hardly have moved into the Highlands because of the problems of food provisioning. Porters were virtually useless for carrying provisions on long-range expeditions, as they quickly ate up all the food they carried. Provisioning by air—through the establishment of base airfields and food stockpiles and then by the use of air drops to supply field parties—was successful in Taylor's 1938 Hagen-Sepik patrol but was extremely expensive and hardly possible except in conjunction with the use of local foods obtained through trade. Money was unusable in the Highlands at this time; Highlanders had no regard for it, and there were no stores or other means by which they could have exchanged money for objects they valued. But the Highlanders were eager to obtain shell, steel tools, salt, and other trade goods Europeans could provide and were more than willing to provide pigs, vegetable foods, or their labor to get them.

The Highlanders had been at the end of long trade routes, over which shells had passed from the coast inland, and they had been paying high prices in pigs and other valuables for their shells. Therefore, when Europeans first arrived carrying among their trade goods several varieties of valuable shells, the Highlanders quickly made known their tremendous desire for shell wealth. Leahy had not been prepared for this demand and did not have enough shells for trading on his first prospecting expedition in 1930. On his expedition in 1932 and 1933 he carried in abundant stores of shells, which were augmented by supplies flown up from the coast when the Bena Bena airfield was finished. These he used to purchase food from the Bena Bena and, later, as trade goods on his explorations to the west. Because of his experience with the Bena Bena demand for shell and his knowledge, gained from an aerial reconnaissance, of extensively cultivated valleys to the west, Leahy stated that he and his exploration party "had no misgivings about the food supply, and instead of carrying food we took shell money with which to pay for it" (Leahy and Crain 1937:152). Taylor, in charge of the administration part of that expedition, was equally sure about their being able to purchase food with trade goods along the way and wrote that "excluding 100 lbs. of rice for use in an emergency, native rations were not carried, as we were quite confident that an abundance of native foods could be bought with shell money, the currency of the inland people in New Guinea, or with knives and axes" (Taylor 1933).

Leahy and Taylor's confidence was not misplaced; they were able to purchase abundant food supplies for themselves, their police escort, and their carriers and at times were embarrassed by the large amount of vegetable food and pigs offered. Salisbury (1962: 114–115, 123) provides an interesting insight into these transactions from the Siane point of view. The Siane were mystified about why these newcomers would offer good shell valuables for "things of no account" like vegetable foods and thought that they must indeed be getting the better part of the deal from the Europeans. Then, when the newcomers thought they were purchasing pigs, in Siane eyes they were actually taking part in a traditional wealth transaction. To the Siane these transactions involved slaughtering pigs in honor of the visiting Europeans, who then made appropriate presentations of shells and other valuables in return. Those who killed the pigs and received the valuables were the local big-men, and it seems that Taylor and other patrol officers who followed him and engaged in these transactions were considered to be of equivalent status and were called big-men (*we namfa*) by the Siane.

One thing the first Europeans traveling west of Goroka did learn immediately was that mother-of-pearl shell (usually called *gold lip* or in Pidgin *kina*) was the primary shell valuable west of the Asaro Range. Subsequent patrols and the permanent government stations that were later set up began importing these shells in great quantities, and they soon became popular among the Bena Bena and other Goroka Valley people, who had seen little mother-of-pearl shell in precontact days, and came to rival in popularity the egg cowrie, their traditional paramount shell valuable. As late as 1949, after the introduction of money, a patrol officer working in the northeastern end of the valley could still write:

> The gold lip shell speaks all languages and I suppose is the natives most treasured possession. They take precedence over everything and are a leading passion. I noticed that some had been skillfully mended but large or small, broken or otherwise, they possess great value in native eyes. (Corrigan 1948–1949a)

The supply of shells became a major concern for the administration, for without them the maintenance of government stations and patrols in the Highlands would have been tremendously difficult. The administration therefore entered the shell-buying business in a big way. Egg cowries, money cowries, nassa shells, green snail shells, and bailer shells (the latter two being popular primarily west of Goroka) were bought from European traders and New Guineans along the north shore and on Manus, New Britain, and other offshore islands. Mother-of-pearl shell was apparently first sought in the Papuan Gulf, the traditional source, but supplies were found to be scarce. Manus Island mother-of-pearl shell was tried but was found to be lacking in quality by the Highlanders, who were very discriminating as to color and the incidence of worm holes in the shells. Finally, a major source of supply for quality shells was located on Thursday Island, an old pearling center in the Torres Straits between New Guinea and Australia. Particularly in the postwar period, Thursday Island shells were imported into the Highlands in great quantities, coming up to Goroka and other Highlands centers in chartered DC-3 transports.

Just as the Highlanders thought they were getting the better part of the deal out of trading food for valuable shells, so did the Europeans regard these transactions as tremendous bargains. For example, Father Ross, who founded the Catholic mission at Mount Hagen, records with some nostalgia that in the mid-1930s a bailer shell costing him twenty-five cents would buy a 200-pound pig and that twenty-five cents worth of cowries and nassa shells would bring a ton of sweet potatoes (Ross 1969:61). Although exchange rates were adjusted as European-imported shell became more plentiful, shell was still highly valued in the immediate postwar years in Goroka and was used almost exclusively by the administration to buy food and to pay workers until mid-1947, when money was introduced. Taylor recalls using shell during this period to buy quantities of sweet potatoes and other vegetable foods sufficient to feed a thousand or so men working in Goroka and also for regular wage payments to hundreds of laborers. The going rate of exchange for a mother-of-pearl shell was one medium-size pig or three months' labor, and five small cowries would buy fifteen pounds of sweet potatoes.

Shell was, of course, only one of the many trade items accepted by Highlanders. Salt, twist tobacco, beads, face paint, cloth, leather belts, and, for a time, crockery (worn like shells) were used, as were steel tools—axes, knives, machetes, and shovels. The utility of steel tools was not always immediately recognized by the Highlanders, however. Leahy reports that in 1930, just southeast of Goroka:

> At one place we found an ultraconservative *lapoon* (old man) who had a positive prejudice against such modern innovations as steel hatchets. I offered him one for a pig, but he showed me his much heavier stone axe with obvious pride, his attitude being, 'what was good enough for grand-pa is good enough for me.' Seeing no convenient piece of wood about for a demonstration of the hatchet's superiority, I tried him with a strip of tambu shells, sewn on bark, and he accepted eagerly before I had a chance to back out. Shell being the recognized currency, I told Dwyer we had found the original 'hard money man.' (Leahy and Crain 1937:65)

Taylor had a similar experience with a man in the Wahgi Valley, except that he was able to note a shift in attitude once the utility of a steel axe had been established. As he related the incident to me, he offered the man a steel axe in exchange for a stone one, but the man refused and asked for five cowries instead. Taylor gave him the cowries for the stone tool, and, with an eye to educating the Wahgi people on the value of metal tools, he threw in the steel axe also. When he returned to the same area a few months later, the people, having discovered the superiority of steel over stone, besieged him with requests for axes.

Once the utility of steel axes and other metal tools was established, a steady demand for them developed in the Highlands, although they do not seem to ever have had the same appeal that mother-of-pearl and other highly valued shells enjoyed. In 1949, for example, a patrol officer working in the Upper Asaro region found that "steel is in fair demand but it is of very secondary consideration in comparison to gold lip" (Corrigan 1948–1949b). Nonetheless, the use of steel tools was to have far-reaching consequences in Gorokan society, which, in conjunction with the tremendous inflation in circulating shell wealth and the freedom brought about by pacification, made the postcontact efflorescence of the traditional wealth-exchange system possible.

Salisbury has documented how the introduction of steel tools among the Siane led to a marked expansion in their wealth-exchange activities in *From Stone to Steel* (1962). The Siane groups Salisbury studied were first contacted in 1933 but were left alone and uncontrolled until 1945, when ANGAU patrols moved in to stop the spread of dysentery; even in 1952 and 1953, when Salisbury made his study, they were still isolated from day-to-day contact with Europeans. These Siane groups received some steel axes from the first patrols of the early 1930s, but from then until 1945, and probably for some years thereafter, steel reached them largely through trade with Goroka Valley people, not through trade with Europeans. This situation allowed Salisbury the rare opportunity of analyzing the impact of a technological innovation on people who remained largely isolated from direct contact with Europeans.

Steel axes began to be common among the Siane in the mid-1930s. At first, through wealth exchanges with groups closer to European sources of supply, they flowed mainly to the big-men, who treated them both as a valuable to be used in further exchanges and as a tool. Gradually, however, as more axes reached Siane territory they became universal among adult men; their use in wealth presentations diminished, and they became more of a tool than a valuable.

The steel axe, like its stone predecessor, was a man's tool, and the benefits of its superiority went mainly to the Siane men, not to the women. According to Siane informants, the steel axe was at least three times as efficient in cutting wood for clearing gardens and fence-making—the main male subsistence tasks[6]—and Salisbury (1962:118) estimates that by using steel axes a man needed to spend only 50 percent of his time at subsistence tasks, as opposed to 80 percent when he had relied exclusively on stone tools. The time saved could have been used to make larger gardens and produce more food or to build bigger and better houses, but it was not.

A major portion of the time saved from subsistence work went into the myriad of activities involved in arranging, promoting, and participating in wealth exchanges. The tempo of exchanges apparently did not accelerate, as this was governed by presumably stable maturation rates—of pigs to be slaughtered, youths to be initiated, and daughters to be married off. But the time spent on individual exchanges, the number of participants, and the amount of valuables presented did increase. For example, marriages, which previously had involved mainly the immediate members of the bride's and the groom's lineages and one or two big-men from each side, became clan affairs in which all members of the two involved clans joined for a mass celebration and exchange of valuables. As markedly greater numbers of shell valuables were available by this time, the wealth presentations were greatly inflated. Established big-men had more to present, and ambitious but poor men, who previously might not have owned sufficient shell valuables to participate, now were able to contribute to the presentations. Salisbury (1962:119) also suggests that pig production may have been increased at this time to accommodate the appetites of the larger numbers of participants in exchanges and to match the inflated shell component of the presentations.

This boom in the traditional exchange economy enjoyed by the Siane was also experienced by the Goroka Valley people, only apparently earlier and with more intensity. The valley people were in direct and more or less continuous contact with the succession of Europeans—prospectors, patrol officers, missionaries, and Allied troops—who made their headquarters in the valley and therefore received a steady supply of trade goods sooner than other groups, like the Siane, who were outside the radius of direct contact.[7] They were also in a position to receive greater quantities of shell, axes, and other trade goods; they used these both to intensify their wealth-exchange activities and to trade with outlying groups for pigs and other valuables not provided by Europeans, which could then be used to further increase the size and scope of their wealth exchanges. This steady supply of trade goods therefore allowed the valley people to exert some leverage over more distant groups in trading and exchange relations, causing an imbalance in the flow of traditional valuables that may have resulted in, among other things, a net inflow of women—purchased by or attracted to the people closest to the new sources of wealth—into the valley (Salisbury 1956).

One other reason why the valley people experienced an earlier and more intense boom in the wealth-exchange sphere than outlying groups is simply that they were pacified first. As mentioned, peace brought its benefits, among which were more time and freedom to devote to arranging, preparing for, and participating in wealth exchanges. Peace also, in a sense, prevented time saved by using steel tools in subsistence tasks from being diverted into war activities, as apparently had happened among the Siane. There, because technological change had preceded pacification, warfare activities had increased along with wealth activities as more leisure time had become available. Between 1938, when steel tools were apparently in common use, and 1945, when control started, fighting had intensified among the Siane on such a scale that Salisbury (1962:119) felt that the wars "would have rapidly devastated the whole Siane area" if the administration had not intervened. Once pacified, however, the Siane were free to turn their full attention to wealth-exchange activities, as the previously pacified valley people had done before them.

GOROKA ON THE EVE OF DEVELOPMENT

The events and developments recounted in this chapter bring us up to 1947, a crucial date in Gorokan economic history, for in that year money was first systematically introduced into the local economy, and soon thereafter the first trade store and the first coffee plantation were started there. Although local economic development really did not get under way until the early 1950s, these events mark the Gorokan entry into the cash economy and the end of the initial contact and control phase of Gorokan history.

Fortunately for the Gorokans, their initial relations with Europeans were, on the whole, more invigorating than embittering to them. The traumas of contact and pacification, of missionary conversion efforts, and of the war were not so great as to shatter their society or to demoralize them so as to make them withdraw from any new opportunities further modernization might bring. They seem, in fact, to have been eager for more change, particularly in the economic sphere. They were already enjoying a boom economy in their traditional wealth-exchange system as a result of new and better tools, enforced peace, and vastly increased supplies of shell valuables—all brought about by European contact and control—and they were looking forward to any further changes that promised them new wealth, either of a traditional kind or of a modern nature. On the eve of development the Gorokans were perhaps uniquely predisposed by their initial experiences with the outside world to take a chance on anything new offered them with the promise that it would increase their economic well-being.

3
Money and Cash Crops

Although coffee was to be the key crop in the postwar commercial development of Goroka and private European interests were to be the prime movers in the coffee industry there, the first steps toward introducing Gorokans to the cash economy were taken by the administration before definite prospects for commercial development had emerged.

The use of shells and other trade goods had been indispensable for opening up and establishing control over the Highlands, but by 1947 the administration's continued reliance on trade goods to buy provisions and pay workers was coming into question. As Jim Taylor, then district officer at Goroka in charge of the entire Highlands region, recalls the situation, two main factors favoring the substitution of money payments for trade goods were at work: sentiment was building up, both inside and outside the government, that the administration was unfairly exploiting the Highlanders and preventing them from progressing into the cash economy by not paying them in money; and trade goods, particularly shell and steel axes, were becoming harder for the local administration to obtain in the ever-increasing quantities demanded by the Highlanders.

At this time only a few of the more sophisticated Gorokans, like an enterprising man named Apo Yeharigie, who had worked for administration officers before and during the war, were aware of the use and nature of money. Apo, for example, had sold vegetables to Allied units stationed in Goroka during the war and was selling vegetables to the administration at this time. Apparently, however, his case was unusual. The overwhelming majority of Gorokans had little idea of money's utility or worth and wanted payment in trade goods, not cash, for their vegetables and labor. Taylor was therefore most concerned that, if money were to be introduced, some means be instituted to enable the Gorokans to immediately exchange their money payments for desired goods. Taylor's ideas on this subject, as expressed in his monthly report to Port Moresby, were:

> I must stress again the fact that the position is most unsatisfactory. If it is intended to place the Highlands on a cash economy, the use and value of money can only be made obvious to the people when they are given the facilities to spend it. (Recently a Chimbu native demonstrated to Mr. A. D. O. Costelloe his estimate of money by making a gesture of casting a 10/- note [$1.00] into the fire). At present a native cannot convert his cash to goods, and therefore, logically, he demands payment in goods, in shell, steel, salt etc. To enable the machinery of trade to run smoothly supplies of shell, steel and salt etc. must be built up at the District Store, or alternatively in Government Trade Stores.[1](1947)

Taylor was unable to make arrangements to restock the district stores with trade goods or to start government-run trade stores, but he did make a personal effort to educate the Gorokans working or living around the station on money matters. Taylor related to me that he had a table covered with a blanket set up outside district headquarters. Notes and coins of various denominations were spread out on the blanket, and the whole display was covered with a pane of glass. Taylor's policeman then explained the use of money to the assembled people for several days and also demonstrated how it could be used to purchase goods in a special store set up temporarily for the use of policemen. (The latter were mostly coastal New Guineans, long accustomed to the use of money, who received their pay in cash and in rations.)

This instruction proved to be inadequate. The people did not really learn what money was worth; and with virtually no money in circulation and no permanent trade store where it could be used to buy goods, there was no way these brief instructions could be reinforced by practice. In late 1947, when Taylor made his first mass payment of money wages, it was therefore poorly received; some of the workers, according to Taylor, "burst into tears, threw the money on the ground and demanded shell instead." Since Goroka had no

Money and Cash Crops 41

trade store, Taylor was forced to explain at length that indeed money had value and to urge that it be saved, with the promise that when a trade store was opened it could be used to purchase desired items.

Further cash payments were made in late 1947 and early 1948 for wages, vegetables, and land sales, including $2,880 paid to men in the Upper Asaro region for building a section of the Daulo Pass road over the Asaro Range. But it was not until June 1948 that the first permanent trade store was opened in Goroka and the people could begin to convert their money to goods.

By 1948 restrictions on prospectors and other nonadministration personnel had been lifted for Goroka and other controlled areas of the Highlands. One of the first men to take advantage of this was Jim Leahy, the older brother of the prospector Mick Leahy, who was interested in starting a coffee plantation in Goroka. While negotiating for land he set up a small store alongside the Goroka airfield and stocked it with goods flown in by chartered DC-3 from Lae. His venture found immediate acceptance, and a rush for his goods quickly developed as Gorokans converged on the store with their hoarded cash to buy trade goods. At this time Taylor recalls seeing men from the Upper Asaro, whom he had paid off some months previously for their roadwork, come running into town to buy goods carrying their pound notes aloft, clamped in the ends of split sticks. Quoting from his diary, Leahy told me he sold $1,016 worth of goods—mostly axes, other metal tools, and shells—in the first five days of operation before his stock was exhausted. He then returned immediately to Lae for another DC-3–load of goods, which he sold out (for $1,024) in a single day, for word of his store had spread throughout Goroka and people were waiting at the airstrip, cash in hand, for his second load of goods.

One witness to these hectic first trading days at Leahy's store swears that some shrewd Gorokans assumed the role of middleman from the beginning by buying extra trade goods and then taking them to rural areas for resale (or exchange with traditional goods) at a profit, or by simply buying up a stock of axes and shells, waiting until Leahy's supplies were exhausted, and then selling them at a high mark-up to customers arriving after Leahy had sold out.

The degree of monetization of Gorokan society at this time was, of course, only slight. Leahy's was the only trade store in Goroka for another year or so, and it was not really until the 1960s, when Gorokan incomes started to rise with their coffee sales and when Gorokans themselves started to build village trade stores in great numbers, that the use of money became widespread. Well into the 1950s shell and other trade goods could be used as currency, particularly in outlying areas, as well as among immigrant plantation workers from other parts of the Highlands, many of whom preferred shell to cash payment for wages.[2] Even Apo, the enterprising vegetable gardener, on occasion was forced to ask for payments in green snail shell because of the demands of his wives, who coveted these attractive shells which became very fashionable in Goroka during the late 1940s and early 1950s. Nonetheless, despite the slowness of the spread of money, Taylor's introduction of cash payments and Leahy's building of the first trade store did serve to initiate the monetization of Gorokan society, a process that gained momentum as soon as cash cropping was started in Goroka.

COFFEE INTRODUCED

Coffee has been grown in New Guinea since the turn of the century, although most, if not all, of the early plantings were of robusta coffee (*Coffea robusta*), a type primarily adapted to low-lying areas below 1,500 feet elevation. The first important planting of arabica coffee (*Coffea arabica*), the type of coffee adapted to higher altitudes and the one that is now cultivated in the Highlands, took place in 1928, when the Mandated Territory's department of agriculture set out a small arabica plantation at Wau in the mountains near the Bulolo goldfields in the Morobe District (Dwyer 1954:2). Although the plantation was subsequently sold to a settler, the department remained interested in arabica coffee and in 1937 used seed taken from that plantation to plant experimental coffee plots at the newly established Highlands Agricultural Experiment Station at Aiyura, thirty miles east of Goroka. The trials at Aiyura, which continued throughout the war years, proved that coffee flourished in Highlands conditions, a finding that was not lost on Jim Leahy, who has the distinction of having started the first coffee plantation in Goroka as well as the first trade store.

Soon after Leahy opened his store, he obtained a small plot of land five miles west of the airfield, a holding that eventually grew to include two hundred forty acres. In December 1948 he obtained his first coffee seeds from the agricultural experiment station at Aiyura and set out a nursery to grow seedlings. A year later, in December 1949 and January 1950, he planted his first seedlings. These efforts, which were more in the form of a tentative experiment than anything else, marked the beginning of the Goroka coffee industry.

Actually, Leahy was not the first to plant coffee in Goroka. Lutheran missionaries had planted some around their mission station in the 1930s (Barrie 1956:1), and during the latter years of the war ANGAU officers had had the men of several villages around the airfield and in the Bena Bena area lay out coffee gardens (Ewing 1944–1945). However, neither of these efforts had resulted in the commercial development of coffee. Not many trees had been planted around the mission station, and the berries appear to have been processed into coffee by mission personnel for local consumption only. A few New Guinean teachers of the mission had coffee planted at several locations around the valley, but no provisions for processing and marketing the product were made. Some villagers did take the initiative and plant their own coffee, using mission seed. But they were attracted by the bright red berries and the dark green foliage of the trees, and planted them as ornamental markers along the borders of their gardens, rather than as commercial plants. Some of the ANGAU-inspired coffee gardens, which amounted to perhaps five to ten acres in all, were bearing by 1947, and Gorokans started to take the berries into the government station to exchange for trade goods. The berries were then processed by station hands into ground coffee, which was issued to policemen and laborers in lieu of the usual tea ration. But sales of coffee were minor compared to those of vegetables, and this arrangement did not develop into any sort of a commercial marketing system that could have stimulated coffee growing on a large scale. It was really the pioneering efforts of settlers like Leahy and the later extension work of agricultural officers that resulted in the Gorokans' becoming major coffee producers.

While his brothers Mick and Dan were prospecting at Bena Bena and points west in the 1930s, Jim Leahy stayed behind in the Bulolo goldfields area to run a contracting business and work a small gold claim in order to provide his brothers with a steady flow of money to keep them in the field. On several occasions he did fly up to the

Highlands to visit his brothers and while there was attracted, like so many of the Europeans when they first sighted the upland valleys, by the area's agricultural prospects. During the latter part of the war, when he was an ANGAU officer attached to the Aiyura Agricultural Experiment Station, Leahy became interested in starting a tea plantation in the Highlands after the war. A visiting Dutch agriculturist with experience in plantation agriculture in the former Dutch East Indies talked him out of this idea, explaining that tea required a large capital expenditure to set up an economically viable estate and the necessary processing factory, and recommended that he try coffee instead. Experiments had already shown that coffee grew well at Aiyura, and the Dutch agriculturist pointed out that coffee would be an ideal crop for a man like Leahy with little capital, because it could be grown economically in practically any amount and because coffee processing machinery was relatively simple and inexpensive.

Accordingly, Leahy became interested in trying coffee in the Highlands, and when restrictions were lifted on the commercial activities of Europeans in the area he set about looking for a suitable site for a plantation. His first choice was Mount Hagen, where his brother Dan had settled and planted a little coffee, but the poor air service there discouraged him. He next considered Goroka, because it had the best airfield in the Highlands and frequent air connections with Lae, and in early 1945, after a frustrating two-week wait for an aircraft to take him out of Mount Hagen, he definitely decided for Goroka. It was a wise choice, for it was not until 1964 or 1965 that the Highlands Highway was completed to the point where coffee could be trucked to Lae; until then all coffee had to be airfreighted to Lae or Madang, and Goroka not only had the best air service but was closest in air miles to these ports.

In March 1950, when Leahy saw that his first seedlings were taking, he transplanted the remainder from his nursery, bringing his total coffee acreage up to twelve. As his coffee trees began to flourish, other Europeans living in or passing through Goroka became interested in growing coffee. Jim Taylor was one of the first to follow in Leahy's footsteps; he resigned as district officer to start his own plantation and settle permanently in Goroka. He was soon followed by several other men—ex-prospectors, ex-aviators, and other "old New Guinea hands"—who wanted to settle down and try their luck at coffee growing.

The administration was not then encouraging alienation of land from indigenous ownership in the Highlands, and only about a half-dozen plantations were started from 1948 to 1951. The plantations were all small; the total area alienated only amounted to about three hundred fifty acres (Howlett 1962:222). These plantations were also undercapitalized. None of the owners had substantial savings, so, since there were no local credit facilities, they were forced to raise vegetables to be airfreighted to coastal centers, to operate trade stores, or to take up some other sideline in order to make sufficient money to pay their workers and to keep themselves going for the first three years or so before their trees started bearing.

SETTLERS AND LAND ALIENATION

The trial period ended abruptly in 1952. In May of that year the administration publicly opened the Highlands to applications for land alienations (Read 1952c:440), and the following July Leahy harvested his first coffee, which he sold in Australia for seventy-three cents a pound (almost twice the 1968 price). When news of Leahy's success spread, Europeans seeking to start plantations rushed into Goroka and other favorable Highlands areas, initiating a land boom that soon had repercussions in Port Moresby and Canberra.

The administration in Port Moresby sent Ian Downs, then acting assistant director of the Department of District Services and Native Affairs, to Goroka to look into the developing boom. "Goroka," he reported, "is already a township and the atmosphere is about as feverish as that of the pre-war gold-finding days." The difference, as he put it, was that it was "not a gold rush but a land rush" that was underway (Downs 1952). This land rush, with which Downs was later to become involved personally, resulted in the alienation of dozens of agricultural properties in Goroka totaling 3,550 acres between 1952 and 1954, a tenfold increase over the acreage alienated during the previous three years (Howlett 1962:222). Although this was still a small area compared to the total area of Goroka, the incongruity of allowing such rapid alienation of land to continue (or, as many Europeans wanted, to accelerate) in a densely populated area and at a time when decolonization and expropriation of European plantation holdings were the coming thing in the world, did not go unnoticed, particularly by the critics of the administration of New Guinea and of the New Guinea policy of the Liberal-Country party coalition then in power in Canberra.

In Australia, for example, critical comments began to appear in the major newspapers: a geographer was reported as warning that continued rapid European development in New Guinea could lead to "a second Kenya"; a missionary was cited as raising the possibility that "Mau Mau type terror might soon break out" if European interests were allowed precedence over those of New Guineans; and a Labour party leader attacked the whole concept of allowing land alienations for European plantations (*Sydney Morning Herald* 1954: January 20, p. 8; January 29, p. 4; February 12, p. 2).

The warning about a second Kenya was particularly apt. Before the war, as successive patrols had come upon more and more fertile upland valleys, the phrase *a second Kenya* was commonly used, often with the express recommendation that the New Guinea Highlands one day become a center for European settlement, following the model of the White Highlands of Kenya (*Pacific Islands Monthly* 1939).[3] By the early 1950s the prospect of extensive European settlement was more than just a possibility. Coffee was a proven crop, fetching prices high enough to bring exclamations about "brown gold," and the hundreds of thousands of Highlanders formed the huge labor pool so necessary for the plantation development of a labor-intensive crop like coffee. The conditions therefore seemed ripe for the making of another White Highlands. But this was the 1950s, not the 1920s, a fact that the Mau Mau uprisings then occurring in the original White Highlands of Kenya served to underline.

Accordingly, in late 1953 the New Guinea administration, under orders from Canberra, called for a temporary halt in new land alienations, and in 1954 a new policy governing land alienation was announced. Prior to this change alienation in Goroka had been handled in an ad hoc and highly personalized manner. Extensive negotiations between the prospective settler and the group that was to sell the land generally preceded any official investigations by the administration of the land being offered. Negotiations often involved discussions of future benefits the landholding groups would gain if they sold their land. These included the receipt of trade goods and money in exchange for foodstuffs and labor, the use of the settler's boar to upgrade local pig stock, and the lasting friendship of the settler, who would show the local people how to develop their land. Once the bargain was struck, the settler applied to the administration in Goroka for the land. If the administration was satisfied that the group who wanted to sell the land did indeed own it and could spare it, the alienation was normally approved. Then the administration purchased the land from the group and leased it for ninety-nine years, without any competitive bidding, to the settler who had negotiated its alienation.

The new policy that Paul Hasluck, minister for territories, proposed was specifically designed to avoid such settler-initiated land alienations. The basic premise that no land should be alienated "unless the Administration, in its own judgement, considers that the land is neither essential now, nor will be essential in the future, to meet the needs of the natives themselves" (Hasluck 1954:525), which had supposedly always applied to land alienation, was reiterated in this formulation, but the procedures for selecting land to be alienated and for choosing the lessee were changed. The Lands Department of the territory was to select, on the basis of a land-use plan prepared in consultation with relevant government departments, those lands which could be alienated, and these were then to be advertised to all interested parties and opened to competitive bidding.

This land policy stopped the Goroka land rush. Those properties on which negotiations had been started before the 1953 freeze on new land applications were allowed to be alienated, but of the applications made after the new policy was put into effect only two were approved, the last one being in 1957 (Howlett 1962:225). Rigorous application of the principle that any land alienated must be surplus to the future as well as the present needs of the group reserved, in effect, virtually all the good land of Goroka for the Gorokans. An estimate was obtained from the Department of Agriculture that 3.3 acres of land were needed per capita for living space, subsistence gardens (including fallow land), livestock, timber, and cash crops. Then the population of each local group was projected over the ninety-nine years of an agricultural lease, assuming a yearly increase of 1.5 percent except where census data indicated a higher rate of growth. The resulting population projection, multiplied by 3.3 acres, was then matched to the land holdings claimed by each group to see if any groups would have sufficient land at the end of the ninety-nine-year lease period to allow alienation of some portion of it to a settler. Given the already fairly dense population of Goroka and the assumption of population growth at even the modest figure of 1.5 percent per annum, it can readily be seen why land alienation was effectively stopped by the application of the principle of respecting the future needs of indigenous landowners.

For example, according to the procedures described above, a village of 200, which needed 660 acres, would grow to include 874 men, women, and children ninety-nine years hence and would then require almost 3,000 acres—over four times the amount of land needed at the time any land alienation would be considered. Given these projections of Gorokan needs, only a few land-rich groups could be judged to have surplus land available for alienation, and in most cases the land involved was too inaccessible, mountainous, or otherwise unsuited for European coffee plantations.

After bitter initial opposition to the new land policy in Goroka (*Pacific Islands Monthly* 1955), the settlers there gradually came to realize they had little to gain from a continued inflow of new settlers and the alienation of more and more Gorokan land for new plantations. A sufficient number of plantations were already established or were being started in Goroka Valley and the small adjacent valleys just east of Goroka to justify the organization of efficient processing, transport, and marketing services. And, since the problem of world overproduction of coffee and possible future difficulties in marketing New Guinea's growing crop could be foreseen, the argument that it was in the established settlers' interest to prevent the opening of new plantations was easily accepted. Furthermore, some of the settlers realized that sooner or later political changes might bring demands that their estates be returned to Gorokan hands and that the fewer their number, the easier it would be to avoid expropriation (Rowley 1965:121).

THE PARTNERSHIP CONCEPT

At this time many of the European settlers of Goroka were advertising what they thought were unique and exemplary relations developing between themselves and the Gorokans. They saw themselves as aiding Gorokans to enter the money economy by promoting the general development of the region through starting the coffee industry and by directly providing the Gorokans with employment opportunities, a market for their surplus vegetables, and an example to follow in growing their own export crops. *Partnership* was the term they used to describe this allegedly developing relationship, a relationship they contrasted to that prevailing in coastal plantation areas, where, according to their analysis, the development of large plantations dependent primarily on labor brought in from elsewhere and essentially divorced from the economy of the local people had resulted in minimal local development and much bad feeling between Europeans and New Guineans.

This concept of partnership had its most vociferous spokesman in Ian Downs. Downs, who had been transferred to Goroka in late 1952 to be district commissioner for the Eastern Highlands District and who had stayed on after his resignation in 1955 to develop a large coffee estate in the Upper Asaro, wrote in the 1954–1955 annual report for the Eastern Highlands District:

> The European settlers are a force for good and are so far removed in outlook and tradition from the prejudices of the average coastal plantation manager that they are entitled to respect and our [the administration's] reciprocal help. . . . It can be recorded that the average European settler has developed a conscience in respect of the native situation. I find this a very remarkable feature and one which has to be fostered and developed constantly because it has within it the means of creating a new tradition in the relationships between European settlers and an indigenous people. The idea of Partnership is not new but the means and circumstances of creating a genuine and sincere Partnership between Europeans and natives very seldom exists. This is probably the only place in the world at the present time where the circumstances actually exist for sincere partners to be created. (1954–1955)

This statement, however paternalistic it might now appear, was in line with Gorokan thinking at the time, for many Gorokans were anxious to have settlers living in their midst and were actively seeking out buyers for their lands. Gorokans besieged administration officers with requests for buyers, and many groups approached Europeans directly or through intermediaries with offers of land for sale.

Why were Gorokans so eager to sell land? Since they had been enjoying a European-fostered boom economy in their wealth-exchange system and had just been introduced to money and its uses, they were at once optimistic about the continued economic benefits of associating with Europeans and anxious to explore the new opportunities offered them by the cash economy. As local opportunities for earning cash were then largely limited to working for the administration or selling them vegetables, Gorokans—particularly those distant from administration headquarters—were attracted by the idea of bringing European settlers into their midst, who would then be local sources of money and trade goods. In so doing they would receive an initial sum of money from the land sale (paid them by the administration) and then would have the opportunity of working for the settler and selling him surplus vegetables.

But the prospect of immediate cash payments for their land and an assured market for their produce and labor were not the only attractive features of European settlement. The money earned from land sales, from produce sales, and from working for a settler hardly brought the Gorokans anything compared to the wealth enjoyed by Europeans, and more than a few Gorokans realized this. They wanted to know the "real" formula for earning money and obtaining the goods with which the Europeans seemed so liberally endowed and thought that if a European would settle near them they might learn the secrets of the white man's affluence. Some cargo cult thinking was undoubtedly present here, although "rational" thinking about wealth production seems to have dominated over beliefs that European goods, or *kago* (cargo) in Pidgin, could be obtained by ritual means. European settlers and administration officers, alike, did all they could to encourage rational thinking about wealth production: they told the Gorokans that the Europeans' wealth was the end product of *hatwok* (hard work) and that in a rural area like Goroka they had a chance to emulate the hard work of Europeans by growing their own export cash crops.

Some European settlers today claim that Gorokans were most shrewd about the value of European plantations—as sources of cash and as demonstration plantations—and point out that land was offered for sale in such a way that European settlement was dispersed, so that each local group had its own settler and a chance to benefit by his presence. Although there may well be some truth in this theory, it ignores an additional motive in Gorokan land sales—that of using the Europeans' desire for land to make use of disputed and previously unexploitable land between hostile groups.[4] In precontact times a stretch of land between enemy groups was often a no-man's-land, virtually subject to instant dispute if one or the other group tried to clear a garden or graze pigs upon it. As the Australian-enforced peace did little to render these lands exploitable, for rarely could traditional enemies agree on dividing or sharing such land, many a Gorokan group hit upon the idea of selling off the no-man's-land adjacent to its territory. The group thereby gained cash from otherwise unusable land, brought a European settler to its doorstep, and bested its traditional enemies, particularly if investigating administration officers never discovered the disputed nature of the land and awarded none of the purchase price to other claimants (Read 1952c:442–449). The net result of this one-upmanship between traditional enemies was indeed a dispersal of that scarce commodity, the European settler, although, if the above argument holds, intergroup hostility must receive more credit for the result than any conscious and coordinated development-oriented planning by the Gorokans.

It is apparent, then, that the land rush of the early 1950s was not solely a one-sided, European affair; Gorokans as well as Europeans had their eyes firmly set on profiting from partnership. While the settlers were after cheap land, labor, and produce, the Gorokans were out to make a profit on furnishing these and were anxious to learn something of European productive techniques in order to obtain a direct and more rewarding access to the wealth the outside would have to offer. How well did each group fare in its expectations? There can be no question that most European settlers did well: before the clamp-down on land alienations thirty of them were able to obtain agricultural leases in Goroka, ranging in size from 36 to 410 acres (Howlett 1962:229–230), and with the aid of cheap labor many of these men established profitable coffee plantations, thereby laying the foundation for today's prosperous European coffee industry. But, how about the Gorokans? How well did they fare? Without bringing this account forward to include a discussion of contemporary Gorokan-settler relations, some answers may be offered for the early development period of the 1950s.

In terms of immediate monetary rewards it appears that Gorokan desires for wealth were only partially satisfied. According to the anthropologist Kenneth Read (1952c:443), who witnessed many of the early land sales, Gorokans were initially excited by the payments of several hundred dollars in notes and coins presented them by administration officers. However, he also noted that since several hundred persons often shared in the proceeds, most received "little more than a few shillings" and consequently there was "invariably some disillusionment when the sale had been completed and the proceeds distributed." Gorokan laborers were used extensively to develop plantations, but conflicts with plantation owners over wages, work attendance, and other issues resulted in their being replaced by more tractable workers from Chimbu and other remote areas of the Highlands, who were then walking the roads of Goroka in search of work. Although some local people—mostly women employed seasonally to harvest coffee—continued to work for plantations, the virtual withdrawal of Gorokans from plantation work left vegetable sales as the main way they could earn money from plantations. Gorokans did manage to make some money in this way during the first years of development but lost most of their market when plantations started relying primarily on imported rice, instead of sweet potatoes and other local vegetables, as the main staple for feeding their workers.

Small per-capita payments for land and the loss of jobs and outlets for their vegetables left the Gorokans somewhat disillusioned with the settlers, a feeling that was heightened when disputes over trespassing and the depredations of village pigs eventually broke out between most plantation owners and their Gorokan neighbors. A patrol officer investigating the resultant discontent in 1957 recorded the following statement from a Gorokan complainant:

> a. Europeans who wish to settle on our land are initially very friendly to us who own, or have rights to, the land they wish to have.
> b. After they have the land, and have planted their gardens, and built their houses, they do not seem to like us any more. They do not let us near them.
> c. They do not give us enough pay for food which we sell to them.
> d. They shoot our pigs. (McArthur 1956–1957)

From this testimony, from other statements gathered during the same investigation, and from the similar complaints I heard from Gorokans ten years later, it is clear that the personal relationships

Money and Cash Crops 53

with settlers that the Gorokans thought they were entering into when they sold their lands seldom turned out to be satisfactory to them. Except for a few men like Jim Taylor, whose efforts will be recounted shortly, settlers tended to disregard promised or implied obligations toward the land-selling groups, and when conflicts arose they generally reacted by cutting all personal bonds with those groups. Settlers defend their behavior by claiming that demands made by land-sellers were often unreasonable and beyond anything they had agreed upon when negotiating for the land. Whether one sympathizes with the settlers or with the Gorokans in these cases, the outcome was the same—a general estrangement between settlers and neighboring land-selling groups, a condition that was often exacerbated when the plantation was resold to another planter or a company, with whom the land-selling group could claim no personal bond.[5]

If, then, the Gorokans were generally disappointed with the returns from selling their land, labor, and produce and disillusioned with what they thought would be personal and reciprocal relationships between themselves and the settlers, can it be said that they gained anything substantial from the intrusion of the latter on their soil? The answer to this question must, I think, be yes. The settlers built up a coffee industry that provided Gorokans with a ready-made and highly profitable opportunity to enter the market economy as producers of export crops, not just as laborers or suppliers of foodstuffs for immigrant laborers. And it is clear that European plantations did in fact serve as demonstration plantations that stimulated Gorokans, who had never before witnessed primary production for the world market, to emulate European production techniques. It may of course be argued that the administration could have built up the coffee industry itself through government-sponsored plantation, processing, and marketing organizations and could thereby have provided the necessary stimulus for the Gorokans to enter the industry, but the fact is that the administration did not do so.

The crucial role of agricultural officers and administration officers in carrying out extension work designed to get the mass of Gorokans to plant coffee and then maintain and process it properly should not be ignored. Nevertheless, the point remains that settlers started the coffee industry largely on their own and that, as extension workers and administration officers testify, it was their pioneering activities that served to awaken the interest of Gorokans in coffee and thereby to make extension work easier.[6] For example, R. Carne, the chief agricultural officer working in Goroka during 1954 and 1955, has told me that he "supposed that extension work would have been more difficult if there had been nothing for the people to see" but that with European plantations operating before their eyes the people "knew there was something at the end of the road—at the end of the rainbow." F. Kaad, who as assistant district officer worked with Carne in introducing coffee among the Gorokans, is of the same opinion and also believes that the fact that the first three top administration officers stationed in postwar Goroka—James Taylor, George Greathead, and Ian Downs—all resigned their jobs to take up coffee growing confirmed to the Gorokans that it was surely an important and profitable activity.

The rapid creation of a highly profitable cash-crop industry in their midst gave the Gorokans a commercial opportunity shared by few New Guinean groups. The Gorokans had land to spare—not all was needed for subsistence, and only a small portion had been alienated; they had plenty of manpower, particularly since pacification and steel tools had reduced male labor requirements; and now they had a crop that could easily be planted, tended, harvested, and sold for considerable profit. Despite some settler sentiment against having Gorokans grow coffee themselves, in general the European coffee industry was prepared to buy Gorokan coffee. The settlers had the market contacts for selling coffee overseas, they had the equipment and know-how to process the Gorokan-produced coffee to the stage where it could be sold and exported, and they had the trucks to drive around the countryside to buy the coffee from Gorokan producers. Given this local marketing and processing system built up by the settlers, the crude but extensive network of roads laid down by the administration (using Gorokan labor), and a cheap and efficient airfreight system (based on DC-3 aircraft which, after unloading their inbound cargos of materials and supplies for the administration, could be chartered at low rates to carry coffee to Madang), once Gorokans started growing coffee they were able to sell it easily and get a price high enough to stimulate them to plant more and more.

A few European settlers were also directly responsible for getting the Gorokans to plant coffee. Many of the settlers had promised to aid land-selling groups and individuals to grow coffee or start other potentially profitable activities when they were negotiating for their lands, and some of these men did carry out their promises by actively helping Gorokans get started as independent coffee growers.

Jim Taylor was one of these men; his role in helping a Gorokan, Khasawaho (Baito) Heiro, become one of the first major New Guinean coffee growers is an outstanding example of what some of the propaganda promoting partnership envisaged. Baito had served with the police during the war and afterwards had become Taylor's personal servant when the latter was district officer in Goroka. When Taylor resigned to take up land next to Baito's village, Baito stayed in his employ and became the foreman of his work force. Once the plantation was well under way, Taylor gave Baito coffee seedlings, helped him to plant them on Baito's land, and encouraged Baito to tend them as he had learned while supervising Taylor's laborers.

Everything went well; the seedlings flourished and in 1957 yielded a harvest that brought Baito $4,000, an unheard-of amount of money for a Gorokan—or practically any New Guinean—in those days. Baito was, of course, overjoyed with his financial success and proud of the association with Taylor—a man of considerable local prestige because of his early patrols in Goroka in the 1930s and his role as the top administration officer for the entire Central Highlands after the war—that had made it possible. To advertise his success, as well as his association with Taylor, Baito set up a sign on the edge of his property that bordered the main road, which read, freely translated from the mixture of Pidgin and English in which it was printed:

> KHASAWAHO HEIRO
> FIVE THOUSAND TREES
> BAITO IS THE FOREMAN
> FOR JIM TAYLOR, FARMER[7]

The example set by Taylor was followed by a few other settlers, although in most cases I know about, the aid given and the results obtained were not as spectacular as in Baito's case. To be sure, some settlers gave away seeds and seedlings or simply allowed Gorokans to pick up fallen berries to use for seed or to dig out seedlings sprouting naturally in the plantations, but others were not so generous. A few men exploited the Gorokans' interest in the new crop by selling them seedlings. Some other settlers, primarily among those who had come to Goroka after the initial pioneers, turned a cold shoulder to Gorokan requests for growing coffee. Their attitude was logical enough: if Gorokans started growing coffee, they would cease to offer their services for even casual labor at harvest time and would lose interest in providing plantations with cheap vegetables. In addition, it was feared that wholesale coffee planting and production by Gorokans would lead to marketing problems as New Guinea's crop came to exceed the amount that Australian and other overseas buyers would take.

However, even if other settlers were uninterested or opposed to following Taylor's example in aiding Gorokans to grow coffee, the very presence of these settlers, their anxious search and sometimes frantic negotiations for agricultural land, and their extensive and—when the coffee started bearing—obviously profitable efforts to grow coffee could not but help to alert Gorokans that here indeed was one of the secrets of European wealth and to stimulate them to try their hands at coffee growing.

4

Gorokan Economic Growth

Although the establishment of a European coffee industry in Goroka set the stage for coffee growing by Gorokans, large numbers of them did not start growing coffee until the administration took an active role in promoting the crop. Except for a few men who, like Baito Heiro, received direct assistance from European settlers, most would-be Gorokan coffee growers had to wait until the Department of Agriculture, Stock and Fisheries (DASF) began to offer extension services in 1953 before they could find out enough about coffee to grow it properly. Although this extension effort was modest in scale, it was tremendously successful—so successful that within five years Gorokan coffee planting and production had gained such momentum that extension workers found themselves unable to keep up with the demands for their services, and the DASF was forced to worry more about overproduction of coffee than about helping Gorokans to grow it.

EARLY EXTENSION WORK

Prewar New Guinea had seen many an unsuccessful effort by the administration to promote cash-crop production through compulsory planting. Fortunately, in the postwar years a more modern extension philosophy, one based on demonstrating new crops and giving technical assistance to those who volunteered to grow them, prevailed, and the Gorokans, as well as other New Guineans were able to benefit from the services of trained agricultural officers sensitive to their needs and prepared to work with them to promote the cultivation and production of cash crops.

An early statement of the principles that were to guide coffee extension work among the Gorokans was made in 1950 by Aubrey Shindler, the director of the Aiyura experimental station and the man who trained many of the first extension workers in coffee planting and cultivation techniques. Shindler's statement came in response to a report on development prospects in the Highlands submitted by an agricultural officer stationed there briefly during 1949 and 1950 who first maintained that the Highlanders were too backward to voluntarily take up cash crops and advocated a program of compulsory planting, and then declared that a European agricultural officer would not be able to stand the pace of the constant patrolling needed, in his estimation, to make the people plant and tend new crops. Shindler's (1950) comments on these assertions were that although:

> ... the backwardness of the people may make extension work difficult ... as the officer begins to understand the people ... he should make rapid headway. ... If we take the steps of bringing our superior force to bear ... then they will not see the necessity for cash crops but only the necessity to avoid new crops ... by force or cunning of their own. I would suggest that a large degree of assistance would be more efficacious than a mild degree of compulsion. ...

And, that:

> To succeed in extension, it is absolutely necessary to keep the sought-for innovations in front of the people who are to adopt them. To do this there are two means, the demonstration at Administration centres to which people are attracted and by patrolling through an area. ... The primary result of the patrolling must be to set up an attitude of mind in the people, mainly as a result of the example set by patrolling officers. ... Such an interesting life should certainly please many a European.

The first man to put these extension principles to work in Goroka was Robert Cottle, who arrived there in 1952. Cottle, who had first seen New Guinea as a belly-gunner in Liberator bombers during the war, had just finished serving two years under Shindler at Aiyura when he was sent to Goroka to be the area's first agricultural officer.

His assignment was, however, to promote passion fruit, not coffee, as a cash crop among Gorokans.

In 1951 Cottees Passiona Ltd., an Australian firm specializing in drinks and other preparations made from passion fruit, began having difficulty obtaining passion fruit from Kenya, its principal overseas source, because of political troubles there and started looking around for a new overseas source in order to avoid sole reliance on the few Australian growers of passion fruit. Cottees learned that passion fruit was already growing in the New Guinea Highlands, having apparently been introduced there by the missionaries, and decided to set up an experimental plant in Goroka to process the pulp for shipment to Australia. The plant was opened in mid-1952 under the supervision of George Greathead, who had resigned earlier as district officer in order to start a coffee plantation. As the quality of the product made from the passion fruit that Gorokans had in their gardens was satisfactory, Cottees directed that nurseries be set up and that seedlings be distributed among Gorokans for mass planting. At this point DASF sent Cottle to Goroka to help promote the distribution and planting of seedlings.

This Cottle did, but he soon realized that only a few Gorokans could participate in the passion fruit industry and that other cash crops had to be introduced to serve a wider range of people. Passion fruit was a feasible crop for Gorokans living near the processing plant or along the few miles of road in the sub-district, but it was uneconomical in areas far from the plant or the road because of its low value per weight (a cent or less per pound to the producer). People from distant villages could certainly grow passion fruit, but no buyers could reach them, and the effort of carrying bags of passion fruit on journeys of several days to buying points would greatly reduce or eliminate any profit. Cottle therefore declined to promote passion fruit beyond a close radius of the processing plant and the road and chose, on his own initiative, to promote coffee in the remote areas of Goroka and in the Chimbu region. As a pound of coffee beans was worth at least twenty to thirty times as much to a producer as a pound of passion fruit, Cottle reasoned that coffee was the better crop to promote in areas where human porterage was likely to be the only feasible mode of transport for some time to come.

Cottle had few resources at his command other than a load of coffee seed, the services of a few New Guinean assistants, and a small quantity of trade goods and hand tools. A typical patrol to promote coffee began on the west side of the as-yet-unbridged Asaro River. There he would hire carriers—using money or trade goods for wages—to carry boxes of seed and tools and would set out on foot to cover villages from the west side of the river to well into the Chimbu country. On his first patrols through the area Cottle says he spent most of his time talking—explaining what coffee was, how it was grown, and how much it would bring in cash or trade-good equivalents. If at the end of these discussions, which often went late into the night, one or two men would volunteer to give coffee a try, the following day Cottle and his New Guinean assistants would distribute seed to the interested men, show them how to prepare ground for a nursery, and then demonstrate how to plant the seed and tend the nurseries until the seedlings were ready for transplanting the following year. If his talks brought no positive response from a village, Cottle simply moved on to the next one without attempting to demonstrate anything or to force anyone to plant coffee, for he knew that progress could only be made with people who volunteered. He also knew that there were many villages in the Eastern Highlands to cover and that if the people of one village were unresponsive, he could usually find responsive individuals in another along the way.

In most areas Cottle had little difficulty in finding men willing to experiment with coffee. Most of the men who volunteered to set out these first DASF-sponsored nurseries and coffee plots were already acquainted with coffee, either from the early Lutheran- or ANGAU-sponsored attempts to introduce the crop or from the more recent activities of the European settlers who were then busily acquiring land and planting it in coffee. Many had either tried to exploit old plantings commercially or to set out new coffee plots on their own, and as their attempts had been largely unsuccessful, they were most anxious to obtain Cottle's expert advice and aid. This is particularly true for central Goroka, which Cottle had bypassed in his initial coffee extension work because the area was well situated for passion fruit growing and marketing. The many requests for his services from central Gorokans forced Cottle to offer these people advice and aid in coffee planting, and by early 1953 he had established a string of coffee nurseries that extended from Bena

Bena well into the Chimbu region. After the village nurseries were established, Cottle returned to each area and, with the help of Gorokan assistants, helped interested men select proper land, clear it, and then plant coffee seedlings and shade trees on it. By late 1954 a number of the most ambitious men in each area had set out model plantations with the aid of Cottle and his assistants, and other men had made innumerable small plantings of coffee.

Intergroup rivalry played a role in the spread of coffee cultivation throughout Goroka; agricultural officers active during the early development of the Gorokan coffee industry have told me that one means they used to spur coffee planting among lagging groups was to compare their performance unfavorably and in public with those of more progressive groups. However, this use of invidious intergroup comparison does not mean that agricultural officers encouraged communal ownership of coffee plots. In particular, both R. S. Carne and J. W. Barrie, who succeeded Cottle, strove to avoid any type of planting wherein ownership or use of the trees would be vested in a group rather than an individual. Each had had previous experiences elsewhere in New Guinea where a village or a kinship unit, working as a group, had planted and unsuccessfully tried to exploit some commercial crop, and both wanted to avoid repeating these unsatisfactory attempts at communal cash cropping in Goroka.

Barrie, for example, had started his career as an agricultural officer in New Guinea in the Morobe District, where he had been influenced by administration officers who wanted to compile a good record of the number of cash crops planted by the people in their district, and who assured Barrie (then newly arrived in New Guinea) that local society was communal and that therefore the most expedient course, and the one most in tune with local custom, was to have a whole village plant and exploit cash crops as a group. But although Barrie found that he could get the Morobe villagers to plant coconuts, coffee, and other cash crops, organizing the proper maintenance and exploitation of the plantations was another matter. In most cases the people could neither be cajoled nor forced into maintaining and exploiting them in the communal fashion envisaged by the administration officers who had advised Barrie. Strife among villagers over who was to maintain the plantings and then over who had harvest rights soon broke out, rendering these plantations virtually unexploitable and leaving a bad taste in the mouths of both the villagers and the agricultural officers about communal cash cropping. Carne had had a similar experience before coming to Goroka and, in addition, had been fortunate in having been able to tour cash cropping areas in Africa before taking up his post in Goroka. In Africa he had received the universal advice, born of local experience, to avoid communal ventures and to concentrate on individual plantings.

In seeking to promote individually controlled coffee plots in Goroka the agricultural officers were actually following local precedents in land use, for the growing and exploitation of sweet potatoes and other subsistence crops was largely an individual matter for a man and his wife or wives. The agricultural officers did realize, however, that in traditional Gorokan society there was an important element of cooperation and pooling of resources, and they sought to tap this without violating the principle of individual coffee plots. The formula they hit upon was simple, effective, and congenial to the Gorokans: coffee nurseries, where seedlings were grown for distribution to individual planters, became a group responsibility, and the subsequent planting, caring for, and exploitation of the coffee trees were an individual responsibility.

The coffee nurseries established at central locations could be called communal in that they were cleared, planted, and cared for by the people of the surrounding area, who typically represented a traditional clan, subtribe, or tribal group and who were used to acting together in work and on military and ceremonial occasions. According to Barrie, the tie between the local community and the coffee nursery was really forged when a sign identifying the nursery with the group was put up in front of each nursery for all, including erstwhile enemy groups, to see. The cut-out ends of gasoline drums were used as signboards; on them the agricultural officer would print the name of the traditional group, and then a local artist would, according to Barrie, paint an abstract design to symbolize the group. (These designs, as described to me by Barrie, appear to have been similar to the designs painted on the *gerua* boards worn by Gorokan dancers during feasts and exchanges.)

The signs marking each nursery elicited the element of group pride so important to Gorokans; they were tangible symbols of a group's progress, evident to members of the group themselves as well as to members of other groups, and hence served to reinforce local interest in coffee and to spur competition between groups for the establishment of nurseries. A similiar device was used by DASF officers to stimulate individual Gorokans to clear and plant a sizable coffee plot. (A one-half acre plot, with about three hundred trees, was the minimum size desired by the DASF; many Gorokans exceeded this minimum.) Once a man had planted seedlings taken from his group nursery, DASF personnel would count his trees and erect a sign on his plantation on which were printed the man's name and the number of trees he had planted. Although few Gorokans could read or count into the hundreds, they were able to identify the name and the relative size of the printed number, and competition to plant the largest number of seedlings, and hence to have the largest number painted on one's sign, served to spur individual coffee planting efforts.

That only individually controlled coffee plots were promoted does not mean, however, that groups did not work together to prepare and lay out plantations. Three main forms of collective effort were employed to clear land and plant coffee. First, a reciprocal work team, composed of men who would work on each member's plot in turn, was used by many groups as an efficient way to utilize collective labor for the arduous tasks of clearing, digging holes, and planting the hundreds of trees in each man's plot. Second, in some areas, as along the fertile banks of streams and rivers in the Bena Bena region, a large group sharing rights to the land would join together to clear and plant the land (Howlett 1962:91–92). Then, once the land was planted, separate plots would be allocated to individuals for exploitation. Third, an important man—usually the one who had taken charge of the group nursery—employed his clansmen to prepare and plant his own coffee plantation without any apparent direct reciprocity or payment. These planting efforts, which often involved plantations of several thousand trees, worried DASF officers, who considered that they either bordered on the communal or represented blatant exploitation of labor by an important man. It is fortunate that the DASF officers did not interfere with the large plantings, however, for they represented a development crucial to the emergence of a self-sustaining drive for economic growth among the Gorokans.

How these important men perceived the potential for coffee and then were able to combine land, labor, and, in some cases, capital in the form of cash savings derived from other commercial enterprises to start the first major Gorokan-owned plantations is treated at length in the next chapter. Here it is important to emphasize that these coffee entrepreneurs were not lone individuals acting in isolation from their social milieu. While these men were certainly interested in gaining personal status and wealth by becoming major coffee growers, they also saw to it that their clansmen and neighbors followed their example and also took up coffee cultivation.

The Gorokan Coffee Boom

At first not all Gorokans were interested in this new crop of coffee. Some simply had no idea of what coffee was, and even among men who knew a little bit about coffee there was apparently some skepticism of the whole idea that coffee beans could be exchanged for money, which in turn could be used to buy goods. Others, particularly during the early stages of coffee's introduction in Goroka, were absolutely opposed to the crop, considering it a wasteful, if not dangerous, plant to introduce. A few of Baito Heiro's clansmen, for example, warned him not to plant coffee lest it kill all their pigs. But these skeptics were convinced of their error when no increase in pig deaths occurred as Baito planted, grew, and harvested his coffee, and they started to plant coffee themselves after they saw how much money Baito received for his first harvest. In fact, as the efforts of Baito and the other early coffee planters began to pay off, their clansmen and neighbors (including jealous enemies) sought to emulate their success by planting their own coffee. This effort by Gorokans to follow or compete with the first coffee entrepreneurs led to mass plantings throughout Goroka that soon assumed boom proportions.

This Gorokan coffee boom was unexpected; few Europeans, in or out of the administration, had thought that coffee growing would catch on so quickly. Within a few years after extension work had started, the demand for aid and instruction began to outpace the ability of agricultural officers to provide extension services. Even as early as 1955 the director of DASF in Port Moresby complained to the government secretary concerning the nascent coffee boom in Goroka and other Highlands centers: "it is impossible for the present staff to keep up with demands for assistance sent in by natives. More staff is urgently needed there to direct and supervise

Gorokan Economic Growth

the coffee activity in the area" (Dwyer 1955). Despite the staff increases in Goroka that followed this plea, the Gorokan demand for extension services continued to exceed DASF's ability to provide service.

The situation became acute during the coffee planting season of the wet months of late 1957 and early 1958. Not enough seedlings were available from DASF-sponsored nurseries to meet the needs of Gorokan coffee growers or would-be growers. In some areas people had prepared land and dug holes for up to four times as many seedlings as there were available; when they realized that there were not enough seedlings to go around, they clamored for seeds and assistance to start more nurseries to grow sufficient seedlings to fill their planting needs. In reporting the rising Gorokan interest in coffee, D. J. Kingston (1958), the district agricultural officer, could therefore write with some satisfaction that "the native people of the Goroka Sub-District have shown a great desire in 1958 to increase the planting of coffee as a cash crop" but had to admit in his next sentence that "due to the increased demand it was physically impossible to give these people as much departmental assistance as in previous years. The supervision alone of the preparation and planting of the number of nurseries that the people requested could not be completed during the wet season."

Because he realized that he and his staff could not begin to cope with the accelerating Gorokan demand for assistance unless some new strategy of extension work were devised to enable the DASF staff to serve more people, Kingston switched the emphasis in extension work from direct instruction and aid at the village level to the demonstration of all phases of coffee culture at centralized locations in Goroka to serve large, multivillage groups. These field days, as they were called, were well attended: nine of them held in Goroka and surrounding areas during the first quarter of 1958 drew an average of more than eight hundred growers each. If these attendance figures and the subsequent expansion of Gorokan coffee planting are any indication, the field days served their purpose in keeping up Gorokan interest in coffee and in stimulating continued planting efforts.

But, as the growth of coffee planting continued among the Gorokans and other Highlanders, the DASF became worried about overreliance on coffee and the possibility that the growing world surplus might make it difficult to market New Guinea's crop if planting and production were allowed to expand further. After a DASF conference on coffee held in Goroka in 1959, orders were issued to agricultural officers in Goroka and elsewhere to temporarily reduce the emphasis on coffee and to cease active encouragement of new plantings until accurate marketing forecasts could be made (Montgomery 1958–1959). In 1961, according to what W. Conroy, now director of the DASF, has told me, the ban on active encouragement of new plantings was made permanent and a definite decision was made to switch extension activities from coffee to promoting other cash crops, such as passion fruit, peanuts, local vegetables, and livestock, primarily cattle and pigs.

This ban on further encouragement of new plantings stemmed from restrictions New Guinea had to accept as a condition of joining, with Australia, the International Coffee Agreement Organization. In joining this organization New Guinea and Australia were considered to form one production/consumption unit, and New Guinea thereby earned the right to sell on the world market at favorable prices upheld by the agreement organization as much coffee as Australia consumed (regardless of whether Australia bought all of New Guinea's coffee). As New Guinea's production was then less than Australia's consumption, this gave growers an assured market for their coffee. The agreement organization required, however, that New Guinea take steps to reduce the expansion of coffee production by, first, banning any further alienation of land for European coffee plantations and, second, ceasing active extension work designed to spread coffee growing among New Guineans. Although extension workers were allowed to continue to aid New Guineans in the maintenance of their coffee plots and in coffee processing and sales, joining the International Coffee Agreement Organization meant the end of the active phase of coffee extension work.

However, by the time these restrictions went into effect in the early 1960s, the Gorokans and other Highlands coffee growers had entered into a period of self-sustaining growth; they knew by then how to set out their own nurseries, transplant the seedlings, and bring the maturing coffee trees into production. The early and mid-1960s were actually the period of greatest growth in Gorokan coffee plantings. In 1962 a census of coffee trees indicated that the

Gorokans had already planted almost two million coffee trees, and censuses from 1963 to 1965 (after which coffee censuses were not made) revealed an annual increase of around a half-million trees (Table 1). These figures, even though they probably, according to DASF officers, represent underenumerations, indicate how much momentum had developed in the Gorokan coffee boom by the mid-1960s.

TABLE 1. Coffee Trees Planted by Gorokans in Goroka Sub-District to 1965.

Year	Number of trees planted
To 1962	1,956,000
1963	481,000
1964	419,000
June 1965	582,000
TOTAL	3,438,000

By the late 1960s the bulk of the Gorokan plantings had begun to bear, and Gorokan coffee production began to be a significant part of New Guinea's total coffee production. By the fiscal year 1967–1968, for example, the DASF estimated that Gorokans produced 2,500 tons of parchment coffee, or more than 12 percent of all the coffee produced (by both Europeans and New Guineans) in New Guinea that year (Table 2). In the fifteen years from the time the DASF had first started promoting coffee, the Gorokans—a people isolated from the outside world until the 1930s and not even acquainted with money until the late 1940s—had become major producers of export crops for the world market.

In terms of tons of coffee produced, and in terms of the Gorokan share of the total New Guinea production, the Gorokan achievement is impressive. However, it must be remembered that these figures represent the combined efforts of many thousands of Gorokan

TABLE 2. Gorokan Coffee Production and Income.

Fiscal Year	Tons of Coffee[1]	Coffee Income	Population[2]	Cash Income Per Capita
1954–55[3]	1+	$ 360	45,800	$ 0.27
1958–59[3]	100	40,720	49,700	1.36
1960–61[4]	143	63,420	51,600	1.61
1961–62	400	177,410	52,500	3.96
1964–65	910	384,385	55,700	7.37
1965–66	1,110	464,640	57,000	8.50
1967–68	2,500	1,047,500	60,000	15.79

1. Parchment (unhulled) coffee.
2. Estimates from Goroka Sub-District Office.
3. Estimates from Howlett (1962:101).
4. Statistics for this and the following years are taken from estimates in DASF, annual reports on Goroka. Tonnage and income figures are estimates only, as no record is kept of actual production and income.

coffee growers. Figured on a per-capita basis the Gorokan production yields (in 1967–1968) a yearly income of fifteen dollars or so for each man, woman, and child (Table 2). Per-capita cash income among the Gorokans, even if we allow another ten dollars or so per person for revenue derived from market vegetables, passion fruit, peanuts, other cash crops, livestock, business enterprises, and wage labor, is therefore not all that impressive in itself. Twenty-five dollars a year is indeed a low per-capita cash income, putting the Gorokans well down on any scale, even one that would include other underdeveloped countries of the world.

But any attempt to compare the Gorokan economic situation with that prevailing in many other underdeveloped countries in terms of per-capita cash income would have to take into account one crucial feature of the Gorokan experience. Unlike many economically stagnant peasant societies, Gorokan participation in the market economy has been marked by greatly increasing rewards. While Gorokan cash income may be low, the rate of increase has been high; from a few cents in the early 1950s, per-capita cash income has risen in quantum jumps to around twenty-five dollars—an increase of a hundredfold or more in a decade and a half. This steep increase has been as impressive to the Gorokans as it would be to any analyst; their experience of constantly increasing cash rewards has given them a confidence in their ability to make money and in the cash economy itself that is perhaps rare among low-income people around the world.

CONSPICUOUS INVESTORS

Just as the Gorokans were beginning to plant coffee, Ragnar Nurkse, a distinguished economist, published *Problems of Capital Formation in Underdeveloped Countries.* One of the problems he stressed related to the supposed demonstration effect of consumption standards current in affluent countries on consumption behavior in underdeveloped countries. Nurkse posited:

> When people come into contact with superior goods or superior patterns of consumption, with new articles or new ways of meeting old wants, they are apt to feel after a while a certain restlessness and dissatisfaction. Their knowledge is extended, their imagination stimulated; new desires are aroused, the propensity to consume is shifted upward. (1953:58–59)

The outcome, in terms of capital formation, of exposing people in underdeveloped areas to new and higher standards of consumption is therefore, according to Nurkse's reasoning, that the people will spend so much of their money on new consumption goods that little or nothing will be saved for investment. Nurkse's analysis leads to the inevitable conclusion that the demonstration effect will tend to prevent citizens of underdeveloped countries from making significant contributions to local capital formation.

If Nurkse had waited a few years before publishing his analysis and could have seen how the Gorokans were using their newly earned coffee money, he might not have been so pessimistic. Certainly, the Gorokans envied the Europeans' wealth and sought to buy European goods when they started to earn money, but they were selective and restrained in their purchases. If we may divide the purchases Gorokans made when they first started using money, into consumption goods, on the one hand, and capital goods, on the other hand, their ability to pass up consumer goods, save their money, and then invest it in productive assets is striking. If anything, the Gorokans have been more impressed by the capital goods of the Europeans than by the consumer goods and have sought to emulate European investment, rather than consumption, behavior.

The demonstration effect has indeed been at work in Goroka, but not in the way foreseen by Nurkse.

BUSINESS FIRST

Bisnis, the key Pidgin term in Gorokan commercial thinking, has a wider range of meaning than its English progenitor. To the Gorokans it means any revenue-producing activity or any investment made to produce revenue. Market gardening, coffee growing, operating a trade store, investing in a truck, or building up a cattle herd are all examples of *bisnis* in Gorokan terms, for they are activities that make money, or promise to do so.

If any people could be adjudged to be business-minded, it would be the Gorokans. To reach this conclusion one need only overhear their conversation—in Pidgin or in one of the vernaculars—and note the frequent and stressed use of the term *bisnis,* or to look at their record of investing their meager cash resources in what they consider to be profitable, or potentially profitable, *bisnis* activities.

Gorokans were investing small amounts of money, derived mainly from wage labor and the sale of vegetables or land, in capital goods well before they had any coffee revenue for larger-scale investment. Steel axes, knives, and shovels were among the most popular goods sold in the trade stores operating in Goroka during the late 1940s and early 1950s. Jim Leahy recalls, for example, that most of the goods he sold in 1948 when he opened Goroka's first trade store were tools and that the Gorokan demand soon outran the supplies available in Lae, forcing him to search as far away as Rabaul on New Britain for steel tools to sell to his eager Gorokan customers. And it is probably not stretching the point to say that the purchase of shells, the second most popular commodity sold in the early trade stores, was also an example of Gorokan investment orientation, for these shells were used as personal investments, designed primarily to increase one's status through their display and exchange. If this suggestion that shell valuables may be classed as capital goods seems strained at this point, it will not seem so farfetched as the discussion of the motives behind Gorokan investment behavior unfolds.

Planting and tending coffee, of course, required the use of the tools Gorokans had to purchase, and as their coffee trees began to bear, Gorokans were forced to make further capital investments for processing the coffee. While many of the small growers got along, at least in the early stages of the development of the Gorokan coffee industry, with pulping their coffee berries by hand (or with their teeth), fermenting the pulped berries in hollowed-out logs, and then drying the cleaned beans on any board or flat surface that was available, the bigger growers, who had some cash saved from previous commercial ventures, invested in pulping machines, concrete or wooden fermenting vats, and raised wooden drying racks.

Those administration and agricultural officers who were promoting coffee growing were pleased at the willingness of these men to invest in processing equipment and hoped that when Gorokan coffee started bearing well all the growers would put some portion of their earnings into processing equipment, wire fencing, and other equipment needed for efficient coffee production and other agricultural development. However, they and the members of the European business community in Goroka actually anticipated that much of the Gorokans' coffee money would be spent in trade stores for clothing, pots and pans, imported foodstuffs, and other consumer goods. They had little inkling of and made no preparation for the interest in *bisnis* investment that was to develop as soon as the Gorokans started making money.

What Baito Heiro, Taylor's protégé, did with the four-thousand-dollar payment for his first coffee harvest in 1957 should have alerted the local Europeans that the Gorokans had more than consumer goods in mind when it came to spending their coffee money. Baito wanted to use his to buy a four-wheel-drive Land Rover utility truck (which, along with the jeep, was about the only available vehicle capable of operating on Goroka's primitive roads). He therefore ordered one from England, which after being landed at a coastal port had to be airfreighted into Goroka, for the road link to the coast was not completed then. Baito did not want the Land Rover for just his private use; he wanted it to give rides to his clansmen and others who had helped him get started in coffee, to carry paying loads of passengers and freight around Goroka, and simply to show off his success by being the first Gorokan *bisnisman* to own and operate a commercial vehicle.

Trade stores actually preceded commercial vehicles as the first major post-coffee business investment of the Gorokans. By 1958, the first year for which records are available, five Gorokan-owned trade stores were licensed. As more and more coffee money became available, the number of Gorokan stores multiplied rapidly. By 1967 447 such stores were licensed (Table 3), and as some Gorokans operated stores without bothering to get licenses, the actual number of Gorokan-owned stores was probably higher. Using just the licensed figure, it is evident that there was one trade store for about every 130 persons in 1967, a ratio which is not deceiving, for the *tredstoa* (trade store) had by then become as much a fixture of the Gorokan village as the men's house had been in the past.[1]

TABLE 3. Gorokan-owned Trade Stores Licensed in Goroka Sub-District.[1]

Year	Number of licenses	Year	Number of licenses
1958	5	1964	95
1959–60	no data	1965	290
1961	8	1966	338
1962	20	1967	
1963	49	(as of May)	447

1. Figures were obtained from trading-license records held in the sub-district office in Goroka.

Although Apo and a few other Gorokans purchased commercial vehicles in the late 1950s, because of their high cost, vehicles were not purchased in quantity until the mid-1960s, when coffee revenues began to increase significantly (Table 4). By 1967 they were buying commercial vehicles—ranging from small pick-up trucks or utilities costing less than $2,000 to medium-sized trucks and buses in the $3,000 range and even a few heavy-duty trucks costing more than $5,000—at the rate of four or five dozen a year. (The exact rate is difficult to determine, as some Gorokans buy and register their trucks in the coastal port of Lae.) Despite the frequent breakdowns and poor maintenance that were keeping many of their vehicles off the road, at least sixty to seventy commercial vehicles were being operated by Gorokans in 1967.

TABLE 4. Gorokan-owned Commercial Vehicles Registered in Goroka Sub-District.[1]

Year	Number of Vehicles Registered	Year	Number of Vehicles Registered
1963	5	1966	58
1964	17	1967	
1965	42	(as of May)	68

1. Figures were obtained from the Motor Vehicle Registry office in Goroka and do not include Gorokan vehicles registered in Lae. No reliable data are available for before 1963.

These figures would seem to indicate that Gorokans are fairly well served by their own vehicles (even though there is not yet, as is true of trade stores, one per village), a conclusion that can also be reached by watching the constant movement of local vehicles on Gorokan roads, particularly on market days, when Gorokan utilities, trucks, and buses ply the roads to and from rural areas and the town.

Unlike the Gorokan adoption of coffee growing, which owed so much to direct administration aid as well as to the encouragement of some settlers, the movement to own and operate their own stores and commercial vehicles was largely an independent Gorokan development. They saw the need for stores and trucks themselves and in most cases started their enterprises without outside aid or encouragement. Until recently Gorokans received virtually no government or private aid and financing for setting up their businesses; in fact, many of the Gorokan pioneers in business say that administration officials looked askance at their efforts and tried to discourage them from investing in nonagricultural enterprises, arguing that their money was better spent on improving their land, developing new crops, building modern houses, and buying modern furnishings and clothes.

Fortunately, in the early 1960s the DASF realized that the Gorokans were interested in investing in new enterprises and had the money to do so. To tap this investment potential and to try to inaugurate commercial livestock production, they first set up a program to build up small commercial herds of cattle and later started to promote small commercial piggeries. Cattle projects, especially, seem to have caught the interest of Gorokans and have become a major investment interest for some groups rich in grasslands.

One other type of business investment that Gorokans have begun experimenting with is restaurants. Trade store owners, in particular, noted that there were transient New Guineans about who wanted meals and had the money to pay for them, so they started putting up small restaurants which catered to these men and any local people who wanted to buy meals. By 1967 there were at least two dozen small restaurants operating in Goroka, including a few well-built European-style structures equipped with modern stoves and refrigerators and featuring full meals of meat, rice, sweet potato or other local vegetables, and tea, served with bread and butter.

All these enterprises, including the DASF-sponsored pig and cattle projects, have been almost wholly financed by the Gorokans themselves. Although since the inauguration of the Papua and New Guinea Development Bank in late 1967 the credit situation for New Guineans has begun to change, before then New Guineans received little in the way of loans from trading banks, business firms, and the Native Loans Development Board (the Development Bank's predecessor). When New Guineans have gone into business for themselves, it has largely been with their own money (ToRobert 1967). Gorokans are no exception to this general statement; they have had to rely primarily on their own savings for their investments. A conservative estimate of investments made during the year from May 1966 to April 1967 indicates that Gorokans invested at least $180,000 in buying commercial vehicles, building and stocking new stores, buying coffee processing equipment and other agricultural tools, starting cattle and pig projects, and building and equipping restaurants (Table 5). Of this total I estimate that less than $10,000 came from external credit sources (Table 6).[2] In other words, at least 95 percent of Gorokan investments during this period were self-financed.

POOLING MONEY

Where did you get the money to build your store? I asked this question of scores of Gorokan store owners, as well as many Gorokans operating trucks, cattle projects, and other enterprises.

TABLE 5. Gorokan Investments, May 1966 to April 1967[1]

Item	Number	Cost
Commercial vehicles	45	$130,000
Trade stores	100	20,000
Coffee growing and processing equipment	?	15,000
Cattle and pig projects	?	12,000
Restaurants	3–5	3,000
TOTAL		$180,000

1. These are my estimates based on trade store and motor vehicle license records, on DASF records of cattle and pig projects, and on investigations of selected enterprises.

TABLE 6. Investment Loans to Gorokans from External Sources, May 1966 to April 1967[1]

Source	Number	Amount
Trading banks	7[2]	$3,800
Native Loans Development Board	0	0
European firms and individuals	?	5,000
TOTAL		$8,800

1. These are my estimates derived from interviews with officials of the institutions involved and with European and Gorokan businessmen.
2. This total includes two vehicle installment-plan loans that were arranged, but not actually financed, by local banks.

With few exceptions, the answer was the same: "It came from coffee."[3] But this was only a partial answer, for except for a few individuals like Baito, who enjoyed substantial windfall profits from large coffee holdings, the majority of Gorokans could not finance their business ventures solely from their own savings. As per-capita coffee earnings for 1966–1967 (the year for which total Gorokan investments were estimated) were under ten dollars and overall cash earnings were less than twenty dollars, it was obvious to me that Gorokans must have devised some means of raising capital to finance enterprises too costly for most single individuals to undertake.

Most Europeans in Goroka, both from the administration and

the business community, that I spoke with about the problem theorized that Gorokans were able to make substantial investments because people from whole villages, clans, or even larger groupings would put their money into a common investment pool to finance a communal venture. The most outstanding example they could cite involved the people of Watabung, who had put together a large investment fund and presented it to Bimai Noimbano, an entrepreneur whose case will be considered in detail in the next chapter, for the purpose of buying a truck to be used to take coffee out of their area and bring supplies into it. As the estate of Bimai, who died in 1966, was just being inventoried when I arrived in Goroka, I was able to secure solid information on this case by consulting a notebook in which Bimai's helper had recorded the names of all contributors, the amounts they had contributed, and their clan or village affiliations. In the notebook nineteen village or clan groups were represented by 784 Watabung men and women (plus a few outsiders residing in Watabung), who gave an average of $3.31 apiece in individual donations that ranged from $0.10 to $100 to form an investment pool of $2,597.

This is the most impressive example, considering the number of contributors and the wide range of social groups involved, that I found of the Gorokan practice of forming investment funds, a process they term *bungem mani* (pooling money). While I found this Gorokan facility for pooling money unusual in view of the apparent difficulty so many low-income peoples around the world have in combining their savings for investment, the Gorokans thought little of it. To them it was a natural way to obtain the capital to finance the businesses they wanted to start. One perceptive Gorokan businessman, who realized that I found their ability to pool money unusual and sought some explanation, discussed it with me in terms of the traditional practice of clansmen of pooling their pigs, shells, and other valuables to present to another group. Just as we collected our valuables together in the past for exchanges, so today do we pool our money to start businesses, was his explanation. Pooling money appeared, then, as an adaptation of traditional wealth-pooling behavior to meet modern needs, a view which subsequent research tended to support and one which sets modern Gorokan investment behavior firmly in the traditional social context from which it developed.

However, upon investigating case after case of businesses financed by pooled funds, I found it to be an exaggeration to think of them all as communal enterprises—as "clan stores" or "village trucks," for example. My investigations revealed that, in the first place, the typical number of people pooling money for a venture was small—around a half-dozen—and, in the second place, although most of the contributors were generally drawn from a common traditional group, the enterprises were usually under the control of one or two leaders, not the whole group.

Data from a survey undertaken in 1968 of the contributors to fifteen commercial vehicles bought by people in the Lowa and Bena Bena census divisions may be cited to back up these points (Table 7). This survey revealed that the mean number of contributors per vehicle (which ranged in price from $200 for a battered old Land Rover to $3,800 for a new heavy-duty truck) was only 7.4 and that ten of the fifteen vehicles had 6 or fewer contributors each. And, although the survey also revealed that most of the contributors were indeed from a single subclan, clan, or tribal group,[4] it also showed that most vehicles had one principal contributor, who put up 50 percent or more of the purchase price. Upon questioning contributors about their vehicles, it usually was revealed that the principal contributor was considered the *papa bilong bisniska* (owner of the commercial vehicle) and that although he might allow one or two other contributors (particularly those who had contributed large amounts of money themselves or who were particularly forceful men) some say in the management of the vehicle, he appeared to exercise a degree of personal control over the vehicle that would disqualify it from being considered a village truck in any literal sense.

The modest number of contributors per vehicle and the considerable amounts ($1,100 per vehicle on the average, with a range of from $60 to $3,100) put up by principal contributors indicated in this survey would seem to contrast greatly with the data on the Watabung case of pooled money. The apparent difference between the two situations diminishes somewhat, however, when we consider that Bimai Noimbano allegedly added $418 of his own money to the Watabung investment pool to bring it to just over $3,100 and that the two situations probably represent different stages in the evolution of Gorokan capital formation practices.

In the early 1960s, when the Watabung people pooled their money to buy a truck, they had very little cash on hand, for only some of their coffee plantings had begun to bear. Financial necessity therefore forced them to join together in a large group to raise the necessary capital. The vehicle survey done in the Lowa and Bena Bena areas deals mainly with vehicles purchased recently, when the people involved were getting considerable amounts of money from their fully mature coffee plantings. Differential cash resources would therefore seem to explain much of the contrast between the two situations and would also seem to suggest, as do investigations of selected enterprises, that as Gorokans became more prosperous the number of contributions to investment funds decreased, the share per individual increased, and principal investors who made large, if not majority, contributions came to the fore.

A survey undertaken in 1967 of twenty-five trade stores in the Lowa and Bena Bena areas revealed a pattern similar to that of the vehicle survey as to the number of people pooling their money to make up the initial capital (Finney 1969:42–44). The mean number of contributors per store was 5.1, a figure somewhat less than that for vehicles—as one would expect, given the lower initial outlay involved in building and stocking a store ($275 on the average, with a range of from $12 to $1,300). Of the twenty-five stores surveyed, I found only one that even remotely approached the European conception of the village trade store. It had been started by two men who solicited funds from most of their fellow villagers, which meant a total of about twenty-five men and women. However, the two promoters did not run the store as a communal enterprise; in fact, so individualized was their management that the store building—a large and substantial structure of timber and galvanized iron sheets, which had been purchased with the pooled funds of the villagers—had been partitioned into two halves. Each promoter had taken over one half in which to store and display his wares and to trade for his own profit.

MOTIVATION

Why have Gorokans shown, to use the language of the economist, such a high propensity to invest? This question brings us into the area of motivation, usually considered the domain of the psychologist. Here, however, I want to look at the motives behind Gorokan

TABLE 7. Contributors to Some Commercial Vehicles Purchased by Gorokans from the Bena Bena and Lowa Census Divisions.[1]

Vehicle Number	1	2	3	4	5	6	7	8	9	10	11	12	13	14	15
Number of contributors	2	2	2	2	2	3	4	4	6	6	9	15	17	18	18
Price in dollars	2,600	2,500	2,080	1,900	450	290	3,500	700	2,450	200	1,830	3,200	2,255	3,800	964
% of price paid by principal contributor	92	80	96	53	56	93	86	57	57	30	40	31	53	29	21
% of secondary contributors from same subclan as principal contributor	0	100	100	100	100	50	67	33	100	100	22	53	31	78	35
% of secondary contributors from same clan as principal contributor	0	100	100	100	100	50	67	33	100	100	67	100	62	83	88
% of secondary contributors from same tribal group as principal contributor	0	100	100	100	100	50	100	100	100	100	67	100	94	89	94

1. Vehicles 1, 9, 10, 12, and 14 are from the Bena Bena census division; the remainder are from the Lowa census division.

investment behavior with data derived from my essentially sociological observations and interviews with Gorokan businessmen.

Kisim winmani (to obtain profits)[5] was the most frequent response by Gorokan businessmen to my questions as to why they started their stores, bought their trucks, or initiated other enterprises. However, upon further questioning and detailed investigations of specific enterprises, it became obvious to me that making money was only part of the motivation behind Gorokan investment. At least two other motives can be isolated, which, for purposes of discussion, may be covered by the terms *service* and *prestige*.

The service aspect of Gorokan enterprises, particularly in the case of the first stores and trucking ventures to be started in a region, should not be underrated. A store can be a valuable asset for villagers, particularly those who live far from town or the main highway, for with a store close at hand they can easily buy an axe, salt, cloth, or whatever they want without taking a long walk into town or down to the highway. Similarly, a truck is a most useful investment for people who live off the main road and who are not served by any regular means of transportation, for they can use it to haul their coffee to coffee mills, to carry their vegetables to the market, and to take back goods from the town. When the Watabung people collected money for a truck to be purchased and operated by Bimai Noimbano, they primarily had its service aspect in mind. At that time their area was visited infrequently by coffee-buying trucks and other vehicles, so they had difficulty in selling their coffee and in getting transport to Goroka or other centers. The people keenly felt the need for transport, were willing to put up the money to buy a truck, and wanted Bimai, the most experienced businessman in the area, to operate it for them so they could obtain access to outside centers and markets.

The quest for the prestige gained by owning and operating a store, a trucking venture, or some other enterprise is probably the most important investment motive to consider in understanding the Gorokan propensity to invest. Gorokans have a passion for investing in commercial ventures, and, in general, the bigger and more visible the capital asset, such as a five-ton truck or a modern roadside store, the more attractive and prestigious is the investment to the Gorokans. In contrast to the American nouveaux riches of the turn of the century whom Veblen characterized by their habits of conspicuous consumption, the newly wealthy Gorokans stand out as conspicuous investors.

The prestige factor in Gorokan investment behavior is particularly apparent in their desire to own and operate commercial vehicles. Baito Heiro's purchase of a Land Rover in 1958 was the first outstanding example of this penchant for conspicuous investment in vehicles; Baito used the Land Rover not only to carry passengers and freight around Goroka, but also to drive as far as Kainantu in the east and the Wahgi Valley in the west to advertise his success as an accomplished *bisnisman*.

When I arrived in Goroka for the first time early in 1967, the Gorokan leaning toward status-motivated investment in commercial vehicles was particularly striking, for they were then in the midst of a truck-buying spree. While the prosperous European coffee planters and businessmen, as well as a few highly paid European government employees, were buying Mercedes-Benz sedans or other luxury automobiles to impress their colleagues and enhance their status, Gorokans who could have afforded such "prestige cars" were putting their money out for four-wheel-drive utilities (particularly the Japanese counterparts of the British Land Rover), light and medium trucks suitable for local service, and heavy trucks suitable for long hauls between the Highlands and the coast. The Gorokans were not buying private automobiles and were not interested in doing so.[6] It was the commercial vehicle, the *bisniska* as they call them, that counted in their scale of values.

Gorokans planning to buy a truck will tell you with obvious pride of their plans; what kind of truck they will buy; how much it will cost; how much of the price they have already accumulated either in special bank accounts earmarked for buying the truck or in hiding places in their village; and who will contribute funds to meet the final cost. Then, when the truck is purchased, the very act of buying is made dramatic. For example, a man with a truck bank account will withdraw all his funds in cash and then triumphantly plunk the notes down on the truck dealer's desk. Or, in the case of a rural group who have been saving money at home, a procession of villagers will come into town, head straight for the dealer's office, and then deposit hundreds of dollars in ten-cent pieces on the counter, which the dealer must then spend hours counting while the villagers stand around awaiting the final tally and the announcement that they have enough to buy a truck.

Once all the money is delivered and the truck is officially purchased, the next important step is to paint in bold letters on one of the doors the name of the *papa bilong bisniska* and the name of the village or clan he and the other contributors hail from. Once it has been properly identified, the new *bisniska* can usually be seen around the countryside loaded down with clansmen of the proprietary group, rather than paying passengers, for all to see, particularly those groups who bought last year's model or who haven't yet bought trucks.

The same element of group pride and invidious comparison between groups that played a role in spreading coffee planting a decade earlier was at work in 1967, spurring the Gorokans to buy trucks and make other conspicuous investments to enhance their status. The two situations were alike, except that competitive investment activity was not being promoted by the administration and it received, save from truck dealers and others selling capital goods to Gorokan investors, scant encouragement from the European business community. Indeed, many of the latter seemed to consider the whole idea of Gorokan business investment to be either a waste of money or a misguided attempt to break away from sole reliance on cash-crop production and to challenge the commercial hegemony of European store owners, truckers, and other businessmen.

5

Business Leaders

Of all the students of entrepreneurship, it is Schumpeter who is most emphatic about the crucial role played by the entrepreneur in economic development. To Schumpeter (1949) the entrepreneur is not just an owner or a manager of a business. Nor is he just an investor risking his capital in some enterprise. In essence, Schumpeter's entrepreneur is an innovator whose pioneering commercial efforts promote general economic development. He is a man who, in perceiving hitherto unrecognized opportunities and in exploiting them by introducing new goods or production methods or by opening new markets or sources of supply, lifts the economy from a state of stagnation to one of growth. Although Schumpeter, who formulated his concept of entrepreneurship in 1912, primarily had in mind the pioneering innovators of Europe and North America who contributed so much to the formation of the modern industrial economy of the West, his thinking has application elsewhere—even in New Guinea.

An amendment to Schumpeter's concept of innovation is required to realize the utility of his entrepreneurial theory in New Guinea and other developing countries. The entrepreneurs of Goroka are not original entrepreneurs in the sense that they have introduced entirely new goods or procedures into the world economy. Rather, they are imitative innovators who have taken crops, technology, and commercial structures developed elsewhere and adapted them to their own society. Just because they are imitators, however, does not mean that their entrepreneurial role has been minor. As

Hoselitz (1963:163–164) points out, the adaptation of elements from developed countries can have a developmental impact on the economy of a less developed country, analogous to that of the efforts of the original pioneering entrepreneurs in the industrial countries of the West. Although starting a coffee plantation, a store, or a trucking venture might seem routine procedure, for a people like the Gorokans, who are just emerging from a subsistence economy, they represent considerable innovation. To take land from the subsistence cycle and then organize manpower to clear it and plant it in coffee was a new and daring step for the first coffee growers, as was their later investment of newly earned coffee money into retail sales and trucking ventures. The Gorokans who took these first, innovative steps in commercial enterprise provide classic examples, albeit in an exotic milieu, of Schumpeterian entrepreneurs at the forefront of economic change.

A word about terminology is necessary before starting our analysis. *Bikfela man bilong bisnis,* the Pidgin term Gorokans use to refer to the entrepreneurs in their midst, could be rendered as "big businessman." But, "business leader" is both a more accurate translation (*bikfela man* = big-man, or leader; *bilong bisnis* = of business) and a more apt one, for these men are not simply big businessmen.[1] They are men who have led their fellow clansmen and tribesmen to take advantage of the opportunities made available to them through their recent linkage with the cash economy.

Ten Business Leaders

In order to understand more fully the role business leaders have played in Gorokan economic change, soon after my arrival in Goroka, I selected ten business leaders for intensive investigation and then focused a major part of my research on their careers, their enterprises, and their relations with other Gorokans. The ten men were selected on the basis of repute; they were the men whose names repeatedly cropped up in discussions with a wide range of Gorokans as being the main business leaders of the area. Nine of them come from Goroka proper. The tenth, who lives just over the eastern border of the sub-district, was included because he was well known in Goroka, where he centered much of his trading activities.

If the commercial assets of the ten business leaders are compared with the general distribution of assets among all Gorokans, the

TABLE 8. Assets of Gorokan Business Leaders.

Name	Coffee Trees	Trade Stores	Trucks	Cattle	Restaurants
Sinake Giregire	24,000	1, (1)[1]	1, (2)	6	0
Akunai Rovelie	18,000	0	2	0	0
Apo Yeharigie	12,000	0	1, (1)	0	0
Bin Aravaki	7,800	(1)	(1)	0	0
Soso Subi	7,500	1	2, (1)	0	0
Wale Kabiliha	6,900	2	1, (1)	0	1
Bimai Noimbano[2]	6,700	(1)	4	20	0
Bono Azinapfa	5,100	1	1	4	1
Sabumei Kofikai	2,000	1	1	14	0
Hari Gotoha	1,400	1	2	10	0

1. Numbers in parentheses indicate trade stores now closed or trucks no longer operating.
2. As of his death in 1966.

distinctive position of these *bikfela man bilong bisnis* is immediately apparent. Whereas the average coffee holding in Goroka contains about 450 trees, the plantations of business leaders average slightly more than 9,000 trees apiece, about twenty times the general mean (Table 8). Similarly, the participation by business leaders in other major enterprises—trade stores, trucks, cattle projects, and restaurants—indicates their commercial prominence. Although it would be difficult to estimate their net incomes, most business leaders gross over $4,500 yearly from their commercial activities, and several probably bring in well over $10,000 a year from their coffee plantations and other ventures. Even if we consider that a considerable proportion of their gross may go toward operating costs and other expenses, there can be no doubt that business leaders are far better off than the average Gorokan. In an area where per-capita cash income is in the vicinity of twenty-five dollars per annum, the financial position of these business leaders is outstanding.

The business leaders' reputations are therefore solidly based on personal wealth and control of extensive assets, but that is not all. Part of their renown comes from economic leadership apart from the enterprises they direct personally. Most of them have been the first in their clans or tribes to engage in large-scale coffee production and other commercial ventures, and their lead has inspired others to follow them. All have been free with advice and sometimes considerable aid to others wanting to plant coffee and start businesses, and at least one of them, Sabumei Kofikai, has earned his reputation as a business leader primarily from the service he has rendered his fellow Gorokans. His work as a DASF employee in introducing coffee throughout Goroka has contributed far more to his being known as a *bikfela man bilong bisnis* than his own personal commercial accomplishments. Gorokan business leaders are proud of their inspirational and tutelary role in promoting local economic development, a process they call *kirapim bisnis* (business development) or *kirapim ples* (local development). And, to foreshadow the analysis of their political ambitions that is offered later, it should be added that most of them do not hesitate to brag about their economic leadership and to make political capital of it if they can.

"What did you do before you planted coffee?" was a question I asked all the business leaders, in order to elicit details of their early careers that might help explain their subsequent commercial success. This inquiry, the main findings of which are summarized in Table 9, revealed that all the business leaders had occasion, through schooling, work experience, or both, to become acquainted with European ways before they began to plant coffee, to a degree unusual for Gorokans of their generation. Six had attended administration or mission schools, four of them for six or more years. All had worked for Europeans in public or private employ, or both, before starting their commercial careers. Significantly, many of them had held jobs as schoolteachers, agricultural assistants, medical assistants, or personal servants, which allowed them a degree of personal contact with Europeans and insight into their behavior that was denied the ordinary Gorokan, who remained in his village or at most worked for a while as a plantation laborer.

To illustrate just how extensive an exposure to Europeans and European ways some business leaders had before they started planting coffee, we can look briefly at the early careers of Apo Yeharigie and Sabumei Kofikai, two of the most widely experienced Gorokan business leaders.

Apo Yeharigie, the vegetable farmer mentioned earlier because he was demanding cash payment for his produce at a time when other Gorokans were satisfied with trade goods, is the oldest of the business leaders, having been born around 1915. Apo also had the longest continuous exposure to Europeans. As a youth he had attached himself to Mick Leahy's prospecting party when Leahy was working in Bena Bena during 1932 and 1933. After Leahy had left Goroka, Apo tried to make himself useful to patrol officers working in the area. One of these, A. F. Kyle—who was later killed by the Japanese while he was a coast-watcher on New Ireland (Feldt 1967:70)—hired Apo as his personal servant and took him down to Madang when he was transfered there in the late 1930s. When Kyle left Madang just before the outbreak of the war, he got Apo a job with another patrol officer, John R. Black, who had done much of the patrol work in the Eastern Highlands during the mid-1930s. Apo served Black as a combination personal servant, confidant, and assistant during the tense wartime years, first in Madang, then in Goroka, and finally in New Britain.

According to Black, Apo proved invaluable in keeping him in

TABLE 9. Experience of Gorokan Business Leaders Before Cash Cropping.

Name	Years of schooling	Type of private employment	Type of public employment
Sinake Giregire	8	mechanic	helper at agricultural station
Rovelie Akunai	9	. . .	schoolteacher, clerk, prison guard
Apo Yeharigie	. . .	servant	. . .
Bin Aravaki	1	. . .	supply carrier on patrol expeditions, policeman
Soso Subi	. . .	. . .	headman (*luluai*), asst. headman (*tultul*)
Wale Kabiliha	6	servant	medical assistant
Bimai Noimbano	. . .	plantation laborer (coastal)	helper at agricultural station
Bono Azinapfa	1/2	servant	headman (*luluai*)
Sabumei Kofikai	8	. . .	schoolteacher, agricultural assistant
Hari Gotoha	. . .	servant	. . .

touch with dissident movements among the New Guinean policemen and the Madang people on the eve of the Japanese landing along the Madang coast, in aiding him to withdraw safely from the Madang coast inland over the Bismarcks and into the Goroka Valley, and then in helping when Black was made senior ANGAU officer in the area to set up an early-warning system for Japanese air and ground movements directed against the Highlands. In addition, Black says he relied heavily on Apo to act as an informal intermediary between the ANGAU administration and the Gorokan people and to keep conflicts down at a time when a Japanese thrust toward the Highlands seemed imminent.

Later in the war, after the threat of a Japanese invasion of the Highlands had passed, Apo was able to render further service in another crisis—the Highlands dysentery epidemic. Because of his sophistication, Apo was chosen to act as the main contact man between the army medical personnel and the Gorokan people. After a crash course in the cause and treatment of dysentery, Apo was given the task of making his home village of Seigu, located just east of the present township of Goroka, into a model village: proper latrines were constructed, and all refuse was buried to stop flies from breeding and carrying the disease, and all infected people were treated with sulfa drugs. Then Apo and a medical team toured the countryside to explain to the Gorokans, many of whom were apparently convinced that the disease was a result of sorcery, what caused dysentery, how it was carried, and how its progress could be stopped by undertaking village sanitation measures, and, for affected people, by taking sulfa drugs.

By the end of the war, Apo, after more than ten years of working for miners, patrol officers, and ANGAU personnel, in Goroka, on the Madang coast, and as far afield as Port Moresby and New Britain, had learned much about Europeans and their ways. Apo's experience with Black during the war was probably particularly crucial for expanding his understanding of the outside world, for Black had assigned him tasks of considerable responsibility. In addition, Black says that he took pains to instruct Apo about modern technology, about cash crops, about money and its value, and about the possibility of applying this knowledge profitably in postwar Goroka. Apo was therefore uniquely qualified for a Highlander of his time to become one of the first Gorokan entrepreneurs.

Sabumei Kofikai, although he is about ten years younger than Apo, also has had extensive experience with Europeans dating from the early 1930s. As a young boy Sabumei tagged along with patrol officers and their police escorts as they moved through Bena Bena, his home area, and adjacent regions, and he became one of the first Gorokans to learn Pidgin. In 1935 or 1936 Sabumei was sent by a patrol officer, who recognized his potential, to a newly opened administration school at Kundiawa, now the headquarters of the Chimbu District. There Sabumei picked up some English and the rudiments of a primary education, and in 1939 he was sent to the Malaguna Technical School, near Rabaul in New Britain, for further training to enable him to become a teacher.

The war interrupted Sabumei's schooling; when the Japanese invaded Rabaul in 1942, he and many of the other students fled into the bush but were soon captured and forced to return to Rabaul to work as domestic servants and laborers until 1945, when Rabaul was retaken by the Allies. After the war Sabumei returned to Goroka, where he taught school for several years. Then, because his English (partially forgotten during the war, when he had had to learn Japanese) and other skills needed upgrading, he was sent to Sogeri High School, near Port Moresby, for a special two-year course designed to raise the proficiency of New Guinean teachers.

Upon completion of the course in 1951, Sabumei was sent back to the Highlands, where he taught school in both Goroka and Chimbu until he resigned in 1953 to join the DASF. At that time Australian teachers and better educated teachers from coastal areas were beginning to staff schools in the Highlands, and the director of education in Goroka, realizing that Sabumei's limited training would block his advancement as a teacher, recommended that he be taken on by the DASF in Goroka to serve in some capacity where his training, linguistic skills,[2] and local knowledge would be of more use. Sabumei found his true calling with the DASF. He was made foreman of the extension work crew and instructor of Gorokan agricultural trainees and in general served as the chief liaison between European agricultural officers and the Gorokan farmers. His services were invaluable in implementing the DASF extension program for introducing coffee among the Gorokans.

As is apparent in Table 9 and as will become more evident as the careers of some of the other business leaders are discussed, the "modern" experiences of Apo and Sabumei are not entirely unique among business leaders. All of them have had some experience in working for or dealing with administration personnel or private European employers, which it could be argued, proved to be an asset in the postwar period, in that it gave them more insight into "modern" market opportunities and ways of exploiting them than was shared by their fellow villagers, who had had slight or insignificant contacts with Europeans.

If this reasoning is correct, it might seem logical to consider the business leaders to be the first representatives of a modernized elite to emerge from the mass of Gorokans. However, I would argue that, although these men have undoubtedly used the modern skills they acquired through schooling or work experiences in exploiting market opportunities, they have done so in their own home areas and in a manner which, if not judged to be traditional, could at least be classed as neotraditional. These business leaders all returned, after some experience with the outside world and new ideas, to their home villages to start commercial careers which in style, if not content, have followed the model of the career of a traditional big-man. This is not to maintain that traditional big-men have become modern business leaders; indeed, that is a virtual impossibility, since the traditional big-men of precontact times are now dead or too old to lead active economic lives. What is maintained is that modern business leaders follow the style of traditional big-men in seeking and achieving eminence. They, like their predecessors, are ambitious and opportunistic men, and they have been attracted to European school and work experiences as much for the advantage to be gained in furthering their personal careers as for the immediate rewards of knowledge or pay. In this circumstance the exploitation of modern opportunities is not opposed to traditional achievement behavior but combines with it.

The ability of business leaders to combine traditional and nontraditional methods to their advantage is apparent in their commercial undertakings. They have all exhibited, for example, a facility for obtaining land, labor, and capital and for combining these in their enterprises in ways involving both traditional and modern operations. How they mix the traditional and the modern can be illustrated by considering the early careers of those business leaders who were the first in their home areas to plant coffee on a large scale.

Established leaders, particularly those who also held the administration-appointed office of village headman (*luluai*) had the edge on other Gorokans when it came to starting large plantations, for it was they who were usually placed in charge of coffee nurseries and who could command, by virtue of their status as a big-man or administration-appointed leader, or both, the labor of their fellow clansmen for clearing and planting large tracts of land. Despite this advantage, however, not all established leaders became major coffee producers and business leaders. Most did indeed plant some coffee, but only a few really exploited their position to the fullest to achieve commercial success. Of these commercially oriented men, two stand out—Soso Subi and Bono Azinapfa—for their ability to combine traditional leadership, administration-sanctioned leadership, and innovative behavior in the cash economy.

Soso Subi was born around 1920 into the Asaroyufa clan, a group then in control of some of the land on which the present township of Goroka is located. His childhood, though marred by the death of his mother in a tribal war, was typical of a youth in precontact Goroka; and the coming of the first Europeans in the early 1930s, sometime before his initiation into manhood, does not seem to have directly affected his early life. Although Soso, along with other Asaroyufa villagers, grew vegetables and worked for the Allied forces who built and manned the Goroka airfield on the edge of Asaroyufa territory, he remained tied to his village during the war. Though he preferred to stay in his home area rather than travel or work elsewhere as so many other young men at that time were doing, Soso was interested in becoming associated with the Europeans, who now ruled the Highlands. Soon after the war he accepted an appointment as assistant headman (*tultul*) and became Asaroyufa's headman about 1950, by which time he was also established as a big-man in the traditional sense.

Soso was one of the first Gorokans to seek out Robert Cottle for advice on coffee when the latter arrived in Goroka in 1952 to initiate agricultural extension work there. Soso showed Cottle the sixty-odd trees that had already been planted by the Asaroyufa people and asked his advice on how to tend and harvest them. He also asked Cottle about the possibility of planting more coffee, and, as Soso seemed to be able to command the necessary land and labor, Cottle jumped at the chance; under Cottle's direction Soso and his clansmen cleared and planted a large nursery and prepared ground for transplanting the seedlings the following year. When the seedlings were ready for transplanting, Soso did not hesitate to take a lion's share for his own use or to employ his followers as unpaid laborers to help him plant his personal coffee plot, the nucleus of what was to develop as one of the first of the large Gorokan-owned plantations.

Bono Azinapfa is another traditional big-man and administration-appointed headman who used his position to help launch his commercial career. He was not one of the first of the big coffee growers, however, for he did not begin planting coffee in earnest until 1958, several years after Soso and a few other Gorokan pioneers had started their plantations. His late entry into coffee growing is to be explained mainly by the fact that he lived in a remote area along the northeastern border of Goroka that was off the beaten track until the late 1950s as far as extension work or European plantations were concerned.

Bono was born in the late 1920s or early 1930s, just as prospectors were beginning to explore the eastern edge of the Highlands. His traditional upbringing was interrupted just before the war, when he enrolled as a student in a Seventh Day Adventist mission school. When the war came, however, the school was closed, leaving Bono with less than a year of formal education. When the Allied build-up in the Goroko Valley started, Bono walked over and began a career as a personal servant, first for Allied officers and later for administration officers, that was to last into the 1950s. During his servant days in Goroka, Bono was still not cut off from his home village; he hosted his clansmen when they came to town, and whenever he could get time off he would walk home or hitch a ride there on a jeep or truck. He not only kept up his ties with his home village but managed to become known as a big-man there as he matured; in the mid-1950s he was appointed headman for his village and moved back there permanently.

Once Bono was settled, he started a modernization drive, getting his clansmen to build roads, and—following the advice given him by a European settler whom he had helped to gain land near his village—to lay out a coffee nursery and prepare ground for coffee planting. Like Soso, Bono planted the bulk of the seedlings in his own plantation using his clansmen as unpaid laborers.

Bono, like Soso, could be charged with having used his position as headman to obtain free labor. Headmen at this time were required to organize their clansmen and others in their areas of jurisdiction to build and maintain roads and to carry out other public-works projects ordered by the administration, and, as we have seen, they were also requested to supervise coffee nurseries for agricultural extension officers. That some headmen took a large share of the seedlings grown in communal nurseries for planting in their own plantations and used their clansmen as essentially unpaid workers to clear and plant their plantations could easily be considered corrupt exploitation of the office of headman except for the following considerations. These headmen were also regarded as traditional leaders by their clansmen, who believed they stood to gain by helping their leaders to become successful coffee growers. Group prestige was at stake; clansmen would be willing to help their leader to become wealthy because his success would enhance the group's status vis-à-vis other groups. And some hardheaded economic reasoning was also involved. First, by helping their leader, clansmen felt that they themselves would be able to learn about coffee and later would be able to use their experience in setting up their own plantations. Second, by helping their leader they stood to gain, like followers of a traditional big-man, from the leader's largesse. A successful coffee grower was in a position because of his comparatively high income (which could run into several thousand dollars a year) to reciprocate, or *bekim,* to use the Pidgin term, their followers' aid by presenting them with gifts of food, cash, or traditional valuables. Gorokans freely talk about such reciprocal arrangements between big-men and their followers. For example, Bono proudly explained to me his relationship with those clansmen who had helped him get started in the following words:

> When these people are in need, I give them some money because they helped me with coffee. All right, now I help them well—by buying some food when they are short, by buying meat, buying rice, and by giving pigs at a feast.

Other Gorokan coffee entrepreneurs did not have the advantage of being headmen to help them launch their careers. Nonetheless, many were able at some stage in their commercial careers to call upon traditionally recruited labor to aid them in planting and exploiting their coffee. The most impressive example to offer in this context is that of Bimai Noimbano, one of the first Gorokans to try to plant coffee on a large scale and, until his death in 1966, the undisputed economic leader of his home area of Watabung.

Bimai was born about 1920, the son of Nemavera, a famous Siane warrior—the man who challenged Taylor's patrol as it moved through Watabung in 1932 and who was shot dead by Taylor. Bimai was not, however, born in his father's village, for Bimai's mother had been banished by the Kindeimarofa group (Bimai's father's clan) before his birth for having violated the postpartum taboo on sexual intercourse and having become pregnant too soon after the birth of her first child. Bimai's mother had sought refuge with her sister, who had married into the Yamei clan. There Bimai was brought up as the foster child of Noimbano, his mother's sister's husband and an important man of the clan.

According to Robert Kapo, Bimai's nephew and adopted son who is now an employee of the DASF, Bimai first became interested in cash crops when he went to Manus Island as a plantation laborer in 1949.[3] From Manus Bimai moved to Aiyura, where he worked briefly as an agricultural trainee and learned more about cash crops, including something about coffee. When he left Aiyura, he took with him some coffee seedlings and seed to plant in Watabung. Although some people today credit Bimai with stealing these from the experiment station, Kapo says that Bimai was given them by the station manager Aubrey Shindler, who made a practice of furnishing departing employees and agricultural trainees with seeds and seedlings of various cash crops and encouraging them to use their new knowledge to plant and cultivate them in their home villages.

Bimai returned to his home village in Watabung around 1951 and planted his coffee seed and seedlings on a steep hillside high above the village. They failed to take hold, apparently because of the cold and exposure, so Bimai switched his attention to raising chickens, for he had also brought back a rooster and two hens from Aiyura. He soon had a small but thriving chicken business, finding a cash market for his fowl among passing Europeans and among a few local people who had money from working for European plantations or the administration. He then turned his attention to coffee again and sent some young boys to walk to Aiyura (more than seventy miles away by foot trail and road) to obtain a new supply of coffee seed. With these new seeds he started a coffee nursery, on lower ground this time, but still could not get the seedlings to grow properly.

At this point, in late 1952 or early 1953, Cottle passed through Watabung on his first agricultural patrol to the area, and Bimai asked him for professional help. Cottle was delighted to find anyone in such a remote region who knew something about coffee. With Cottle's aid, Bimai was able to set up a nursery and, a year later, to lay out a model plantation and successfully transplant the seedlings. Although Bimai was not yet considered an important big-man, the people apparently recognized him as a potential leader in the cash economy, and they willingly provided all the labor for the nursery and for his plantation.

Apo Yeharigie, whose early career has already been reviewed here, is another business leader who was not a headman when he began. He was, however, in a particularly advantageous position to recognize and exploit commercial opportunities, for, as we have seen, he had been associating with Europeans from the time Mick Leahy was prospecting in Bena Bena to the end of the war, an experience which gave him considerable insight into modern ideas and technology.

After the war Apo decided to return to his home village of Seigu to try his hand at making money. Apo was spectacularly successful; by the late 1950s he was one of the wealthiest of Gorokans and was better off than some struggling European settlers. When I arrived in Goroka in 1967, Apo seemed more legendary than real, particularly since I was told that he had just retired, leased his coffee plantation to a European, and gone off to the seashore to live with three of his seven wives on a small island off the port of Madang. Conflicting tales were then circulating around Goroka about just how Apo had achieved success; most knowledgeable people, European and Gorokan, knew that Apo had done well in vegetable farming, gold mining, and coffee growing, but none was sure just how he had managed to succeed in these enterprises.

To try to straighten out the details of his career, I finally decided to fly to Madang where I rented a canoe to take me out to Apo's island retirement home. There I found him relaxing in an attractive thatched house, which served as a combination dining room and bar for him and his entourage. Even though I was a total stranger, Apo was willing to talk. Evidently he was used to such inquiries and launched into a brief narrative, touching on what he felt were the highlights of his commercial career. These bear repeating, for even if they represent a highly selected view, they illustrate how Apo, like so many Gorokan entrepreneurs, visualized commercial success as a result of investment, profit-making, and then reinvestment of profits, in a series of successively larger enterprises.

According to Apo, he returned to Goroka after the war with $14 in savings. He used this money to buy garden tools and seeds and started cultivating European vegetables for sale to European personnel stationed in Goroka, and New Guinean vegetables for sale to the administration for provisioning their workers, hospital patients, and prisoners. After a few years he claims he accumulated $238 in profits (he always quoted exact amounts), which he used to fly to Kainantu to buy picks, shovels, and other equipment needed to prospect and pan for gold and to finance prospecting trips around the Eastern Highlands for himself and a crew of workers. After a few years working alluvial gold deposits, primarily in the Lufa area southeast of Goroka, Apo came back to Seigu with an accumulated profit of $1,060. There, following technical advice offered by an extension worker, Apo says he planted 9,923 coffee trees (again he quoted an exact figure), using his savings to buy tools and hire workers for clearing and planting.

Akunai Rovelie is another of the Gorokan coffee entrepreneurs who was neither a big-man nor an administration-appointed official when he started to plant coffee and who used cash savings to pay laborers to clear and plant his lands. Akunai, who was born in the early or mid-1920s, had an early career virtually identical to that of Sabumei Kofikai, the Gorokan coffee extension worker. Akunai was one of those Gorokan youths who tagged along with the patrols that moved through Goroka in the early 1930s and who picked up a fair knowledge of Pidgin from the New Guinean policemen on those patrols who used him as an interpreter. Akunai's precocity earned him a chance to attend the government school at Kundiawa in the Chimbu region and then, along with Sabumei Kofikai, a place in the Malaguna Technical School near Rabaul on New Britain. Akunai's wartime and early postwar career was also like that of Sabumei. He was caught by the invading Japanese, forced to work for them, and released by the Allies, and then he worked briefly as a prisoner-of-war-camp guard and a government clerk before returning to teach school in Goroka. Again like Sabumei, he was subsequently sent to Sogeri High School near Port Moresby for two years to improve his English and then returned to teach, first at Kundiawa in Chimbu and then at the Okiufa school, a few miles west of Goroka township.

Once back in Goroka he started growing market vegetables for sale to Europeans, and when he saw the possibility of making much more money by growing coffee than he could as a schoolteacher (a job which only paid a few dollars a week) and a part-time vegetable grower, he quit his job to go into the coffee business. As Akunai had ancestral ties in the area and was recognized as a potential economic leader by the traditional big-men, who controlled land allocation there, he was able to obtain a large tract of land adjacent to the school for his plantation, and with the aid of paid workers he was able to lay out a plantation which has since grown to about twenty-four acres, making it the second largest Gorokan-owned coffee plantation.

Sinake Giregire of Gimisave Village on the border between the Lowa and the Upper Asaro census divisions is the youngest of the first generation of Gorokan coffee entrepreneurs that we have been considering here, having been born about 1937, some years after European contact. When he was eight years old, Sinake enrolled in the local Lutheran mission school. Because of his obvious intelligence, two years later he was sent to the Lutheran mission headquarters in Finschhafen on the Morobe coast to continue his education at the Lutheran school there. Sinake progressed well in his studies at Finschhafen and became fairly fluent in English. However, when he was thirteen years old a near-fatal attack of malaria forced him to leave school and return to the healthier and relatively malaria-free Highlands. Sinake never went back to school. Instead, after recuperating at home for several years, he took a job as a mechanic's helper with a small airline operating out of Goroka. He remained with the airline for three years before quitting to take a job at the Aiyura experiment station. Sinake stayed there only briefly, for even though he was then only about twenty years old he was anxious to go into business for himself.

His first venture was a hand-operated pit saw, which he set up in the hills around Kainantu to make timber planks to sell to the administration. He was fairly successful and at one time employed ten laborers to cut down the trees and saw them into planks. However, as the price he was receiving for his timber brought him only minimal profits (he had to compete with power-equipped European sawmills), after a year or so Sinake abandoned the timber business for gold prospecting. With a crew of a half-dozen or so workers Sinake began panning for gold in stream beds from Kainantu to Watabung and enjoyed enough success that he soon accumulated the money to return home and start a large coffee plantation. In 1955, before he went to Kainantu, Sinake had tried to start a coffee plantation at his home village of Gimisave but had been handicapped by his youth and lack of status and could only get enough land and help to plant a small plot. In 1958, after winding up his business ventures in Kainantu, Sinake returned to Gimisave as a man who, though still young, had proved his business ability and had accumulated $1,800, which he was willing to invest in a coffee plantation. Impressed by his accomplishments, his clansmen were willing to allocate him a large tract of land, and with his savings he was able to buy tools and hire a dozen laborers from the Chimbu area to clear the ground, plant the seedlings, and care for the maturing coffee trees. This plantation now extends over about forty acres, making it the largest Gorokan-owned coffee plantation, if not the largest one owned by a New Guinean anywhere.

A man like Soso, the first coffee grower mentioned in this section, and a man like Sinake would seem to represent very different types of entrepreneurs: one started his career as a mature leader, a traditional big-man and a headman, who could easily command village labor for his own uses, while the other began as a young man lacking in traditional or administration-sanctioned status who went out and accumulated capital in various business ventures in order to finance his coffee plantation. However, the apparent differences in the way Soso and Sinake started their careers should not be given too much weight, lest they obscure the subsequent convergence of their entrepreneurial styles and the status levels they achieved upon becoming successful coffee growers. For example, largely through his leadership in coffee growing, Sinake came to be accepted as a big-man despite his youth, and he later became a political rival to Soso in the struggle to become Goroka's first elected member of the House of Assembly. Furthermore, once Sinake had proved himself as a coffee grower, he was able, in the style of a traditional big-man, to recruit workers from among clansmen who by this time had become his followers and who would work for Sinake without his having to pay them regular wages.

Other Gorokan entrepreneurs who started out using cash wages to employ laborers also found that as their success became apparent they were able to recruit clansmen to work for them, offering them, as Soso and Bono did from the beginning, leadership and reciprocal gifts instead of regular wages. Even the most modern-appearing of the Gorokan coffee entrepreneurs, Apo, used quasi-traditional means to operate in the market economy. Apo used tambu shells secured in New Britain while he was in the employ of Black and other shells obtained during his sojourns on the coast to purchase land rights for his coffee plantation, to trade for goods and pay workers, and also to obtain wives. His wives, reputed to number ten in his heyday, were actually the backbone of Apo's labor force in his market gardening and coffee growing activities. His exploitation of the institution of polygamy and the traditional division of labor that allots to women the main agricultural tasks of tending and harvesting crops, was widely admired by other Gorokan men, who envied Apo's success in contracting so many marriages and in getting his wives to work so efficiently for him.[4] However, although Apo was following traditional precedent in using wives as laborers to build up his wealth, he also could not escape the use of modern incentives; he had to regularly present his wives with gifts of cash and European clothing, as well as shell valuables, to keep them satisfied and on the job.

This mixture of the modern and the traditional so evident in the early careers of these business leaders is also characteristic of many of their later commercial activities. For example, along with displaying a marked propensity to invest their coffee revenue in improving and expanding their plantations and in new business ventures, many of the business leaders have shown an ability to call upon the cash resources of their clansmen and others for investment.

The commercial activities of three of these leaders—Bimai Noimbano, Hari Gotoha, and Soso Subi—bear examination to see just how complicated financial arrangements between a business leader and his supporters can become and to get some indication of the quasi-traditional character of many apparently individual businesses.

First, let us look at the commercial activities of Bimai Noimbano. Although Bimai died in 1966, some months before I went to Goroka to make my study, I decided to include him because he seemed, from what I heard about him from Gorokans and Europeans alike, to be the archetype of the *bikfela man bilong bisnis*. There was no difficulty in obtaining information on Bimai. Indeed, his death and, more particularly, the dispute over his estate that was in progress meant that I was able to learn a range of details which probably would not have been available to me had Bimai been alive at the time of my research.[5]

Some details of Bimai's early career have already been related—how he experimented unsuccessfully on his own with coffee and then how with the aid of DASF workers he was able to set out a model coffee nursery and plantation. Although we might think that Bimai, like many of the first successful coffee planters, would have had little difficulty in obtaining sufficient land for his coffee, this was not the case. Bimai's status as an adoptive member of Yamei clan only gave him limited rights to clan land, so in order to obtain enough land to expand his coffee plantings Bimai was forced to buy out the land rights of Yamei landholders with cash payments of around two dollars apiece.[6] With this purchased land and with the coffee seeds and advice furnished by Cottle and his staff, Bimai was able to set out during the mid-1950s three separate coffee gardens with a total of nine thousand trees. (This total was later reduced when landslides ruined some of his plantings.) When these trees started to bear in the late 1950s, Bimai began to have a considerable cash income, unsurpassed by anyone else in Watabung and only rivaled by a few of the major coffee growers of the Goroka Valley.

Bimai was not satisfied with just being a prosperous coffee grower. He continued to raise and sell chickens as he had done before planting coffee, and he also started to breed tilapia fish (furnished by the DASF) for sale to local people and to raise pigs commercially on a large scale. According to his adopted son, Robert

Kapo, Bimai at one time was raising several hundred pigs and was making good money selling these to other Gorokans, particularly to people from the Goroka Valley who had money to spend and needed pigs for feasts and exchanges and to build up their own herds. In the early 1960s Bimai branched out further in the livestock business and started a cattle project in partnership with a cousin, a man who had had experience working with cattle as a DASF employee.

In addition to primary production, Bimai tried his hand at running a trade store and then at buying coffee for resale to coffee mills. Although he did not stay in the trade store business, Bimai went into coffee buying in a big way and became the main coffee buyer operating in Watabung. At the time of his death he had four trucks on the road buying coffee and was easily the most successful of all the Gorokan businessmen who were in coffee buying at the time.

If these few facts were the only information available on Bimai's commercial activities, it would be easy to come away with the impression that Bimai was an example of a modern Gorokan who had successfully broken out of the limiting confines of a traditional society based on subsistence production to become an individualistic entrepreneur operating by modern means in the market economy. But this would be a misguided interpretation, one that would ignore the really crucial aspect of Bimai's career. While it is true that Bimai was an entrepreneur who operated in the modern context of the cash economy and that he was an unusual individual who stood out among the Watabung people, it is also evident that a key element in Bimai's entrepreneurial success was his ability to mobilize the resources of clansmen and others to found and operate his enterprises, a characteristic he shared with other successful business leaders. And it requires examination to see just how much group support was behind his accomplishments.

Like Soso Subi and Bono Azinapfa, Bimai was skilled in appealing to the group—to his clansmen and in some instances to virtually all the people of Watabung—for aid in building up his enterprises. From his clansmen, particularly his age mates and the youths of Yamei, he was able to recruit unpaid workers to establish and tend his coffee plantations. From his clansmen he was also able to secure a steady supply of sweet potatoes to feed his pig herd. In addition, he was able to prevail on some households to take his pigs on their land and feed and care for them until they were ready to be sold. Then, when it came to obtaining money for buying equipment for improving his plantations and processing his coffee, and later for buying trucks and going into the coffee buying business, Bimai was able to supplement his own savings by drawing funds from his clansmen and on occasion from people throughout the Watabung area.

From the beginning many people were willing to support Bimai because he offered them economic leadership. He seemed to them to know something about the workings of the cash economy that they did not, and he was willing to lead the way in trying to grow coffee and start other commercial activities such as coffee buying that promised to benefit the entire community. Bimai realized that he had an obligation to fulfill in leading his clansmen and other Watabung people into a fuller participation in market activities and tried to live up to it. To those who helped him get started in coffee he, in turn, gave help in growing coffee by furnishing them with advice, seeds, and seedlings, and occasionally by loaning them his work force. Although Bimai ran his coffee buying business for a profit, he also tried to see that all the coffee produced in Watabung, particularly by those who had contributed money to him, was purchased and not left to rot by the roadside as sometimes had happened before he had started his service. In addition, when the administration proposed that a cooperative coffee factory be set up in Kundiawa to serve the people of Chimbu and Watabung, Bimai promoted it enthusiastically. He himself put up $2,400 for shares, convinced other Watabung people that they should contribute, and became a director of the cooperative society (Bond 1964:10).

When Bimai died, the commercial organization that he had so successfully built up in effect died with him. Without a leader, without some central big-man, a commercial organization like Bimai's, which depended on one man's entrepreneurial talents, could not survive. By the time I arrived in Goroka seven months after Bimai's death, his various enterprises either were neglected or were being operated at a loss by associates or kinsmen who lacked Bimai's commercial acumen.

Almost immediately upon Bimai's death, claimants came forward to press their claims for all or parts of the estate. Bimai's elder brother, who had been born and reared within the Kindeimorofa clan (Bimai's father's clan), went to Yamei and tried to convince the administration that he, as elder brother of the deceased, had the right according to Siane custom to administer Bimai's businesses until Bimai's elder son, then in school in Australia, came of age. The brother's claims were bitterly opposed by the Yamei people on the grounds that Bimai was an adoptive member of their clan and that his plantations and other enterprises had been built up on their soil and largely with their aid. Prominent among the Yamei claimants was Robert Kapo, whose testimony concerning Bimai's early career I have been citing. In the early 1950s Bimai had adopted Kapo and sent him to school—first to the local government school and then to an agricultural training school in another district—to learn skills that Bimai needed to manage his enterprises efficiently. Kapo claimed that Bimai had wanted him to take over management of his businesses upon finishing school and that he therefore should be given control of them until Bimai's son came of age.

In addition, many Yamei people and others from Watabung who had given Bimai cash contributions for some project or another came forward to claim refunds. Most of the 784 persons who had originally pooled their money to buy a truck and had given that money to Bimai asked for their money back,[7] as did many of Bimai's business associates, who maintained that he had owed them money. The substantial claim of one of his associates merits listing, for it reveals the extent to which Bimai could continually attract financial contributions from a supporter. This man claimed to have given Bimai $1,049 over the twelve years in which he had worked for him, in sixteen separate contributions, which he listed as follows:

1. to help buy a coffee pulper — $30
2. to repair a truck — $20
3. to buy sweet potatoes for workers — $10
4. to pay workers for clearing and fencing a cattle pasture — $110
5. to help buy a Toyota truck — $104
6. a personal loan to Bimai — $60
7. to buy sweet potatoes — $16
8. to help pay for a Land Rover — $168
9. to help pay school expenses for one of Bimai's children — $16
10. to help pay Bimai's workers — $200
11. to pay for a feast for Bimai's workers — $11

12. to buy a bag of rice and a goat and make a two dollar loan to Bimai	$28
13. to help pay Bimai's wife's clansmen for the birth of Bimai's son [one of the transactions between groups that follows the initial bridewealth transactions]	$20
14. to pay for a truck to carry Bimai's coffee to Goroka	$10
15. to help buy a new tire for Bimai's Toyota truck	$20
16. to help Bimai buy another Toyota truck	$226[8]

When I was last in Goroka, in November 1968, two years after Bimai's death, his estate had not yet been finally settled—because of the extensive assets involved, a dispute between the public curator and the Department of District Administration over who had jurisdiction over the case, and the conflicting claims of Bimai's natal and adoptive clansmen. By this time his enterprises were in ruin: all his trucks were broken down or greatly in need of repair; much of his coffee buying capital had been exhausted through mismanagement; his plantations were in poor condition; and his livestock ventures were only partly operative. Fortunately, some of his cash assets had been held in trust by the administration, which planned to use them to satisfy the claims of all those who had given Bimai money. In October 1968 a meeting of Bimai's close relatives, his business associates, and the councillors of Watabung was convened by the administration to hear and pass on all claims. Claims totaling $6,073 were approved; these were to be paid from the cash assets plus what could be gained from selling Bimai's trucks. The remainder was to be held in trust for Bimai's children, and Bimai's adoptive clansmen of Yamei were to be given control of his coffee plantations.

A Gorokan business empire that is bigger and perhaps more complicated financially than Bimai's is that operated by Hari Gotoha and Soso Subi, both members of the Asaroyufa clan. Soso, it will be recalled, was the headman of Asaroyufa who became one of the first major Gorokan coffee growers. Hari, Soso's junior in age and status, did not become commercially active until the late 1950s, when he started a food selling business, which with the help of Soso and other clansmen has grown into one of the most impressive and profitable Gorokan-owned commercial organizations.

In addition to their coffee plantations, the holdings of Hari and Soso include a modern store located opposite the town market,

1. The Goroka Valley seen from the dry grasslands of the Kami Hills.

2. Soso Subi's water-powered coffee pulper.

3. Sun-drying coffee beans before their sale as parchment coffee.

4. Goroka coffee was airfreighted to coastal ports until the Highlands Highway was completed in the mid-1960s.

5. Sinake Giregire preparing land for a sweet potato garden.

6. A Gorokan-owned bus loading passengers at the Goroka market.

7. Observers at an early cattle project in Bena Bena.

8. Hari Gotoha and part of his business empire.

which is the best stocked and probably the most profitable of all Gorokan stores, a well-equipped restaurant located next to the store that caters primarily to town and transient New Guineans as well as occasional Europeans, and two heavy-duty trucks used for local and long-haul work. Together these represent a cash investment of at least $30,000; and if the prime commercial land on which the store and restaurant stand were included in the valuation, the total value of Hari and Soso's business holdings, not including their coffee plantations, would approach $100,000.

When I arrived in Goroka early in 1967, several Europeans singled out the store and the restaurant to me as being among the best-run and most profitable Gorokan enterprises. Most of these European informants believed that the main reason they were so successful was that they were individually owned and operated by Hari, whom they regarded as a young Gorokan who knew how to make a go of things on his own and how to avoid the entanglements of jointly owned and operated enterprises.

Upon meeting Hari and asking about his career, I received essentially the same story of individual ownership. Hari was most emphatic that the store, the restaurant, and the biggest truck were his alone and that he had bought them all with his own money. He even launched into a Horatio Alger story, which he told with great pride, to account for how he had risen so high and so fast in the business world.

"It all started with thirty cents of self-rising flour" was the way Hari's story began. One day in 1959 when he was a young man employed as a personal servant for a European in Goroka, so his story goes, he went out and bought some flour. Using his employer's stove while she was away at work, he cooked up a batch of scones, which he took to the market and sold for a profit. He then reinvested his receipts to buy more flour and other ingredients and soon had a flourishing business going—so flourishing, in fact, that his employer suggested that he resign and devote himself full-time to baking and selling scones. This he did, and after a year he claims to have amassed $600, which he used to put up a small restaurant, where he baked and sold scones and other foods.

Hari says his restaurant was so successful that he was soon able to build a small store and stock it with an extensive line of trade goods with the profits. Then, when the public health authorities made him close his restaurant because of inadequate construction and facilities, Hari says he hired a carpenter and put $5,000 of his savings into a new and modern restaurant, made of all-modern materials and equipped with running water, electricity, a large stove, and a refrigerator-freezer. Later, as more profits came in, he bought one truck outright and invested some funds in another. He also told me he had $8,000 saved up to build a modern store to replace his old one.

Although I did not challenge Hari's tale of individual enterprise, capital accumulation, and investment, I thought it unusual in light of what I had begun to find out about the dealings of other Gorokan business leaders. When I asked other Gorokans about Hari's businesses, they confirmed his story of starting out by selling scones in the market, but a few indicated that Hari's senior clansman Soso and other members of the Asaroyufa group probably helped him finance his ventures. After I became better acquainted with Hari (and after I had eaten many a meal in his restaurant), he modified his story by admitting that Soso had indeed helped him finance many of his projects. This Soso confirmed, saying that he had invested money derived from his coffee plantation and the sale of Asaroyufa land to the administration (for town expansion) in the restaurant, the store, and one of the trucks. Soso maintained, however, that Hari had provided the nucleus of investment funds for each new venture out of profits he had derived from the preceding venture and that, although he, Soso, was a major investor and had a say when it came to long-range plans, he left day-to-day management to Hari.

Investigation of Hari's businesses also revealed a strong clan element behind them. Some money pooled from the Asaroyufa people had apparently been invested in one or more of the enterprises. In addition, the very location of Hari's store and restaurant on Asaroyufa land and the fact that money derived from the sale of Asaroyufa land and the sale of coffee from Soso's plantation (which, as we have seen, was partially built up by clan labor) had gone into financing the investments meant that in a sense the Asaroyufa people could regard the businesses as part of the general resources of the clan, rather than the strictly individual enterprise of one or two of their number.

The methods that Bimai, Hari, and Soso used in building up their commercial interests are not at all unusual for Gorokan business-

Business Leaders

men, although the size and complexity of their operations exceed those of most of the other entrepreneurs. Every Gorokan business leader has at some stage in his career looked to clansmen and other fellow Gorokans to furnish him with resources, monetary and nonmonetary, to initiate and operate his commercial ventures. Without this access to the resources of others it is unlikely that the Gorokan business leaders could have advanced as far as they have in so short a time.

But just because business leaders have been backed by their clansmen and others does not mean that their coffee plantations, stores, trucking services, and other ventures should be dismissed as mere examples of clan businesses or communal enterprises. To so class them would obscure the entrepreneurial drive behind them and the whole course of economic change in Goroka. Business leaders are entrepreneurs in the sense of being innovators and promoters of development; they differ from Schumpeter's entrepreneurs in that they operate with one foot in a traditional (albeit changing) New Guinean society and one foot in the cash economy. This means, for example, that instead of securing risk capital from banks or other financial institutions (which, as we have seen, have largely been closed to them) or from share issues, like an entrepreneur in London or New York, they seek to tap what money their clansmen and other Gorokans can provide. The milieu in which Gorokan business leaders operate may be exotic when compared to the European and American settings that Schumpeter had in mind when he wrote about entrepreneurs, but the essential entrepreneurial function of recognizing new opportunities and organizing resources to exploit them is the same.

Leaders and Followers

Why should Gorokans be willing to provide support for one of their number so that he can build up his business enterprises and achieve a level of affluence far above their own? Why doesn't each man husband his resources for his own use and refuse to contribute to men who are, or promise to be, important business leaders? These basic questions lead us back to the exotic milieu of the Gorokan entrepreneur and open the whole question of relations between leaders and followers in Gorokan society.

Perhaps the most systematic way to approach these questions is to look at leader-follower transactions in the light of the analysis of the high Gorokan propensity to invest offered earlier. Three main motives for Gorokan investment behavior were isolated—the desires for prestige, profits, and service benefits. Although the analysis was offered to explain Gorokan investment motivation in general, from the case histories presented so far it should be apparent that it is equally applicable to questions raised here concerning relations between Gorokan business leaders and their followers, for one of the secrets of the success of Gorokan entrepreneurs has been their skill at mobilizing the support of others by appealing to general desires for prestige, profits, and service benefits.

The Gorokan business leader or aspiring business leader is without a doubt most interested in acquiring prestige—in becoming a big-man, or, to use the Gahuku term, a *man with a name*—and he sees commercial activity as the main way to do so. However selfish and individualistic this quest might seem, it must be remembered that these commercially oriented men are still counted as members of viable traditional groups—subclans, clans, and tribes—and that whatever prestige they acquire because of their commercial success is also shared, partially at least, by the other members of their groups. In this situation men with minimal personal ambition may therefore be willing to support one of their clansmen or tribesmen who promises to become a big-man through commerce by helping him to set out his coffee plantation, feeding or caring for his pigs or other livestock, contributing cash toward his truck or store, or otherwise aiding him to achieve his commercial success and high status. While maximum prestige accrues to the entrepreneur, those who contribute toward his success gain a measure of pride for being the supporters of such a man and for being members of a group that can boast a successful business leader. This situation appears to be the modern counterpart of an aspect of traditional leader-follower relations in New Guinea that has been succinctly portrayed in reference to a Western Highlands group by Bulmer:

> Clansmen take pride in the clan's corporate performance in the Moka [a wealth exchange] and measure this against the performance of other groups. Even socially insignificant men with little or no direct part in the exchanges lend their efforts in preparing the dancing-grounds, building the houses and helping the leaders in the breeding and assembly of pigs. . . . The performance of the leaders of the

clan in the Moka is also seen by its members as the performance of the whole group. (1960:7–8)

Supporting a business leader also promises clansmen more direct and material rewards than simply a gain in status. Clansmen may be willing to aid one of their number to establish a coffee plantation, store, or trucking business because, on the one hand, by helping him they can learn how to participate in commercial activities on their own and, on the other hand, because they stand to gain by using the services he can offer them. The successful coffee entrepreneur is in a position to aid those who helped him get started by showing them, for example, how to grow and process their coffee (and even to loan them labor and equipment to do so). If he has a store, he can provide them with ready access to trade goods, and if he has a truck, he can furnish them with transport for themselves and their crops. A business leader need not give, and seldom does give, these and other services absolutely free to his followers. But even if they are "paying customers" they still usually appreciate the local entrepreneur's role as a leader in promoting the group's participation in the market economy.

In addition to initiating his clansmen into the mysteries of coffee growing and other commercial activities and providing them with the services necessary to enable them to participate more fully in the cash economy, a business leader is in a position to reciprocate to his followers in other ways. He can, for example, stand ready to provide them with food or cash when needed, like Bono Azinapfa. Or he can become the prime contributor within his group to intergroup feasts and to bridewealth payments that the young men of his group must assemble in order to marry. However modern Gorokan business leaders might seem, they are still bound to their traditional groups, and, like the big-men of earlier days, they are a prime source for the goods (which nowadays include considerable sums of cash) necessary for intergroup feasts, marriages, and other occasions when valuables are exchanged.

The career of the late Bimai Noimbano can once again be examined with profit—this time to see how reciprocal relations between a business leader and his followers may be structured. As has been detailed, Bimai's clansmen, and in some instances the Watabung people as a whole, contributed greatly with donations of labor, sweet potatoes, and cash to building up Bimai's commercial empire. Whatever rancor may have developed after his death over the disposition of his estate, there can be no doubt that during his lifetime Bimai was the big-man, in the sense of a modern business leader, of Watabung and that his followers, particularly his Yamei clansmen, were proud to identify themselves with him. When he started to plant coffee, a crop alien to the Watabung people, he was able to gain their support, for they believed that he was showing them a new way to acquire modern forms of wealth. Then, as his coffee plantations began to flourish and he branched out to other enterprises, Bimai was able to maintain their support and to continually attract contributions of labor, vegetables, and cash because he could furnish his followers with needed services (such as coffee buying) and provide the valuables so necessary for the maintenance of intergroup relations.

Watabung informants still tell with pride how generous Bimai was when it came to giving feasts in which great quantities of food were consumed (and in which, after New Guineans were permitted to drink in the early 1960s, large amounts of beer and spirits were liberally dispensed) and in donating handsomely to bridewealth transactions and other exchanges. Bimai reputedly often gave two or three pigs, and, when money entered the exchange system, fifty dollars or so toward the brideprice. Bimai's fame for generosity spread well into Goroka Valley and even reached the ears of European residents. For instance, in commenting on Bimai's spending habits, one administration officer noted that "in many ways Bimai could be described as a philanthropist as he was prone to giving away various monies and throwing numerous parties etc."[9] While such behavior might seem most profligate and unbusinesslike to the outsider, from the perspective of traditional leader-follower relations this generosity can be seen as an essential device which Bimai utilized to keep his followers satisfied and rallied behind him.

To further illustrate the high regard in which business leaders may be held and to indicate the extent to which their fellow Gorokans will support their efforts to consolidate and extend their commercial activities, two recent cases involving the lands exploited by important business leaders can be cited. The men in question are Akunai Rovelie and Sinake Giregire, the two biggest Gorokan coffee producers. In the late 1960s both applied to convert the title of their lands from ownership according to traditional custom to sole proprietorship in the European sense, so that, first, they and their heirs would have an assured title to the land and its improvements and, second, they could use the land as collateral for obtaining bank loans. Since under current legislation an applicant for title conversion must gain the unanimous approval of all people who also have claims to the land in question, the success of both Akunai and Sinake in having the title to their lands converted testifies to the support they could count on from their clansmen and others who were in a position to approve or disapprove their applications. In effect, by gaining approval for granting indisputable title to their lands and the coffee planted on them, Akunai and Sinake received votes of confidence from their fellow clansmen and tribesmen.[10]

Akunai's land is a parcel of twenty-five acres that had been under control of the Megusayufa tribal group in the early 1900s. Akunai's father's father had actually cultivated a portion of it until his death in a tribal fight that was part of a series of defeats that led to the dispersal of the Megusayufa group and the abandonment of its lands. Then Akunai's father fled to Seigu (Apo Yeharigie's village), where Akunai was born and reared until he left to join administration patrols and then later to attend school in Chimbu and New Britain. After the war, when Akunai had returned to the Highlands as a schoolteacher, he says that a delegation of the leading Goroka big-men, a group that included Soso Subi, Makis (a leader whom Read [1965] describes) and a man called Gohonite (whose status as a traditional Megusayufa big-man will be described later) called on him to take up his ancestral lands and plant coffee on them. These big-men were impressed by Akunai's education and experience with the outside world and believed that he should be the man to develop this land, which was then vacant, with a coffee plantation that would be a model for his less sophisticated clansmen and neighbors to follow. Since Akunai did establish a flourishing plantation on the property, an enterprise that inspired other Gorokans around him to try cultivating coffee, when Akunai made his application for title conversion he had no difficulty in obtaining the unanimous consent of local leaders and other parties with ties to the land.

Sinake Giregire's land is about three times the size of Akunai's parcel, and its ownership was much more vulnerable to dispute than Akunai's, since three separate clan segments (including a segment of the same scattered Megusayufa group that Akunai belonged to), who had amalgamated to form one group under the pressures of tribal war just before pacification, could lay claim to it. Sinake, whose father was a leader in the defeated Megusayufa segment involved, originally gained rights over about forty acres of the land in the late 1950s when he returned home from sawing timber and gold mining in Kainantu with enough money to establish a sizable coffee plantation. When he made his application for title conversion ten years later, he claimed this land plus another thirty-five or so acres he wanted to exploit as his alone. That all the key people of the three groups approved his claim is an indication of the high regard in which he was held, as well as, of course, his political skill in convincing followers that activities designed to promote his interest were also in their interests.

Some of the testimony given during hearings on Sinake's application by key men in a position to judge his claim may indicate how his followers were willing to go on record as supporting his claim to the land. One such statement came from a man who stated he was originally

> . . . from Megusayufa in the Gahuku area. I am a close kinsman of the applicant and I have land interest, acc. to native custom, in Yanowa [Sinake's land]. I am clear in my mind that if this application is successful I will lose my rights. But I am happy to renounce these rights of mine in favour of Sinake who has worked to develop the land.[11]

Perhaps the most important testimony supporting Sinake's claim came from Gohonite Gerepaima, the same man who was instrumental in helping Akunai obtain his land. Gohonite, who is the senior surviving traditional big-man among the Megusayufa and the one leader who has the most authority over land matters, stated in his testimony:

> I am a former Luluai and fight leader. In pre-European times my clan intruded on this land Yanowa and for a time my father lived here. The applicant Sinake is educated and he has fenced and developed this land so that it grows coffee and vegetables. Sinake has some claim to this land on traditional grounds of inheritance but now I want to see him get a title to it.

Some of the people from the other groups that had amalgamated with the Megusayufa people who also had rights to Yanowa were willing to give up their land rights only after Sinake paid them compensation. One land claimant from another group said, however:

> I do not claim any compensation from him [Sinake] because he has cared for and educated the three children of my brother from the time they were infants.

In this statement we catch a glimpse of another way a big-man may assure himself a following—by providing for orphaned or neglected children of his group and helping them to attend school by paying school fees, buying them clothes and books, and giving them rides to school. Sinake is widely known for his efforts to get the children of his group to attend school, as well as for his general advocacy of universal education, all of which add to his reputation, particularly among those Gorokans who see education as a passport into the modern world.

Read (1959), in his analysis of traditional leadership among the Gahuku people, stressed that, however much men might strive for power and status, the really successful and universally recognized big-men were those who tempered their desires for personal aggrandizement by being moderate in dealings with others and by not behaving too despotically toward their followers. When I first read Read's analysis some months after I had arrived in Goroka and had started to learn something of the behavior of business leaders there, it struck me as being as applicable to the modern situation as to the traditional one. This impression was heightened by the then-current Gorokan concern over the sudden deaths of several prominent business leaders from Goroka or nearby. These included Bimai Noimbano, who died in the Goroka hospital following abdominal surgery, and Kondom Agaundo, one of the major business leaders of the Chimbu District, who was killed when his truck plunged over a cliff on the Daulo Pass road. Many of the Gorokans with whom I discussed the deaths attributed them to sorcery or poisoning carried out by persons who were envious of the commercial success and high status of the deceased. This theory was even current among high-school students in Goroka, for in an essay written for my wife, who was inquiring about the students' vocational interests, one student volunteered that being a prominent businessman was dangerous, for "whenever a man is becoming rich or popular in the district some of his people quickly get jealous of him and kill him or do other things to make him die."

When I talked this over with agricultural officers assigned to extension work in Goroka, they agreed that fears of assassination, particularly by means of sorcery, were common among the men they knew who were becoming prominent by means of cash cropping, cattle raising, and other enterprises and cited several examples to buttress their opinion. They told me, for example, that after Bimai's death his cousin, a former DASF employee who had gone into partnership with Bimai in a cattle project, abandoned the cattle and fled from Watabung. When they finally found him and tried to talk him into returning to look after the cattle project, he refused on the grounds that Bimai's death and those of other prominent businessmen proved that *bisnis* was just too dangerous an activity.

Another case they cited involved extension work carried out some years previously in a remote area of Goroka. When an agricultural officer made his first visit there, he picked out the acknowledged leaders to be the first to grow cash crops, on the premise that they could easily mobilize land and labor to make model plantations that other men could later copy. All went according to plan during the first few years; cash crops were planted, and the leaders began to make money from their sale. At this point, to the initial astonishment of the agricultural officer, they requested that he change his methods—that he stop paying exclusive attention to them and start extension services for all the people. Their request stemmed, he later learned, from the growing resentment of the mass of people in the area, who felt they had been neglected in cash crop development, and the consequent fear of the leaders of reprisal by sorcery if a program of more even development were not introduced.

Hari Gotoha was the one business leader who was most frank about his fears of sorcery or some other malevolent action against him, should he come to be regarded as a *bikhet* (big-head) who lorded it over his followers and clients and gloated over his commercial success without giving due credit and reciprocal favors to those who had supported him. To avoid any dissidence and the possibility of serious consequences should dissidents decide to act against him, Hari told me that he went out of his way to keep the people satisfied—by contributing to a truck, which he let his clansmen operate primarily for their benefit; by giving people rides on his truck; by giving people in need credit at his trade store; and by not acting too big, and instead trying to, as he put it, *sidaun level* (sit down level) with his clansmen and others with whom he was associated. He also told me that he always tried to play down his personal role in his business holdings (which is, of course, the exact opposite of the way he usually presents himself to Europeans) and to emphasize that:

> They do not truly belong to me; they belong to all the people. That's what I say, they do not belong to me, they belong to all the people who pooled their money—I manage them that's all. I don't brag to the people; it would be no good to say they belong to me, they belong to me, or the people would like to injure me or something.

The wording of the sign over his restaurant provides an example of how he has put these sentiments into practice. Instead of printing *Haus Kaikai Bilong Hari* (Hari's Restaurant) or something similar that would emphasize his ownership, Hari has lettered the sign with the words *Ol Wantok i Gat Haus Kaikai Hia* (Friends Have a Restaurant Here)[12], a wording that avoids a personal reference and advertises the restaurant as being open to everyone.

Further evidence of Hari's concern for allaying jealousy generated by his business success came to light when my wife interviewed a young relative of his, who was about to graduate from high school, about his vocational interests. This student told her that he was planning to go to a school for training cooperative society officers so that he could return to Goroka and start cooperatives among the people of his clan and surrounding clans. Hari, he said, would help him raise capital for the cooperatives, which, according to Hari's reasoning, would give local people a greater sense of participation in commerce and thus serve to drain hostility away from Hari. He was completely serious about this plan and maintained that by starting cooperatives "I'll be saving Hari's life."

BUSINESS AND POLITICS

If the thesis that business leaders have actually carried over the traditional style of big-man leadership into modern life is correct, then we should expect them to be interested in achieving and successful in attaining political, as well as economic, leadership. This appears to be the case; just as achieving renown by the accumulation of wealth and its exchange led to political power in traditional Gorokan society, so does modern political leadership go hand in hand with commercial success. The introduction of the cash economy and new political institutions has not broken the linkage of economic and political leadership personified in the person of the traditional big-man. It has merely given ambitious men a new context in which to achieve eminence. Many of the councillors in the local government councils established by the administration in Goroka are prominent in coffee growing and commerce, and it is from the most successful of the *bisnisman* that the leaders of the councils and the members who represent Goroka in the House of Assembly are drawn.

Today Gorokans can seek two main elective offices: councillor in either the Goroka Town Council, which covers people living in the Lowa, Bena Bena, and Unggai census divisions as well as the town, or in the Asaro-Watabung Local Government Council, which covers the rest of the people of the sub-district; or member of the House of Assembly of Papua and New Guinea representing either the Goroka or the Daulo electorate divisions which follow the boundaries of the two councils. Councils have been operating in Goroka since the late 1950s, and there have been two elections held for the House of Assembly so far—in 1964 and in 1968.

If we examine the political records of the ten men selected for study because of their reputations as business leaders, we see that their high degree of participation in modern political institutions is striking (Table 10). Three of them are in the House of Assembly: Sabumei Kofikai represents the Goroka electorate, Sinake Giregire represents the Daulo electorate, and Bono Azinapfa (who, though he lives outside the sub-district, was included in the study because of his close commercial and social ties with Goroka) represents the Henganofi electorate, located along the northeastern border of Goroka. Four more of the business leaders have been unsuccessful candidates for the House of Assembly, and five of the business leaders (including two who are now in the House of Assembly) have at some time in their careers been councillors. The political participation of Gorokan business leaders as candidates and office-holders is far above the average and marks them out as leading political figures, in the modern sense, in Goroka.

TABLE 10. Candidature and Election to Public Office of Gorokan Business Leaders.

Name	Local Government Council	House of Assembly
Sinake Giregire	councillor (president)	member
Akunai Rovelie	......	candidate
Apo Yeharigie	......	.....
Bin Aravaki	councillor (president)	candidate
Soso Subi	councillor (vice-president)	candidate
Wale Kabiliha	......	.....
Bimai Noimbano	......	candidate
Bono Azinapfa	councillor (vice-president)	member
Sabumei Kofikai	councillor	member
Hari Gotoha	......	.....

That more of the business leaders have been interested in being elected to the House of Assembly than to councils is not surprising, in view of what business leaders think about the relative merits of being a member or a councillor. Election to the House of Assembly is attractive to business leaders because of the high status, relatively good pay and allowances (totaling more than $3,000 in 1968), and other perquisites that accrue to members, whereas the business leaders are less interested in becoming councillors because that job is seen to have comparatively little power and prestige and to require inordinate amounts of time and energy, compensated for at the rate of only a few dollars a month, that would have to be diverted from business and other activities. It may be significant, however, that of the five business leaders who have become councillors, four have served either as the president or vice-president of their councils. Apparently when business leaders do decide to participate in a council, they want to have, and can attain, positions of power.

The three exceptions (Apo Yeharigie, Wale Kabiliha, and Hari Gotoha) to the general rule that Gorokan business leaders seek political office are worth examining. None of the three men was taken aback by my questions as to why he had not run for some office, and it became obvious from further questioning that they all felt they were capable of modern political leadership. Only Apo, because of his retirement from an active life, ruled out the possibility of running for office in the future. Both Wale and Hari considered they might someday be candidates but gave excuses as to why they had not yet entered any elections. Wale rejected the possibility of running for the House of Assembly, at least for the present, as his following would be insufficient to unseat Sinake Giregire, his close neighbor. As for becoming a councillor, Wale said he preferred to avoid wasting his time in a council—particularly, he added, since he already could control all the councillors from his area and get them to represent his views in the council. When I asked Hari about his noncandidature, he replied that so far he had been too busy building up his business interests to be active in politics but thought that perhaps if one of his younger brothers could ever take over day-to-day management of his enterprises he might then feel free to run for office.

The close tie between business and political leadership in Goroka is unusual for New Guinea only in the degree to which business leaders dominate the top elective posts. Elsewhere in New Guinea business leaders do not always appear to be so prominent in politics, although it is evident that success in cash cropping and commerce are among the main accomplishments of many of those elected to high political office. Most of the members of the House of Assembly have some background in growing cash crops and engaging in other commercial activities, and it would appear that commercial success, as in the cases of the Gorokan members, was the outstanding accomplishment before election to the House of Assembly of many (Finney 1968:408; Wolfers 1968–1969). This prominence of businessmen-politicians in the first House of Assembly caught many political observers unawares. Probably because of patterns observed in other emerging nations, where leading politicians were often members of an educated and Westernized elite, divorced from or opposed to private commerce, observers were looking for the emergence of a similar type of elite politician when elections for the House of Assembly were first held in 1964.

For example, those directing a major study of the 1964 election at first paid no systematic attention to candidates' commercial backgrounds and reputations. Instead, in making their initial analyses they focused on the obvious variables of modernization—education, church membership, employment, and professional experience (Bettison, Hughes, and van der Veur 1965:388–422; van der Veur 1964). However, when actual field studies of the elections, like that of Harding (1965), clearly indicated that business experience and reputation were crucial variables in many electorates, the directors of the study were forced to admit that commercially important New Guineans were also prominent in modern politics (Bettison, Hughes, and van der Veur 1965:508).[13]

In Goroka commercial success alone has not, of course, assured election to office, for many men with substantial commercial reputations usually contest important elections. The House of Assembly elections are, in effect, contests between rival business leaders. In the 1964 elections, for example, six of the ten Gorokan candidates (there was one European candidate) were business leaders whom we have been considering in this chapter (Sinake Giregire, Akunai Rovelie, Bin Aravaki, Soso Subi, Bimai Noimbano, and Sabumei Kofikai). The other four Gorokan candidates were minor business leaders, well known for their commercial leadership in their home regions, but not as famed throughout Goroka as the other six.

Each of the candidates in the 1964 elections had a local tribal or regional power base from which he could draw most of the votes cast. Bimai Noimbano, for instance, polled 99.6 percent of the votes cast in the Watabung area (Bettison, Hughes, and van der Veur 1964:427). In this situation, which has by no means been uncommon in New Guinea elections, the only way a man can win is by picking up preference votes in successive recounts. This is possible under the Australian preferential voting system, which prevails in New Guinea. Voters are required to indicate their preferences for all candidates, marking them 1, 2, 3, and so on in order of their choice. If after a count of first-preference votes no candidate has a majority, then the votes for lower-ranking candidates are distributed according to the preferences indicated on the ballot papers until one candidate emerges with a majority.

Sinake Giregire won the 1964 election on preference votes. Even though he was "first past the post" on the first count, he polled only 22 percent of all the votes cast. Fortunately for Sinake, after all preferences had been distributed, he remained ahead of the other eleven candidates and was declared winner of the election. In the neighboring Henganofi electorate Bono Azinapfa was not so fortunate. Although the 8,028 votes Bono gained on the first count in the 1964 elections were more than twice the number polled by his nearest rival, Ugi Birutu, they were only 44 percent of the vote, and when preferences were distributed Ugi Birutu picked up many more additional votes than Bono and beat him by almost a thousand votes. Bono seems to have lost primarily because the electorate was split between two main linguistic-cultural groups, of which Bono belonged to the less populous. Thus, although he gained most of the votes from his own group, his rival Ugi, even though he was not as strong a candidate in first-preference voting, eventually gained most of the votes from the other, larger group and came out the winner (Wolfers 1968). (In 1967 in a by-election held after the death of Ugi, Bono defeated the leading candidate from the other group primarily, it seems, because voters in the other group failed to put down their preferences on their ballot papers systematically.)

In 1968, after electoral boundaries had been redrawn to reduce the size of electorates, Bono and Sinake had less trouble winning election to the house. Although we might argue that both had an advantage in this election because they were already in the House of Assembly, probably the major factor in their relatively easy victories was simply that they were standing in smaller electorates that more closely approximated their primary areas of support. Bono, the major business leader of the Kafe-speakers, who now dominate the new Henganofi electorate, won easily in the first ballot. Sinake, who is the outstanding leader in the Upper Asaro area of the new Daulo electorate (but who has only limited support from the Siane people of the Watabung area, who are also in the electorate) only narrowly missed election on the first ballot by a few hundred votes and won by a wide margin when preference votes were distributed.

The 1968 elections in the Goroka electorate presented a much different picture from that prevailing in the Henganofi and Daulo electorates. Of the sixteen candidates (in an electorate of about 30,000 population) there was no single leader, like Bono or Sinake, who stood out above the others enough to gain a majority or near-majority on the first ballot. Sabumei Kofikai, who was third in the first count, did finally win the election, but only on the fifteenth count, when all preferences had been distributed. Clearly, Sabumei was a compromise candidate (Wolfers 1968–1969:29) who won because he was well enough known and thought of in the area to figure on the ballot papers of many voters as a second choice. Here Sabumei's work in introducing coffee in the area undoubtedly gave him an edge over the other, more parochial candidates—an advantage he capitalized on by campaigning throughout the electorate and by asking all those who knew him to vote "number 2" for him after giving their first votes to their local favorites.[14]

GOROKANS AND THE SPIRIT OF CAPITALISM

The emergence of a dynamic group of Gorokan entrepreneurs would seem to contradict some common assumptions concerning entrepreneurship and economic growth. Many writers have stressed that entrepreneurs commonly arise from marginal, dissident, or reformist groups. For example, Weber (1930), in his famous *The Protestant Ethic and the Rise of Capitalism,* stressed that those responsible for transforming the traditional capitalism of the West into its modern version were representative of a new kind of man, born of the Protestant Reformation and imbued with Calvinist ideas of the necessity of hard work and wealth accumulation, which gave rise to what Weber calls the spirit of capitalism. And Hagen (1962), a contemporary theorist, has posited that when a group suffers a "withdrawal of status respect" through conquest, derogation by a more statusful group, or immigration into a new society, the rage and frustration felt by members of the affected group lead eventually to a social environment conducive to the development of innovative, entrepreneurially oriented individuals. However useful these and similar theories may be in explaining entrepreneurial drive and economic growth among some groups, such formulations would not seem to be directly applicable to the Gorokan case. Although the Gorokans have been subjugated by the Australians, whatever loss of status respect they may have felt has probably been more than made up by the new opportunities made available to them through contact with the outside world. Furthermore, it is clear that Gorokan business leaders are not members of marginal or reformist groups;[15] they spring directly from the mainstream of Gorokan society and have promoted change within that society by using the modern means of cash cropping and commerce to attain traditional ends.

Nonetheless, the thinking of Weber, Hagen, and others who have put forward related theories is relevant to the Gorokan case in one important sense. These writers, like Schumpeter, McClelland, and LeVine—the men whose work has been used to form the theoretical basis for this study—stress the crucial role of human motivation in entrepreneurship and economic growth. The primary difference between their formulations and the explanation offered here lies more in the nature of the historical situations to be analyzed than the theoretical premises employed. For example, Weber was faced with explaining the rise of modern capitalism from what he called traditional capitalism, an economic state in which he maintained that all the economic ingredients—technology, transport, capital, skilled labor, and the like—necessary for the development of modern capitalism had long been present. What Weber did was to point out that it was a change in human motivation, one brought about by the Protestant Reformation and a subsequent reinterpretation of the value of economic enterprise, not any change in material conditions, that added the ingredient necessary to mobilize existing economic factors into a dynamic and rapidly expanding system of capitalism. Weber's thesis needs to be reversed in the Gorokan case; there the motivation necessary for economic growth was present in the traditional setting, but the economic factors were missing until contact with the outside world supplied the cash crops, technology, monetary system, and marketing channels that made it possible for the Gorokans to earn money and start their own enterprises. In Weberian terms, it can be said that the Gorokans already had their own analogue of the spirit of capitalism and needed only linkage with the cash economy to express it.

6

Preadaption, Preconditions, and Cargo Cults

This narrative of rapid economic growth led by emergent entrepreneurs may strike the reader who thinks of New Guinea as the epitome of Stone Age backwardness or as the home of cargo cult movements as the account of a completely exceptional case. But the Gorokan case is only exceptional in that extremely favorable circumstances have allowed the potential for accelerated development—a potential that is, I maintain, present in most New Guinean groups—to be expressed in cash cropping and other commercial activities. Were it not for circumstances favorable to this development, the Gorokans could easily have remained economically backward or have been dominated by cargo cult movements, as so many New Guinean groups have.

PREADAPTION AND PRECONDITIONS FOR ECONOMIC GROWTH

Most of the peoples of New Guinea, despite the geographical barriers and their great linguistic diversity, are culturally similar. In particular, most share the basic Melanesian values and institutions that link wealth, prestige, and leadership. In other words, the Gorokan focus on material goods and on achieving status through economic accomplishment is common in New Guinea. Therefore, it should follow that most New Guinean groups (that is, those with wealth-oriented, achieved status-mobility systems) should have about as much potential for economic development as the Gorokans have.[1]

Recent motivational research in New Guinea on need for Achievement, the main psychological motive that McClelland and his associates have so far identified as crucial to entrepreneurship, supports this proposition. Following LeVine's (1966) contention that societies with achieved status-mobility systems will be relatively high on need for Achievement, R. S. Finney (1971) posited that New Guinean groups with achieved status-mobility systems would, no matter what their level of economic development, exhibit similar levels of need for Achievement. Tests done with high school students from six New Guinea districts with contrasting levels of economic development showed no significant differences in achievement motivation, a probable indication that the district populations have approximately equal motivational potential, as far as need for Achievement is concerned, for entrepreneurial development. (R. S. Finney's research on need for Power, and its relation to need for Achievement and entrepreneurship among these groups, is not yet completed.)

However, despite the general potential for development in New Guinea indicated by both sociological and psychological analyses, it must be admitted that the stereotype of a primitive and economically backward New Guinea is still generally true: most New Guinean groups are still only marginally involved in the cash economy. If the potential is there, why is there so little evidence of successful cash cropping and business activities on the part of New Guineans? In other words, why are there so few Gorokas?

To answer these questions it is necessary to draw a clear distinction between the concepts of preadaption for economic growth and of preconditions for economic growth. I use the former to refer to factors internal to the makeup of a society which, although they have evolved independently from the cash economy, prove adaptive to new economic activities once the society becomes linked with the cash economy. I use the latter to refer to factors external to a society which make the adoption of new economic activities feasible, attractive, and profitable for the people concerned. The remarkable record of growth of the Gorokans can be best explained, in terms of this distinction, by saying that in addition to being preadapted for growth by virtue of their traditional values and institutions, the Gorokans also enjoyed favorable preconditions for growth.

These favorable preconditions bear summarizing here. First, much of Goroka has fertile, well-watered soil, ideal for growing high-value arabica coffee as well as other cash crops. Second, the contact situation in Goroka was relatively nondisruptive; Gorokans were allowed to retain much of their precontact integrity and autonomy, and they also enjoyed an efflorescence in their traditional exchange system brought about by the introduction of labor-saving steel tools, the prohibition on warfare, and the importation of large quantities of shell valuables. Third, European settlers not only introduced coffee and built up transport and marketing facilities for the crop, but many of them encouraged Gorokans to grow and market coffee. Fourth, the administration aided the introduction and exploitation of coffee and other cash crops by developing an extensive network of roads throughout much of Goroka and by providing extension services to the Gorokans. It has been the existence of these preconditions that has allowed the preadaptive features for economic growth embedded in Gorokan society to be expressed in modern economic activities. Without these preconditions the Gorokans might well have remained on the periphery of the cash economy and might have turned to cargo cult activities to achieve progress, as have so many groups around New Guinea who, because of either a lack of basic infrastructure improvements or a lack of stimulus or aid from European settlers and businessmen or the administration, have had little opportunity for economic growth.

In short, my argument is one that would be congenial to the thinking of most development economists. Those New Guinean groups like the Gorokans that have experienced rapid economic growth are generally the ones most favorably endowed with natural resources and with opportunities to put these resources and their own skills to work in cash cropping and other ventures. Those groups that have experienced significantly less economic growth are generally the ones least favorably endowed, both in natural resources and in economic opportunities. This point may seem obvious, but it needs to be stressed, for many Europeans working in or concerned with New Guinea tend to believe that New Guinean groups differ radically in their capacities for economic change. However plausible this view that explains the widely varying records of economic growth among New Guinean groups by the cultural or psychological characteristics peculiar to each group may seem, it must be emphasized that it is based on shaky ground. Those who hold it tend to assume that an economically advanced group is so because its members are basically hard-working and pragmatic and that an economically backward group is so because its members are simply lazy or ritual minded. This is a totally circular view that confuses cause and effect.

THE OROKAIVA CASE

The history of the unsatisfactory involvement of the Orokaiva people in the growing of coffee and other cash crops provides an illustration of how the lack of favorable preconditions for economic growth can act to severely inhibit development in the New Guinea context. The Orokaiva live along the coast and the foothills of the Northern District, which although it lies on New Guinea's north coast is part of the Territory of Papua half of Papua and New Guinea. In terms of environmental conditions this area is well suited to growing coffee (particularly the robusta, or lowlands, type), cocoa, and other cash crops. With that, however, the resemblance to Goroka stops, for the Orokaiva have fared poorly in respect to early contact experiences, relationships with the European commercial community, and administration-provided improvements and services such as roads and agricultural extension programs.

To begin with, like so many of New Guinea's coastal groups, the Orokaiva suffered considerably at the hands of the first Europeans to enter their area. Gold-seekers, who ranged through their territory during the late nineteenth century, and administration officers, who brought the area under control during the first years of this century, treated the Orokaiva roughly, leaving a legacy of bitterness toward Europeans (McCarthy 1959:110). This early trauma was followed by a long period of stagnation that was broken only by the intrusions of administrators, missionaries, labor recruiters, and other interlopers. Unlike the Gorokans, who were helped by both European commercial interests and the administration to enter the cash economy at a profitable level, the Orokaiva gained minimal economic benefits from the European presence in their territory. The few European recruiters, traders, and settlers who worked in and around their territory did little to aid them. There was no dynamic settler community that built up a flourishing cash crop industry like coffee in Goroka in which the Orokaiva could play an active and profitable part. And administration attempts to foster cash cropping were anything but effective. In fact, Crocombe's

(1964) analysis of administration efforts to promote a coffee industry among the Orokaiva reads like a textbook on how not to promote cash crop development among New Guineans.

The Orokaiva coffee scheme was one of the main agricultural projects undertaken by the administration of Papua (then separate from the Mandated Territory of New Guinea) during the years between World War I and World War II. The administration purchased tracts of land from the Orokaiva with trade goods and then forced the local community around each tract to clear the land and plant it in coffee. Participation was anything but voluntary; every able-bodied man between sixteen and thirty-six years old who lived within a five-mile radius of a plantation was required by law to help establish the coffee and then to work regularly at tending it, at harvesting and processing the crop, and then at carrying the processed beans—usually by hand over bush paths—to distant administration collection centers. Failure to work was penalized by three-month jail sentences, which usually were served by working on government coconut or rubber plantations.

Little attention was paid apparently to the profitability of the industry; compulsion rather than monetary rewards made it operate. Profits, in fact, were very low, and little accrued to the Orokaiva workers. Several factors appear to be behind this unprofitability. First, during the 1930s, when the plantations were most active, coffee prices were extremely low because of the world economic depression. Second, the administration provided little in the way of roads and other improvements necessary for the efficient transport, processing, and marketing of the crop. Third, the compulsory labor was not only greatly resented, but it was inefficient, as the workers felt little incentive to do well. This all added up to low profits from the sale of the coffee and low—extremely low—payments to participating workers. Although the yearly payment varied from plantation to plantation, Crocombe (1964:16) calculates that the average payment per worker was only $3.10 per year, much less than could be earned by working on a European-owned plantation.

It is little wonder, then, that the Orokaiva resented the scheme. They felt that the government had commandeered their land and labor to produce coffee which it sold for its own benefit and then had turned around and only given them token payments. Needless to say, the system did little to encourage cash cropping among the

Orokaiva. Indeed, it seems to have had an opposite effect, which persists today. It is probably no exaggeration to state that the seeming lack of enthusiasm for cash cropping shown by many Orokaiva well into the 1960s was in no small part due to their unsatisfactory experience with compulsory coffee growing and with other similarly unsuccessful cash crop schemes fostered by the administration in past decades (Rimoldi 1966:101; Waddell and Krinks 1968:296). Unprofitable cash cropping schemes that are forced upon a people hardly serve to inspire those people to become market-oriented. If anything, they make them distrustful of the cash economy and wary, as the Orokaiva seem to still be today, of committing themselves to major cash cropping or other commercial efforts (compare Rowley 1965:90–127).

SIX DISTRICTS COMPARED

The districts which R. S. Finney (1971) chose for her study of motivation and economic development provide an excellent opportunity to inquire into the role of favorable and unfavorable preconditions in local development in New Guinea. Four of them—Eastern Highlands, Chimbu, Western Highlands, and East New Britain—are among the most advanced economically in New Guinea, while the other two—Madang and Manus—are among the most backward. Yet the people in all these districts seem to be more or less equally preadapted for economic growth, both in terms of values and institutions and in terms of achievement motivation. R. S. Finney's analysis of the relation between preconditions for development and actual development is summarized here to further illustrate how important preconditions are to the realization of the basic New Guinean potential for rapid economic growth.

To facilitate comparison I shall lump the three Highlands districts together as one region, the Central Highlands, since these districts are relatively similar in preconditions for development and in their actual records of development. We are left, then, with four regions to compare—the "advanced" Central Highlands and East New Britain, on the one hand, and the "backward" Madang and Manus, on the other. Since the main source of cash income for the people of these four regions is the revenue they derive from their cash crops, per-capita income obtained from the sale of cash crops provides the best indication of their present economic status. But, as we are

Preadaption, Preconditions, and Cargo Cults

interested primarily in the rate of economic growth and not simply the current level of income, per-capita income figures must be adjusted according to the number of years the people have had to grow and market cash crops, in order to give a more dynamic picture of the economic accomplishments achieved by the populations of the four regions. In lieu of a more precise starting time, the date each region (or major portions thereof) came under government control (by the German administration or its Australian successor) has been taken to mark the opening of the commercial era in each. By dividing present per-capita income figures by the years under government control, a figure representing income per year under control can be obtained. By ranking the regions according to this figure, we can see how much the increasingly affluent people of East New Britain and the Central Highlands are ahead of the relatively poor and economically stagnant people of Manus and Madang (Table 11).

Of the four regions in this comparison the East New Britain District ranks highest in economic growth. This district is dominated by the Tolai people, who make up about two-thirds of its population and produce well over three-quarters of the cash crops grown by indigenous New Guinean growers there. The Tolai live on the Gazelle Peninsula, at the northern tip of the district and the island. Whereas most of the district is extremely mountainous and sparsely populated, the Gazelle Peninsula is relatively flat and heavily populated, with many areas having densities of one hundred or more persons per square mile. Fertile soils, made up largely of decomposed volcanic rock or of recent volcanic ash deposits, cover much of the peninsula (Epstein 1968:2).

The Gazelle Peninsula has been one of the main centers for European commercial activity in New Guinea since the late 1800s. European traders began to be active there in the 1870s, some coconut plantations were established as early as the 1880s, and in 1889, when the German government took over the administration of New Guinea from the Neuguinea-Kompagnie, the colonial capital was established at Kokopo. In 1910 the capital was moved a few miles north to Rabaul, which has been a major administrative and commercial center in New Guinea ever since (Epstein 1968:8–13).

Extensive European plantations were established during the German rule, and by 1914 economic prospects for the area were

TABLE 11. Per-capita Cash Crop Income Rankings for 1967.

District	Total cash crop income[1]	Indigenous population[2]	Total per-capita cash crop income	Years of government control[3]	Annual per-capita income for years of control	Rank order
East New Britain	$2,655,031	91,709	$28.95	68	$0.43	1
Central Highlands	4,161,558	700,826	5.94	20	0.30	2
Manus	99,546	23,126	4.30	55	0.08	3
Madang	260,350	156,375	1.66	55	0.03	4

1. Income figures were derived from Bureau of Statistics (1967) data on production of the main export cash crops (cocoa, copra, coffee and pyrethrum) and from estimates of prices paid to producers, supplied by H. Brookfield (personal communication January 7, 1969).
2. Population estimates are from Bureau of Statistics (1967).
3. For East New Britain, dating from 1899, when the German government established its capital on the northern tip of the island (Epstein 1968:9); for the Highlands, dating from 1947, when the Uncontrolled Areas Ordinance was suspended for much of the area (Howlett 1962:223); for Manus, dating from 1912, when German local government was first established (Schwartz 1962:223); and for Madang, dating from 1912, when control was established along the coast of the district (Lawrence 1964:42). Some hinterland portions of these districts remained beyond government control for considerable periods after these initial dates.

excellent. The plantations were bearing well; good port facilities had been developed at Rabaul; and a road system covered much of the coast and penetrated to the main population centers inland. The plantations and other facilities were taken over by Australian interests after the outbreak of World War I, and, although the capital of the Mandated Territory of New Guinea was moved from Rabaul to Lae on the mainland of New Guinea in 1938, Rabaul and its hinterland remained the main commercial center of New Guinea during the period between the world wars. Now, despite extensive developments on the New Guinea mainland after World War II, the Gazelle Peninsula's combination of good roads, well-developed transport and marketing facilities, and a deep-water port is still unparalled in New Guinea.

Some of the early European activities on the Gazelle Peninsula, especially the sale of arms and the extensive alienation of land, brought considerable hardship to the Tolai people. Later, however, when the German government took over New Guinea, conditions improved for the Tolai, and they began to benefit from the establishment of the copra industry on the peninsula and all the infrastructure improvements that went with it. At first the Tolai people sold their surplus coconuts to European traders and plantation owners, but later, with government encouragement, they began to make their own copra and plant their own coconut plantations. Although the establishment of Australian rule and a severe drop in copra prices during the 1920s slowed Tolai economic growth between the wars, it nonetheless continued. Indeed, during the Depression years of the 1930s the Tolai sought to increase their cash income by investing in copra driers, trade stores, and trucking ventures. However, the Japanese invasion cut this development short, and the Tolai suffered heavy losses during that occupation and the Allied bombings that followed.

In the postwar period the Tolai benefited greatly from a new and dynamic policy toward indigenous economic development carried out by the administration in the Gazelle Peninsula. The Tolai were encouraged to replant their coconut plantations, and an extension program to promote cocoa growing was inaugurated. The Tolai enthusiastically responded to these efforts, and, with the inestimable advantage of having a road system that reached practically every village and gave easy access to the marketing center and port of

Rabaul, they quickly reestablished their position as the leading cash crop producers of New Guinea. They also resumed their interest in other commercial ventures and invested in crop processing facilities, trade stores, and other enterprises, which, along with their cash crop activities, have made them the most affluent group in New Guinea today (Epstein 1968; Salisbury 1970).

The people of the Central Highlands, like those of the Gazelle Peninsula, have enjoyed relatively favorable preconditions for economic growth, judged in terms of natural resources, infrastructure improvements, and market opportunities. The Highlanders, like the Gorokans, have also enjoyed one additional advantage denied the Tolai and many other coastal groups: because the Highlands remained undiscovered for so long, by the time Europeans first entered the area a more enlightened administrative policy had evolved that was designed to minimize social disruption, to control the impact of European commercial interests, and to promote indigenous economic development. Although this policy was applied unevenly in the Highlands, it can be said that, in contrast to most New Guinean groups, the Highlanders benefited more than they suffered from the imposition of European rule virtually from the start. As a result of this unique combination of favorable circumstances, the Highlanders have shown a remarkable record of rapid economic growth, which, in the cases of a few groups like the Gorokans, exceeds that of the Tolai.

The main economic changes among the 700,000 persons of the Eastern Highlands, Chimbu, and Western Highlands districts, which make up the Central Highlands, date from the postwar period and are closely related, as in Goroka, to the development of the Highlands coffee industry. There are other sources of cash earnings for the Highlanders—gold taken from alluvial streams; minor cash crops like pyrethrum, passion fruit, peanuts, and market vegetables; livestock; and, most recently, tea—but none has been as important as coffee. However, as can be surmised from comparing per-capita-income figures from the entire Central Highlands with those from Goroka, it is apparent that not all Highlands groups have participated in the coffee boom as much as the Gorokans. The poorer growth record of many Highlands groups can be explained largely either by a lack of opportunity or by unfavorable environmental conditions. For example, in remote areas where roads have yet to

Preadaption, Preconditions, and Cargo Cults

penetrate, cash cropping is hardly possible, and virtually the only way people can make money is by becoming contract laborers on coastal plantations or by migrating to Highlands or coastal centers for jobs. And even where roads have penetrated an area, if soils are poor (as in dry, grassland areas and rocky, mountainous areas), if frosts occur (as in the upland regions above about 6,500 feet, where some Highlands groups live), or if population densities are too great to allow much land to be used for cash cropping (as in parts of the Chimbu and Western Highlands districts), major cash crop development may not be possible.

Where conditions approximate those found in Goroka, however, rapid economic growth has usually been impressive. This applies to some areas in the Eastern Highlands adjacent to Goroka, to parts of the Chimbu District, and to parts of the Wahgi Valley and Mount Hagen area in the Western Highlands, where because of good soils and rainfall, adequate roads, good transport and marketing facilities, and an effective agricultural extension program, coffee has been developed as an important cash crop for local populations. Where these favorable conditions have been present, one finds ready acceptance of cash cropping, the drive for conspicuous investment in business enterprises, and the vigorous entrepreneurial movements that have characterized Gorokan economic growth (Brookfield 1968; Dicke 1968; Feist 1968; Hughes 1966; Reay 1969: 66–67).

The first example of a backward region to be considered here is the Manus District, which is made up of numerous small islands lying in the Bismarck Sea a hundred or so miles north of the New Guinea mainland. Only about 23,000 persons live in the district, most of them on Manus, the largest island. Manus is a high, continental island, but because of its rugged terrain and the heavy tropical rains that leach its soil it is considered to have limited agricultural potential (Government Printer 1967:40).

Whalers, labor recruiters, and traders began to visit the island in the late 1800s, and several German planters established coconut plantations along the coast around the turn of the century. European-Manus relations were particularly stormy during this early period, and until the establishment of German local administrative control in 1912 the Manus suffered from raids of reprisal carried out by German warships called in to punish them for having killed or injured European traders, labor recruiters, or planters (Neverman

1934:1–16; Schwartz 1962:223). Australian forces took control of Manus in 1914, extended government control throughout the district, and assigned the German plantations to Australian private interests, but they did little or nothing to promote local economic development among the Manus. About the only way the Manus had of making money in the twenties and thirties was to hire out as laborers on local European plantations or to seek work with the administration or private employers elsewhere in New Guinea (Mead 1956:73–74; Schwartz 1962:223–224).

Japanese forces occupied Manus in 1942 but were ousted in 1944 by American troops, who developed Manus into a major staging base for their invasion of the Philippines. Extensive port and shore facilities were built, and thousands of ships and aircraft, as well as reportedly a million troops and naval personnel, moved through the island during 1944 and 1945. This military development greatly impressed the Manus people. They saw huge amounts of material goods, many of which were completely novel to them and some of which they were able to obtain through the high wages paid them by Americans, through gifts, and through the disposal of surplus property after the war. They also saw that the American forces included black troops, who shared the goods and skills of the white Americans to a much greater extent than the Manus had shared the goods and skills of the white Australians and Germans who had ruled them previously. This exposure to new goods, to a generous American administration, and to black Americans made the Manus look forward to a postwar era of progress (Mead 1956:145–164).

Soon after the war the Manus started movements designed to modernize Manus society in order to clear the way for the new prosperity they thought would be theirs. The most famous of these movements, the one led by Paliau Maloat—a charismatic leader who had served as a policeman on administration patrols through Goroka and other Highlands areas during the early 1930s and who now is the member of the House of Assembly for Manus (Maloat 1970)—succeeded in reorganizing many traditional features of Manus life, but its effectiveness was limited by a lack of real economic opportunities and by the emergence of cargo cult thinking, which turned the Manus toward ritual instead of secular reform and cash cropping as the "true" way to achieve prosperity and a new social order (Schwartz 1962).

Although cargo cult activities have died down since their peak in the late 1940s and early 1950s, economic progress among the Manus has not been impressive. Some of the coastal lands have been planted in coconuts, and one small European coconut plantation has been purchased by a Manus group (Crocombe 1965), but these holdings provide only a limited cash income, which is not shared by many inland peoples who have as yet no profitable cash crops to plant in their home areas. The Manus realize that they are in an economic backwater; they want better shipping service to Rabaul and mainland New Guinea ports, they want roads to open up the hinterland, they want new crops and more extension service, and they want aid in developing a fishing industry (United Nations 1968:27–28).

The Madang District is the last and the most economically depressed of the four regions to be considered. Although larger than any of the Highlands districts, Madang has only 160,000 persons, who live in small villages scattered throughout the district. There are no dense concentrations of population as there are on the Gazelle Peninsula or in the valleys of the Highlands. Much of Madang is uninviting; except for a narrow coastal strip with areas of rich alluvial or volcanic soil, it has little immediate agricultural potential. The interior consists primarily of rugged foothills interspersed here and there with swamps and grassland areas, and then the steep and heavily forested slopes of the Bismarck Range, which defines Madang's border with the Highlands districts.

Soon after Germany assumed control of the northeastern coast of New Guinea in 1884, attempts were made to start settlements on the Madang coast and to explore the interior of the region. The first main European settlements were on Astrolabe Bay, where the Neuguinea-Kompagnie tried its first experiments in plantation agriculture. Tobacco plantations employing Chinese and Japanese laborers were started there, but they were abandoned in 1903 because of health and labor problems, leaving a legacy of strained relations between the Germans and the local people, who had been forced to give up their land to the company (Jacobs, in press). After the failure of the tobacco plantations German interest shifted to the area around the port of Madang. From the start local interests there were ignored: large areas of land were alienated for rubber and coconut plantations, and little or no effort was made to bring the people into the cash economy as producers. In 1904 those who had lost much of their land organized an unsuccessful rebellion, and in 1912, when plans for another uprising were discovered, they were exiled and still more of their land was taken from them (Flierl 1927:113–114; Lawrence 1964:34–43; 68–72).

Australian rule ended the worst excesses of the German period, but the new administration still favored European commercial interests over indigenous interests and did little to redress grievances over land or promote cash cropping among the people. After World War II, during which Madang was occupied by the Japanese, Australian policy toward indigenous economic development began to change. Progress has, however, been minimal, because of both the strained European-indigen relations dating from German days and the manifold difficulties of linking the scattered peoples of Madang with the cash economy. There is only one overseas port, the port of Madang, in the district, and only a few roads barely penetrate the hinterland from there.

Given the circumstances surrounding the establishment of German rule and their alienation of land for plantations, the dominance of European commercial interests during much of Australia's administration, and the difficulties of linking a scattered population to the cash economy, it is not surprising that the Madang District has been the site of vigorous and long-lived cargo cult movements (Burridge 1960, 1969; Lawrence 1964). Although the administration has tried to suppress these movements, it has been unable to offer the Madang people much in the way of tangible alternatives; the Madang people therefore remain one of the most economically backward and dispirited peoples of New Guinea.

The four regional sketches demonstrate how closely indigenous economic developments in New Guinea have correlated with the presence or absence of favorable preconditions for economic growth. Where there are fertile soils, where governmental (and, at times, European private enterprise) policies have actively encouraged and aided indigenous involvement in the cash economy, and where profitable cash crops have been introduced and their exploitation made feasible through extension aid and the development of a transport and marketing system that reaches people in their villages, one finds—as in East New Britain and the Highlands districts—that people respond positively to opportunity and quickly become involved in cash cropping and other commercial activities. However, where soils are poor, where positive economic policies have not been implemented, and where profitable crops, extension aid, and infrastructure improvements are lacking or have not been systematically introduced—as in Manus and Madang—one finds that people make little progress toward becoming significant participants in the cash economy.

CARGO CULTS AND THE GOROKANS

New Guinea is perhaps best known in the general literature on modernization and economic development for its cargo cults, social movements in which people seek to gain free access to European goods, or *kago* (cargo). Cargo cult adherents commonly believe that the steel tools, canned food, and other goods with which Europeans seem so liberally endowed were created by their deceased ancestors or by other spirits and that these goods were originally intended for New Guineans, who would have received them had Europeans not intercepted the goods and kept them for their own use. In order to obtain the cargo wrongfully denied to them, cultists often build cargo houses to hold the sought-for goods and sometimes also construct piers or airstrips to receive cargo-laden steamships or airplanes. They then usually carry out a series of ritual acts prescribed by a prophet who promises them that performance of the proper rituals will bring the cargo. Commonly associated with this belief in the coming of cargo is the idea that recipients of cargo will gain equal status with Europeans and may even be able to overthrow their rule.

Lawrence and Meggitt have argued that a basic difference exists between Highlanders and coastal New Guineans in respect to cargo cult activity. They posit that the basic religious and ritual orientation of coastal New Guineans predispose them to cargo cult activities, whereas the Highlanders are relatively immune to cargo cults because of their essentially secular and pragmatic orientation (Lawrence and Meggitt 1965; Lawrence 1967:42; Meggitt 1967b). This is an untenable position. First, the posited sharp distinction in world view between the two groups is not borne out by the enthnographic record—there are pragmatic coastal New Guineans and ritualistic Highlanders (compare Chowning 1967). Second, it is difficult to accept that Highlanders have not had considerable experience with cargo cult activities in the light of the ample evidence of cargo cult movements in the Highlands. And, third, this formulation ignores, or relegates to a secondary role, any relationship between the economic opportunities available to New Guineans and their inclination to become involved in cargo cult activities. The last two points bear elaboration.

The first Highlands cargo cult that I have found mention of in the literature is the so-called Black King movement, which occurred around 1940 near Mount Hagen in the Western Highlands after two Sepik men had spread the doctrine of the original Black King movement, which had previously been active in the Sepik and Madang districts (Simpson 1965:291; Strathern 1970; Worsley 1957:199). According to Simpson, Ninji, a famous Mount Hagen big-man, and several other leaders had a large cargo house built to receive goods—axes, shovels, knives, and mother-of-pearl shells—that were to arrive by airplane to be given out to them. These items were all valued trade goods which the Mount Hagen people had been receiving in small quantities from gold prospectors, patrol officers, and missionaries. According to the cargo cult doctrine, however, these were really goods that had been sent to the Hagen people by their ancestors but had been intercepted by Europeans, who only doled them out in meager amounts in return for produce and labor.

In Worsley's (1957:198–205) review of cargo cult activity in the Highlands (known to him from the literature available in the mid-1950s) two other Highlands movements are mentioned: the Great Pigs movement, which was discovered by an ANGAU patrol in 1946 in an uncontrolled region of the Western Highlands near the Dutch border; and what Worsley calls the Ghost Wind movement, a widespread cult manifested in numerous outbreaks in the Eastern Highlands between 1943 and 1947. In addition to these movements, at least two other apparently independent Highlands movements have been noted in the literature: the Hine movement, which was active in the Wabag region of the Western Highlands in 1945 (Worsley 1959:120), and an unnamed cult that Reay (1959:194–202) reports as having been active in 1949 in the Wahgi Valley of the Western Highlands.[2]

Only one of these cults, the Ghost Wind movement described by Berndt (1952–1953), appears to have affected the people in and around Goroka. This movement apparently started around 1943 in the Markham Valley and then spread into the eastern edge of the Highlands, where outbreaks occurred sporadically for the next four years. Berndt believes that the events that preceded the importation of the cargo doctrine in the Highlands made the people there extremely receptive to the cult. The sound and sight of airplanes flying over their valleys in the early 1930s alarmed the Highlanders, who regarded them as huge and awesome birds, and their astonishment increased when they saw these "birds" come to earth and disgorge red-skinned men[3] and coveted trade goods. Berndt says that these Highlanders then developed the fear that the newcomers had come to kill their pigs and pregnant women and took ritual steps to ward off that danger. Later, as people came to fear the Europeans less, they developed the idea that their dead ancestors would soon return to give them their full share of the riches and goods possessed by the Europeans. These expectations went unrealized, and when the war came and the small flow of European goods that the Highlanders had been receiving was curtailed, they began to believe that Europeans were conspiring to withhold the goods that had been sent to them by the ancestors and spirits. Conditions were then ripe for a series of outbreaks, marked in many cases by shivering and shaking fits caused by the Ghost Wind, that swept into the Eastern Highlands as the full cargo doctrine reached the people.

This cult movement, with some of its characteristic features—the construction of cargo houses, the placement of sticks, stones, and other objects within the houses in the belief that they would be turned into valuable cargo articles, and the use of wooden imitation rifles for drilling and, in some cases, to oppose European patrols—apparently spread westward as far as the southern edge of Goroka. Salisbury (1958), for example, reports that a prophet from Kainantu, the center of the cult movement, spread the cult doctrine to the Siane people and to neighboring Dene tribes in 1947 and succeeded in provoking a number of cult outbreaks among these two groups.

These outbreaks (which were suppressed by administration patrols) among the Siane and Dene appear to have marked the western limit of the spread of the Ghost Wind movement and also seem to be the only cult outbreaks reported in the published literature as having occurred near Goroka. If one were forced to rely solely on published sources, one might therefore conclude that Goroka has had little cargo cult activity. However, the published record can be deceptive, for there are certainly many cult outbreaks in New Guinea that are never recorded in newspapers, journals, and books. For example, in Goroka I heard about the existence, since the Ghost Wind movement, of at least four separate manifestations of cargo cult activities that had never to my knowledge been reported in the published literature. Although I did not systematically inquire about these outbreaks and hence have little oral data on them to report, I was able to find references to two of them when I examined patrol reports from Goroka in the Department of District Administration in Port Moresby after the completion of my fieldwork in Goroka in 1968.

The first cult mentioned in these reports occurred in 1962 in the Upper Asaro census division. O. K. Adler (1962–1963), the officer who investigated the cult, recorded that the leader, a local man, had reportedly dreamed that he was to go to a place near his village to pick up a load of goods intended for him. After allegedly finding the goods, he told others of his good fortune and built a cargo house. His actions and those of two other men who traveled around the area urging people to cease regular work, build cargo houses, and await the coming of cargo stimulated a full-fledged cargo movement. Lutheran missionaries whose followers were involved in the cult were the first to react against it. They toured the area urging their converts to burn the cargo houses and go back to work, apparently with some success, for when Adler arrived on the scene, overt cult activity seemed to have stopped and the people were mostly back at work in their subsistence and coffee gardens.

The second Goroka cult I found mention of in administration reports occurred in 1965 in Sigoma Village in the Bena Bena census division, only a few miles from Goroka township. C. T. Davies (1965–1966), who investigated the cult, gives only a few details about it. Apparently two men, one from Madang and the other a local villager, started the cult and directed the people to build a large meeting house for the whole village, to build a smaller house in which the village girls were to be sequestered, and to carry out rituals that were to make quantities of money appear. Both men,

Preadaption, Preconditions, and Cargo Cults 141

according to Davies, were disciples of Yali, the famous cult leader of the Madang District (Lawrence 1964), and in the prescribed rituals Yali's name was allegedly invoked. The people were told, for example, to repeat the name of Yali and then (presumably while seated) to turn the soles of their feet upward to receive the money.

In addition, I found references in administration records to four other movements that had broken out around Goroka since the war: a 1947 outbreak south of Goroka, which was probably a manifestation of the Ghost Wind movement and may have been the same outbreak reported by Salisbury (Taylor 1947); another, apparently independent movement that was reported in 1947 to have been spreading toward the Lufa area, southeast of Goroka, from the Papuan border (Searson 1947–1948); a 1957 outbreak that occurred just to the east of Goroka (Johnson 1957–1958); and another 1957 outbreak south of Lufa (Burnett 1957–1958). Since not all cult outbreaks are detected and reported by the administration and also since I probably did not see all the relevant administration records, I suspect that the actual number of cult outbreaks that have occurred in and around Goroka exceeds the seven or eight documented cases discussed here. I would estimate that there may have been at least a dozen outbreaks in and around the Goroka area since the war and that other regions of the Highlands have probably experienced a like number of cult manifestations. In short, I find it difficult to believe that there has been a paucity of cargo cult outbreaks in the Highlands.

Neither can one argue that cargo cult beliefs are purely alien imports into the Highlands. Certainly, some individual movements and some specific cargo ideas have spread there from cult centers in neighboring coastal districts. But, although we need not go as far as to accept Salisbury's (1958:74–75) suggestion that cult activity may have been an indigenous, pre-European phenomenon in the Highlands, the evidence seems to indicate, as Berndt has argued in the case of the Ghost Wind movement, that basic elements of cargo cult thinking have been generated within the Highlands. Highlanders, like other New Guineans, have been faced with the problem of explaining why Europeans are so well endowed with exotic goods, and one of the main explanations that has come to mind is that Europeans have somehow learned the "cargo secret" that gives them ready access to goods. Even today, for example, some Gorokan villagers believe, according to essays written by Gorokan high school students, that

> . . . underground caves serve as repositories for goods; that the goods are made elsewhere and are sent to the caves for storage, or that the ancestors dwell in the caves and manufacture goods there; that these goods can be obtained by using secret rituals to pull them directly out of the ground or from rivers that emerge from the ground; and that Europeans—often thought of as spirits of the dead—know these secrets and intercept the goods intended for New Guineans and then bestow them on or withold them from the latter. (R. S. Finney 1971:61)

If, then, there is ample evidence of cargo thinking and of cult movements in Goroka and other parts of the Highlands, can these areas be considered to be any different from Madang or any other coastal area noted for cult activity? My answer to that question is yes, for cargo thinking seems to be much more in the background and actual cult movements seem to be much more short-lived in the Highlands than in the coastal areas noted for cargo cults. Typically, for example, it seems that Highlands cult movements—save perhaps for the Ghost Wind movement—have been marked by brief periods of intense activity, after which they die down and their adherents return to the normal round of daily activities. And cargo thinking, however widespread it may be, does not seem to dominate the thoughts and actions of Highlanders, who, as we have seen, are very much involved in modern, "rational," means of seeking money and European goods. This situation stands in direct contrast to the record of ubiquitous cargo cult activity and the apparent dominance of cargo cult ideology in coastal areas like Madang (Burridge 1960; Harding 1967; Lawrence 1964).

This contrast should not, however, be explained by saying that Highlanders are less dominated by cargo cults because they are basically secular and pragmatic and therefore reject cargo cult doctrines when it becomes apparent that no cargo is immediately forthcoming after ritual efforts have been made to obtain it. A more satisfactory explanation is simply that relatively ready access to the means of earning money and purchasing European goods, not any inherent secularity or pragmatism, has been most instrumental in dampening enthusiasm for cargo cults in the Highlands. Certainly, the Highlanders, in displaying a preference for cash cropping over cargo cult rituals as a way to obtain wealth and cargo, appear to be highly secular and pragmatic. But this is merely a characterization of their actions, not a causal explanation. My own opinion is that, as Lawrence (1966:274–275) seems to indicate in one of his latest statements concerning Madang cargo cults, even people like those of Madang, whose thinking and actions have long been dominated by cargoism, would also choose to abandon cult activity if they had the opportunity to earn enough money to purchase *significant* amounts of valued cargo items. Therefore, to rephrase the argument in terms of the comparative discussion of regional development records, my point is that where favorable preconditions exist New Guineans are likely to resist the pull of cargo cults and turn to intensive cash cropping and other commercial activities.

The cult movement that was reported in 1957 to be spreading from the Papuan foothills of the Highlands into an area south of Goroka provides an example to illustrate how the attractions of new commercial activities can blunt the appeal of cargo cults. I. D. Burnett (1957–1958), the patrol officer who was sent from Goroka to investigate this movement, found that the Gono people, a group located south of Lufa near the border of the Eastern Highlands and Papua, had resisted emissaries from Papua who were attempting to gain adherents to a new cult movement. These prophets, who preached such classic cult beliefs as the idea that Europeans had changed the labels on boxes sent by the ancestors so that they, not the intended recipients, would receive the cargo, were apparently completely rebuffed by the Gono people. According to Burnett, they wanted nothing to do with this cult because they were then "particularly keen to plant coffee" and were looking north to Lufa, where DASF personnel from Goroka were promoting coffee, not south to underdeveloped Papua, for their models of how to participate in the modern world.

This competition between the ideology of cargo cults and that of commercial enterprise should perhaps not be considered solely in terms of competing ways of obtaining European goods. Cochrane (1970) has recently argued that it is status, particularly as related to big-men, that is at the heart of the cargo cult problem in New Guinea and other areas of Melanesia. Cargo cults occur, according to Cochrane, where repressive governmental, missionary, or commercial practices have deprived the people—and particularly their big-men—of status. A cult movement is then seen as an attempt to regain status, and cargo cult leaders are seen as big-men of a new type, who organize their followers in cult movements to compete on equal terms with Europeans, particularly the "big-men" of the administration who rule over them. The desire for cargo takes a back seat in this view; its role is that of a symbol of equal status— a means to an end, rather than an end in itself.

In the light of this argument Gorokans would seem to have litle need for cargo cults. Their rapid and profitable entry into the cash economy and the emergence of business leaders as neotraditional big-men have meant that they have suffered relatively little status deprivation. Business for the Gorokans has been, then, a cargo cult that works. Coffee growing and other commercial activities have given the Gorokans what cargo cults promise but cannot confer— status as active participants in the modern world. Cargo is involved here, but it is cargo of a special kind: trucks, trade stores, and other capital goods whose purchase and possession seem to be of great symbolic, as well as intrinsic, value to the Gorokans. These conspicuous investments have given the Gorokans, and in particular the business leaders who have amassed the profits and directed the pooling of funds necessary to make the purchases, a measure of pride in their own accomplishments that has enabled them to adjust easily, without the help of cargo cults or other social movements, to their abrupt introduction into the modern world.

It is no accident, then, that Gorokan business leaders with whom I discussed cargo cults expressed opposition to them vehemently. They seemed to regard cults as more than just misguided attempts by ignorant villagers to seek cargo. To them, cult activity was both an insult and a threat. Their pride seemed to be wounded by the thought that people might choose cult activities over the commercial activities that they had pioneered, and they seemed particularly upset that cult leaders dared to challenge their authority as *the* modern-day big-men (compare Reay 1964:255). Several of these business leaders have had the chance to express their opposition to cult movements directly, by participating in government patrols sent to put down outbreaks in Goroka and nearby areas. Sabumei Kofikai, who took part in several administration campaigns against cargo cults, attempted to explain to me the logic he used in exhorting cultists to abandon their practices and follow the "true" road to economic development. He stated his position to the people in the following words:

> . . . plenty Gorokans have bought trucks, and some have stores. Now, these did not come from nowhere. They came from hard work—from planting coffee, selling sweet potatoes, planting pyrethrum, selling passion fruit, selling peanuts, and some men work for companies, and some work for the government. All right, money is obtained from these activities, and is well saved—in the Commonwealth Bank or in the Bank of New South Wales—and then, later, when a man wants to start a store, he goes and gets his money and starts the store. Or, whoever wants to start a cattle business, he goes and gets his money from the bank and starts the business.

The message here is plain: work hard, save money, and invest it to be successful. It is a prescription that so far has worked well for the Gorokans and has provided them with a powerful argument against the cargo cult approach to participation in the modern world.

7

Problems and Prospects

Theorists on entrepreneurship, particularly those who emphasize the social, cultural, or psychological factors affecting the supply of entrepreneurship, tend to think in binary terms—to posit, for example, that innovative entrepreneurs are either present or absent in a society and that economic performance will accordingly be either dynamic or stagnant. This stance can be seriously misleading, for it assumes that highly motivated persons can, in effect, conquer all obstacles and ignores what recent empirical studies of entrepreneurship reviewed by Kilby (1971:27–40) show—that even where economic conditions are favorable a lack of technical and managerial skills among entrepreneurs and the influence of traditional values and institutions which, however conducive to the appearance of entrepreneurship, may hinder the operation of efficient enterprises, can greatly impede entrepreneurial performance and economic growth. Here I shall examine some of the most apparent technical and managerial failings of Gorokan enterprises, as well as what might be called structural problems related to the interplay between Gorokan society and the modern cash economy. In addition, I shall review the colonial problems inherent in the continued presence of European businessmen and firms in Goroka.

TECHNICAL AND MANAGERIAL PROBLEMS

In a previous monograph I analyzed the main technical and managerial problems Gorokans were experiencing in the operation of their enterprises as I observed them in 1967 (Finney 1969). Here I

Problems and Prospects 147

shall summarize that discussion, adding some information that has become available to me since 1967.

Gorokans as Coffee Producers

The alacrity with which Gorokans planted coffee and then went on to become the top coffee-producing group in New Guinea has been emphasized in this narrative. But this does not mean that all is well with the Gorokan coffee industry. DASF officers have told me, for example, that because of substandard cultivation practices yields of coffee beans per tree are generally low on most Gorokan holdings and that the cumulative effects of neglect might cause some older plantings to cease yielding altogether.

One could pinpoint the relative lack of technical instruction and aid as the main, if not the sole, reason for the substandard state of many Gorokan coffee holdings, for the DASF now takes only a passive role in coffee extension work. Because of a policy decision to switch Gorokan attention from coffee to other crops, coffee extension patrols are no longer sent out into the countryside. If a grower comes to DASF headquarters in Goroka with a problem, agricultural officers will attempt to help him out, but they will not go out looking for coffee work. Gorokans are therefore not the beneficiaries of an active extension program such as that which facilitated their first efforts to grow coffee during the 1950s. However, I doubt that this lack of readily available information and aid alone accounts for their substandard cultivation practices.

Most Gorokan coffee growers only work at it part time. They may have planted anywhere from a few hundred to a thousand or so trees, which are their main source of cash, but coffee is not their sole agricultural activity. These small growers still raise sweet potatoes and other crops, which provide their basic subsistence. They also keep pigs, for, although shell valuables have been replaced by money in bridewealth transactions and other exchanges, pigs retain their symbolic value, and few men would consider giving them up. Some of these small, part-time growers have model, if miniature, coffee plantations. However, most of their holdings do not appear to be well maintained, and a few are not even completely harvested during the coffee season. Why should this be? Why should some Gorokans apparently neglect their coffee and thereby pass up potential increments to their cash incomes?

The answer, I suggest, lies in the part-time character of their coffee growing. These men are not wholly dependent on the cash economy for meeting their needs; a man and his wife, or wives, can still easily grow most of the food they eat. And neither tax requirements (which vary from four to eight dollars a year and can be waived in cases of hardship) nor the local interest in consumer goods is heavy enough to force Gorokans to put money earning above all else. Although a modest amount of cash comes in handy for supplementary foodstuffs like bread, sugar, or canned fish, for tools, or for meeting obligations in a bridewealth exchange, most Gorokan men are not so tightly bound to the cash economy that a shortage or lack of cash would spell disaster. In this situation coffee trees can be treated like money in the bank. After the trees have been planted and are mature, they yield one major and one minor harvest of beans a year. If a grower does a minimum of maintenance chores—clearing undergrowth between trees and perhaps roughly pruning them—the trees bear fairly well, and he can make "withdrawals" from his private bank to bring in at least fifty to a hundred dollars a harvest for a minimal effort.

But to increase yields significantly and to maintain the trees in full productivity for several decades, a great deal more effort would be required: the ground between trees should be kept free of growth at all times and well mulched to prevent loss of moisture; the trees should be pruned regularly to prevent overgrowth; fertilizer should be periodically applied to prevent soil exhaustion and consequent damage to the trees; and the shade tree canopy should be maintained to insure that enough, but not too much, sunlight penetrates to the coffee trees. Here is where some Gorokans seem to balk at putting out the extra effort; they appear more interested in maximizing cash return per unit of labor rather than per tree or per area of land planted. Hence, when returns per unit of labor begin to fall off as more effort is needed to properly maintain their plantings in order to obtain maximum and sustained yields, these growers apparently decide not to expend the extra, less-rewarding-per-unit labor and seem to be satisfied with lower, but more easily gained, yields.

What is behind this seemingly casual approach to coffee growing? I suspect that three main factors are at work. First, some growers probably planted coffee mainly because other Gorokans had done so, and they felt they had to also lest they lose status. Once their coffee was in and growing well, these men could turn to other activities that interested them more and still have the prestige of being coffee growers (and some cash dividends to boot), even though they paid relatively little attention to their plantings. Second, some growers are undoubtedly cautious men, not willing to put all their eggs in one basket by devoting all their efforts to coffee growing. This is understandable, given the Gorokan experience with declining coffee prices and the DASF advice to avoid overdependence on coffee. If coffee prices were to fall drastically, or if a world crisis made coffee unsalable, these men would suffer little, for they would still have their subsistence crops to fall back on. Finally, it is unreasonable to assume that all Gorokans need be equally motivated to work hard and strive for success in coffee growing or any other activity. A lot of today's coffee growers are men who probably would have been "nonachievers" in traditional Gorokan society—the man with only one wife (or perhaps none), a small garden, few pigs, and no reputation for leadership.

But what about the big Gorokan coffee growers, the men with thousands rather than hundreds of trees—do they share the same problems as the smallholder? In a few cases the answer is yes. Where a man has built up a large plantation but is not committed enough to manage it properly one finds a situation not unlike the casually operated smallholding. Baito Heiro's pioneer plantation is now in a poor state, for example, and yields are far below those obtained in the late 1950s, when his trees first began to bear. Although Baito complains about declining production, he does not seem concerned enough to make the effort to raise production, for example, by carrying out a complete clearing, pruning, replanting, and fertilizing program. According to Jim Taylor, who is still his neighbor and confidant, Baito simply does not have his heart in coffee growing. He spends too much time away from his plantation—visiting, politicking, and attending meetings, feasts, and exchanges—and is not willing to do the work himself or to supervise a work force to carry out the tasks. Baito was an early starter, but he has fallen behind the more ambitious men, who are willing to devote much of their time and energy to their coffee plantations.

Yet, even ambitious large growers have their troubles. While, in general, most of the large growers are relatively well informed about the technical requirements of coffee growing (primarily because they ask and receive advice from the DASF and friendly European planters), many of the plantations owned by these men show signs of neglect. Here the problem is primarily managerial and financial. A large plantation of ten to twenty thousand trees needs a sizable labor force of anywhere from a half-dozen men in the slack season to two dozen or more at the height of harvesting. Although most of the big growers were able to rely on the traditionally recruited services of their clansmen and followers when they were first developing their plantations, once these workers had their own small coffee holdings they usually declined to offer their labor to the big growers —even for cash wages. These growers have therefore found themselves competing with European plantations for increasingly scarce laborers from remote areas of the Highlands where there is little or no cash crop development. Here the Gorokan is at a clear disadvantage. While his European counterpart usually has the ready access to credit from trading banks, wholesalers, retailers, and coffee export firms that is necessary to operate his plantation and meet his payroll regularly, the large Gorokan grower is typically denied credit from these sources. He therefore must rely solely on his savings to cover his costs.[1] When these are exhausted, he has trouble holding an adequate labor force. Frequently this occurs around harvest time, when funds from the previous harvest have usually already been spent, and the consequences can be disastrous, as for lack of labor much of the coffee may have to be left on the trees. Poor financial planning and a cavalier attitude toward workers— particularly toward unsophisticated boys recruited from outlying regions—on the part of some of these large growers exacerbate this situation, but the primary problem stems from the inability of these men to receive regular credit from European-controlled sources that are open to the European grower.

GOROKANS AS RETAILERS

Gorokan trade stores are numerous, and with a few exceptions, such as the substantial stores owned by Hari Gotoha and Wale Kabiliha, they are small in size, inventory, and profits. Many Europeans, upon noting this and listening to tales of financial failure due to faulty merchandising practices or too-liberal credit policies, freely criticize the whole Gorokan trade-store movement and conclude that Gorokans would be better off without their stores.

Problems and Prospects 151

But this view ignores the important service functions of Gorokan stores, as well as the fact that of all their enterprises retail trading is the one in which Gorokans have begun to improve their performance most.

European critics of Gorokan trade stores tend to forget that, while they have easy access to town stores, the majority of Gorokans live too far from town stores or the few European stores located in the countryside to be able to shop at these outlets conveniently. The small village trade store is therefore a useful local asset; it enables villagers to satisfy many of their needs without having to trek to town or some faraway plantation store, and since some credit is usually available it enables the typical villager, who is ordinarily unable to obtain credit from European stores, to make purchases even when his funds are exhausted.[2]

But it is really debatable whether, as many Europeans in Goroka assume, all or most of Gorokan trade stores are unprofitable. Gorokans have had the benefit of a decade of experience in operating stores, and I would estimate that many of their stores are now turning a profit. According to informants, in the first, experimental years of trade store operation, stores often took in less money than was invested in stock and were frequently forced to close permanently if no further investment funds were available, or temporarily until new funds might become available. Careless handling of funds by the store owner or keeper, the theft of funds or stock, and a too-generous and unrestricted credit policy figured in many store failures, but a more fundamental factor in early difficulties stemmed from the problem of buying goods, transporting them to the store, and then pricing them high enough to ensure a profit. In those days a store owner would usually buy his goods in Goroka township at prices equal to or only slightly lower than retail prices. Then he would pay a trucker (then usually a European) to transport the goods to his village. Faced with the problem of pricing the goods he frequently took the prices prevailing in Goroka Township as a guide or otherwise picked a price without taking all his costs into account. Consequently, many a store owner sold his goods at a loss until his capital was exhausted and he was forced to close the store.

Despite early disappointments, Gorokans did persist in operating stores and in founding new ones, and they have begun to learn something of the rudiments of purchasing, transport, and pricing.

In addition, recent innovations in wholesaling have lessened the burden on store owners. As Gorokan retailing has developed, so have European wholesale firms specializing in supplying Gorokan stores. The largest wholesale firm, for example, is a Goroka-based business that has virtually grown up with the expansion of indigenous retailing. Competition between this firm and branch stores of New Guinea-wide firms has led to a modest lowering of the wholesale prices and the provision of two simple, but extremely useful, services to Gorokan retailers. First, wholesalers send out trucks to pick up store owners in their villages, take them to town, and then return them with their purchases to their villages. Second, wholesalers suggest retail prices or provide lists of retail prices calculated to allow a reasonable profit above the cost of stock and operating expenses. Today's store owner can therefore—if he keeps his cash receipts, storekeeper, and credit allocations under control—almost automatically count on making a profit from his store.

Gorokans as Truckers

Of all the Gorokan enterprises, trucking has, in a strict accounting sense, probably been the least profitable. Indeed, it is probably no exaggeration to say that most Gorokan trucking enterprises have lost money and that trucks have so far been a major capital drain for the Gorokans. Although Gorokans have undoubtedly gained important service benefits from having trucks to transport them and their produce, I doubt that a strong case could be made that these benefits outweigh the substantial losses incurred in operating trucks.

Gorokans operate their trucks in three main lines of business: freight hauling (usually for the administration or European firms), coffee buying, and mixed passenger and freight transport that links rural villages with the town. Gorokans have just begun to try to obtain contracts with the administration and with European firms for local hauling and for transporting coffee and other goods between Goroka and the coast. However, as of 1968 none of them had been able to obtain enough work to keep his vehicle constantly occupied either in the area or in the Highlands-coast trade. Gorokans have penetrated the coffee buying business to a greater extent; about a dozen Gorokan truckers work for or in association with European coffee mills as coffee buyers. Although some Gorokans like Bimai

Problems and Prospects

Noimbano have tried buying coffee entirely on their own, few of these independent buyers have been fully successful, and most Gorokans in this business work for European firms. Hauling passengers and freight between villages and the town is actually the main commerical activity of Gorokan truckers. This trade is heaviest on the Wednesday and Saturday market days, when rural Gorokans flock into town to sell produce, meet friends, and buy goods at town stores, but continues at a low level throughout the week. There is, however, not enough trade to go around to all the truckers, and it is doubtful that more than a few of them make much of a profit out of passenger-freight hauling.

But the lack of a large enough market (or, alternatively, the surplus of trucks) is not the only reason why Gorokan trucking ventures are frequently unprofitable. Running a trucking business presents Gorokans with major technical and managerial problems that few of them have been able to overcome so far. In the first place, most Gorokans have had little technical experience: they have been able to buy trucks before they have had any experience with automobiles, motorcycles, bicycles, or even mechanical toys. This means that drivers are apt to shift gears improperly, to allow their engines to overheat, or to fail to keep water and oil levels up. This abuse and neglect, plus the rough state of Goroka's potholed and steeply graded roads, lead to frequent breakdowns and may shorten the life of a truck to only a year or so. In the second place, many Gorokan truckers are largely ignorant of proper management procedures. Few realize that they must carry paying loads at most times to even meet their operating costs and that money must be set aside from gross receipts for repairs and depreciation.[3] These problems tend to be magnified when several major contributors to a truck attempt to exert joint control—sometimes to the extent that each man, no matter how incompetent he may be technically, will take a weekly turn driving the truck and pocketing the receipts. Cumulative neglect resulting from such practices plus the lack of funds set aside for repairs and depreciation drastically shorten the lives of most Gorokan truck ventures. After a year or so, when major repairs are needed or a new truck must be purchased, truck ventures frequently fail because there is no money available to meet costs and because the disillusioned contributors who originally pooled their funds are seldom interested in coming up with another large sum of money.

However, despite the many difficulties and apparent unprofitability of trucking ventures, the picture is not entirely discouraging. Some ventures, particularly those that are strongly controlled by one man, are beginning to be profitable, as proper maintenance and management practices are learned. For example, one man who operates a successful coffee buying business and carries passengers in between coffee harvests, has put over 60,000 miles on his truck. He originally purchased it with the aid of several clansmen but later bought them out to gain sole control of it. He has learned to maintain his vehicle and is careful to put aside a portion of the profits for the day when a new truck will be necessary. He and a few other efficient truck operators indicate that Gorokans can with experience, learn to operate their trucks profitably.

Gorokans as Cattle Raisers

Economic factors favor the expansion of beef cattle production in New Guinea. Much beef is imported from Australia, primarily for consumption by local Europeans, and the demand for beef is growing among New Guineans with money to spend. The administration has consequently chosen to promote extensively the raising of beef cattle, both by Europeans and by New Guineans, in those areas of New Guinea where conditions are favorable. One such area is the Bena Bena grasslands. This large, but relatively sparsely populated area on the eastern edge of Goroka is considered to have an excellent potential for cattle raising.

Gorokans first began to buy cattle from missionaries and European settlers in the late 1950s, and since 1960 they have received considerable help in starting cattle projects from the DASF. However, despite their apparent enthusiasm and extensive aid from the DASF, Gorokan cattle raisers have not yet been markedly successful. Raising beef cattle seems to have presented Gorokans with technical and managerial problems that they have had great difficulty in overcoming. First I will sketch these problems briefly as they were manifested in the late 1960s; more recent developments in cattle raising that show some hope of overcoming the problems discussed here will be described later.

Although DASF policy in Goroka has vacillated between the idea

Problems and Prospects 155

that Gorokans should raise cattle as a basic part of a peasant mixed-farming system and the idea that cattle should be raised in commercially oriented projects, by 1968 the latter idea was the guiding DASF policy. The DASF was then selling cattle from its experimental breeding herd to Gorokans at reduced prices and was aiding buyers to start what it hoped would be successful commercial cattle projects. A DASF survey completed in early 1967 revealed that Gorokans had already bought almost five hundred head of cattle, which were distributed among fifty-eight projects. There was every indication in this survey and from my own observations that cattle had captured the commercial interest of the Gorokans and that groups and individuals were willing to put considerable resources into building up small herds.

But, although exact data were unavailable, it also seemed obvious that most of the cattle projects were not yet viable. Indeed, sales of cattle had been minimal, and some evidence indicated that the projects were losing more cattle through injury and disease than they were gaining through natural increase. Although in part the poor performance of the projects may have been related to a lack of good marketing facilities (the administration slaughterhouse in Goroka was not put into full operation until early 1969), there appeared to be more basic reasons.

The complete novelty of cattle to Gorokans and their consequent gross ignorance of cattle handling procedures are undoubtedly behind much of the difficulty they have experienced in trying to raise cattle. They have not been able to become skilled cattlemen in the short period they have been experimenting with cattle. Injuries and disease may go unnoticed or may be neglected even if detected. Cattle may be held in overgrazed holding pens for days without any supplemental feed, or, at the other extreme, they may be allowed to wander freely over unfenced lands (and sometimes into gardens and plantations, where they can cause considerable damage). Although the DASF has tried to teach Gorokans proper cattle handling procedures, both through extension work and by sending promising young men to a special school for cattle management, as of 1968 the effect of these efforts was limited.

The adoption by Gorokans of proper cattle management practices has undoubtedly been hindered by three features basic to many of their cattle projects. First, there is multiple ownership of cattle herds; because of the high cost of cattle, a herd, and even individual beasts, may have anywhere from several to a dozen or more co-owners. Where there is no strong leadership exerted by a major owner who makes sure that the cattle are well looked after within the limits of his knowledge, multiple ownership can be disastrous—as when a co-owner charged with taking his daily or weekly turn grazing cattle neglects his duties and leaves the cattle in a holding pen. Second, there is the problem of the availability of grazing land. Anywhere from fifty to several hundred acres are needed for a small-to-moderate-size cattle project, which means—except perhaps where a dominant leader is involved in the project—that a group of men must agree to pool their land to form a common pasture. While men may enthusiastically pledge to pool their lands at the initiation of a project, when they realize how much land cattle pasture demands can take out of the agricultural cycle and how much care cattle require, enthusiasm often wanes and landholders withdraw their land from the common pasture and use it for subsistence or cash crops. Third, in some cases where there has been an increase in herd size, cattle owners may decline to sell cattle because they are more interested in enjoying the prestige of being owners or part owners of many cattle than they are in the cash the cattle would bring if sold. Here considerations of status and good management practices are often in direct conflict, for mature nonbreeding stock usually has to be sold to prevent overgrazing, as well as for commercial reasons.

LEARN WHILE YOU EARN (OR LOSE)

Gorokans may be accused of attempting to own and operate businesses before they have any idea of the technical requirements of each enterprise and of the rudiments of commerce. Yet, had they waited until they had been taught the necessary technical and commercial skills, their entrance into the business world would have been long delayed. In fact, most of them would still be waiting.

Unless conditions have changed radically in the past few years, it can be said that adult Gorokans have had virtually no opportunities for instruction in commercially useful skills. Young English-speaking students can attend a new technical school in Goroka and qualified high school students can take courses in accounting, but for the mass of Gorokan adults, few of whom can even speak

English, there are no formal courses. During my stay in Goroka in 1967 and 1968 the only administration resource available to Gorokan businessmen who needed commercial advice and instruction was a solitary business advisory officer, who, since he was charged with serving all of the Eastern Highlands and Chimbu districts, was hardly in a position to give more than cursory attention to those who sought his advice. Although some European businessmen, planters, and tradesmen do take pains to instruct and aid some of their Gorokan workers and neighbors, this informal help is neither widespread nor systematic, and consequently its impact is limited.

Viewed from this perspective, the brash Gorokan approach of starting businesses before they have any concrete idea of how to run them takes on a new light. The Gorokans' only hope of learning business skills has been to risk their money and other resources in starting their own businesses and then to try to learn through experience. While this may seem foolhardy and expensive, it has been the only way open to ambitious Gorokans. The Tolai of New Britain followed a similar course, and now, after a period of apprenticeship not unlike that which the Gorokans are going through, they seem to have acquired enough business know-how to begin to operate their enterprises with a fair degree of efficiency and profitability (Epstein 1970b:17). The Gorokans may be on the verge of a new period in which, as for the Tolai, the costly acquisition of commercial skills is going to pay off. If the learning trend that is particularly evident in trade store operations is any indication, Gorokans could well be on the way to being able to operate the enterprises with which they have been experimenting skillfully and profitably.

Colonialism and the Gorokans

Although there can be no doubt that they have received substantial benefits from the intrusion of European administrators, settlers, and businessmen into their lives, the question is open as to how far Gorokans can progress economically while they are still subordinate to Europeans in social and political fields, as well as in economic affairs.

Gorokans have, of course, made some political progress from the time when they were completely dependent upon and controlled by

European officers of the administration. In 1957 the first local government council was started in the Lowa census division,[4] and soon after that separate councils were inaugurated in all other census divisions except Unggai. More recently these have been merged into two councils: the Goroka Town Council, which takes in the Lowa, Bena Bena, and Unggai census divisions as well as the town, and the Asaro Local Government Council, which covers Upper Asaro and Watabung. All the councillors in these two bodies, except those elected from the town where the European electorate predominates, are Gorokans. In addition to this local level, Gorokans are also represented on the national level: Sabumei Kofikai has been a member of the House of Assembly since 1968, and Sinake Giregire has been a member since 1964 and since 1968 has been the Ministerial Member for Posts and Telegraphs, one of the cabinet posts in the administration to which New Guineans have been named.

Yet, despite these signs of political evolution, Gorokans, like other New Guineans have not yet achieved a significant degree of political autonomy. Just as the Australian government, working directly through the administrator for New Guinea, an Australian appointed by Canberra, firmly controls basic policy and its implementation on the national level, so does the local Australian administration in Goroka—rather than local councils—effectively control the sub-district. The district commissioner for the Eastern Highlands District, who has his headquarters in Goroka, and the officers of the administration who are assigned to the sub-district are the instruments of direct rule in Goroka. To be sure, the councils may have authority in minor matters, but the administration retains the power to make and implement major decisions and to enforce these with a police force having solely—or almost solely—European officers. And, as Crocombe (1968) and Hastings (1969:146) have pointed out for elsewhere in New Guinea, it must be reported that (for 1967 and 1968, at least) even the decisions made and implemented by the councils may be influenced by the administration to such a degree that these bodies at times appear to be mere extensions of the administration.

Race relations in Goroka also continue to operate in a largely colonial framework, despite legislation against discrimination and the increasing sophistication and affluence of the Gorokans. In fact, if Gunther's (1965:406–407) portrayal of the semiegalitarian relations that prevailed between Gorokans and Europeans in the frontier phase of Gorokan race relations twenty years ago is correct, conditions have hardened. As more and more Europeans have moved into Goroka—which by 1968 had a European population of around a thousand—race relations seem to have taken on patterns characteristic of long-colonized plantation areas and the urban centers of the coast. In the terminology of Pidgin, a European is a *masta* and a Gorokan—no matter what his age—is a *boi,* and many Europeans act accordingly. Goroka Township, with its de facto segregated housing, its "club" and other social facilities reserved for Europeans, and other key elements of a racially divided society, is where the colonial master-servant pattern of race relations is most obvious, but no area of Goroka and no mode of interaction between Gorokans and Europeans is entirely free of some element of inequality.

Even in the economic field Gorokans remain, despite their considerable progress, in the shadow of European firms and businessmen. Branches of two Australian banks have, except for a few tiny, administration-sponsored savings and loan societies, a monopoly on banking services in Goroka. Two Australian airlines and one local airline owned and managed by Europeans control air transport to and from Goroka, and all regular bus and long-haul trucking services between Goroka and Lae and Goroka and Mount Hagen are in the hands of European firms or entrepreneurs. Three European-owned firms dominate retail trade in foodstuffs, clothing, hardware, and sundries in Goroka Township, and two European wholesale firms located in town supply most of the goods purchased by Gorokan owners of rural trade stores. In addition, all motor vehicle distributorships, lumber yards, hotels, and other major businesses based in town are European owned. In short, all major commercial firms are owned and controlled by Europeans, not Gorokans.[5] Even in the coffee industry, where Gorokans have made their greatest strides, European firms and businessmen dominate.

Although Gorokans probably now produce more coffee than do the European growers in Goroka, a great gulf still separates the two groups. European plantations are large-scale organizations, which are tending to become even larger as corporations buy up and amalgamate smaller properties and as plantings are extended to the limits of the land leases. European plantations also usually possess their own coffee mills or have their coffee processed in mills with which they are financially associated. In contrast, Gorokan plantations are typically small, and most of the growers sell their semi-processed coffee to European firms, which complete the processing and sell the product to European export firms. The mean size of Gorokan coffee plantations is probably a little less than one acre, while the mean size of local European plantations (which is difficult to estimate because of the many recent amalgamations) is now probably several hundred acres. Even the largest Gorokan holding, the plantation of Sinake Giregire, which in 1970 had about 40 acres of planted coffee, is small compared to the mean size of current European holdings and tiny indeed compared to the largest European coffee estate in Goroka, a holding of about 1,000 acres, made up of several of the original settler plantations that have been purchased and amalgamated by a large Australian trading and plantation corporation.

The apparently inevitable trend of large corporations' taking over plantations and operating them impersonally through hired managers makes a mockery of the idea put forth in the 1950s that plantations in Goroka would be different from those on the coast. Few plantations are now owned and operated by their original owners, and I know of no case in which a settler's heir has taken one over. Those Gorokans who had thought that they were forging a permanent and personal bond between their group and the settler who had bought their lands and his family now find that they have to cope with new owners or managers with whom they can claim no personal bond. Most Gorokans appear to be uneasy about these new bosses, and particularly about the large corporations. Many resent their presence and regard it as a final betrayal of the promises of lasting partnership made or implied when they sold their land.

Aside from this conflict between particular groups and particular plantations, there is a growing general conflict between Europeans and Gorokans as competing coffee growers in a world market marked by declining prices and increasing difficulty in marketing. When Australia and New Guinea joined the International Coffee Agreement, the administration agreed that no more land could be alienated for European coffee plantations and that extension work designed to spread coffee growing among New Guineans was to be

Problems and Prospects

curtailed. However, because many European plantations have continued to plant more coffee on previously unexploited portions of their leases and because many New Guineans have gone on to increase their plantings greatly without extension aid, these restrictions have failed to keep coffee production down, and in 1968 New Guinea's coffee production, running at about 18,000 to 19,000 tons a year, began to exceed Australia's total coffee consumption. New Guinea and Australia, treated as one unit in the agreement, had therefore become a net exporter of coffee instead of a net importer and were forced to start negotiating for a quota to market any coffee produced above Australia's consumption.

In 1968 European growers there were worried that New Guinea might not receive a favorable quota and that it might become difficult to market a portion of the New Guinea crop. They therefore were warning Gorokans and other New Guinean coffee growers to cease planting coffee and to diversify into other crops such as passion fruit and market vegetables. However, as Gorokans could see for themselves that European plantations were not cutting back on production and that many with land to spare were planting more coffee, this advice was considered by many to be an example of European duplicity. The long decline in coffee prices since the highs of the 1950s served to reinforce this judgment, for a popular Gorokan interpretation of falling prices is that they are an attempt on the part of European buyers and processors to cut Gorokan profits.

But the Gorokans, despite their subordination to Europeans in political, social, and economic spheres, do not appear to be in a great hurry to achieve self-government or independence. For example, the United Nations visiting mission of 1968, after discussing questions of future political status with the Goroka Town Council, reported:

> . . . all speakers told the Mission that the Territory was not ready for self-government. Mr. John Akunai [Akunai Rovelie] . . . said that a great deal of development was taking place but much more was needed. They needed higher technical schools, better roads and bridges, and a great deal of money invested in business in the Territory. When they had sufficient economic development then they would be ready for self-government and would ask for it. Other speakers stated that the Government should not "push" the people

into self-government too soon, before they were able to handle their affairs themselves. When they were prepared for this they would request it from Australia. (United Nations 1968:44–45)

The opinions expressed in this quote seem to be fairly representative of the Gorokan views on the subject that I encountered during 1967 and 1968. In fact, they seem to be representative for all the Highlands as well as Goroka. If anything sets Highlanders off from coastal New Guineans, it is this question of self-government and independence, for, while many articulate coastal New Guineans have recently begun to advocate self-government, if not outright independence, as soon as possible, the Highlanders have been virtually unanimous in their opposition to rapid political change. They want to stay under Australia's tutelage a while longer before setting out on their own. This split between the two groups has given rise to the popular stereotypes of coastal radicals and Highlands conservatives.

In Goroka, if not in the rest of the Highlands, this apparent conservatism appears to be a compound of several elements. Gorokans are sure that they do not yet have enough modern technical and organizational expertise to rule themselves, and they feel that they have yet to master all the economic techniques needed to operate the local economy. They are also afraid that self-government or independence will mean an end to Australian aid—a view that some Australians like to promote—and they do not want to lose the new schools, roads, bridges, medical facilities, and other goods and services that have been provided them. And they are more than a little afraid that an early end to Australian rule would merely result in their falling under the control of coastal New Guineans, who because of their superior educational qualifications would probably dominate the civil service of an autonomous New Guinea. Some Gorokans even say that they are ready to wait a generation until their children are educated before they are willing to take a chance on self-rule.

But conservatism on constitutional questions does not necessarily mean that Gorokans are economic conservatives in the sense that they want no change in the way the development pie is now being divided unequally between Europeans and themselves. For example, whereas in previous years Gorokans were willing to let Europeans acquire large tracts of land to start plantations and take the lead in other economic enterprises, now they are wondering why they themselves cannot initiate or actively participate in the operation of large-scale ventures.

The concept of partnership, in the sense that it was used in the 1950s, is a dead letter today. Unlike in the 1950s, when Gorokans were anxious to allow Europeans to acquire large tracts of land for coffee plantations in order to stimulate development, now Gorokans are more confident of their own abilities and want to initiate new ventures themselves. In recent years Europeans have been putting pressure on various landholding groups in Goroka to sell or lease on a long-term basis large areas for a tea estate and factory in Upper Asaro and for cattle grazing lands in Bena Bena. But they have run head on into this new mood among Gorokans, a mood born of the confidence gained in almost two decades of active and profitable commercial experience, and because of it they have been unable to strike any bargains. If anything, European requests for large tracts of land for tea and cattle have served to alert the Gorokans to new economic opportunities and to make them want to exploit these opportunities themselves.

In 1967 and 1968 some Gorokans were excited about the possibility of growing tea, particularly since coffee prices were then declining and they were receiving advice not to expand their plantings further. These Gorokans knew that a tea industry was already established in the Western Highlands, where the first tea just then being produced was considered to be of high quality and was fetching good prices overseas. But they also knew that the way the tea industry was organized in the Western Highlands was not entirely satisfactory to the people there. To start the tea industry the administration had invited European firms to lease large areas of land (from the administration, which had purchased them from the local people) and to establish tea estates of several hundred acres with a processing factory on each estate. The local people had a chance to participate as producers, but only on certain terms. Small blocks of alienated land surrounding each nucleus estate were allocated to a few of them for tea growing, and they received some help toward growing tea on their own lands. The people around each nucleus estate soon realized that the Europeans had by far the largest stake in the tea industry and that, furthermore, either because of collusive agreements between tea estates or because of transport problems (tea has to be processed immediately after picking to assure a high-quality product), they were at the mercy of the local nucleus estate as far as tea-buying prices and practices were concerned. Many of the Western Highlanders who had become involved with these tea estates, as either land sellers or small-scale tea producers, or both, were therefore not very happy about the resultant organization, which seemed to them to favor the interests of European tea estates over their own (Reay 1969).

In the light of what they had learned from Western Highlanders about the disadvantages of the nucleus estate method of developing tea and their own disenchantment over the promised lasting partnership between Gorokans and European coffee plantation owners, those Gorokans most interested in starting a local tea industry wanted it to be a primarily Gorokan, not primarily European, industry. In 1967 and 1968 they were talking among themselves about putting up several hundred thousand dollars, derived from their own pooled savings and an administration loan, to build a tea factory that would process tea to be grown on their own lands. (European plantations that wanted to switch from coffee to tea or to grow tea on unexploited portions of their lands were to be welcomed into the scheme.) However, they were receiving little support from administration officials, who pointed out to them that it was doubtful that any part of Goroka, even the relatively wet Upper Asaro region, had the ideal rainfall conditions for tea and that a European nucleus estate was necessary in order to maintain an even production of high-quality tea.

Although no administration aid has been forthcoming for the initiation of a Gorokan tea industry, this has not stopped Sinake Giregire, one of the prime proponents of such an industry, from experimenting with tea. Early in 1968 he purchased a large number of young tea seedlings and had them transplanted into a special experimental nursery established on his land. When I left New Guinea late in 1968, he told me that he had been offered a large sum for the maturing seedlings from a European tea estate that was just getting started in the Kainantu area. However, when I saw him in Canberra in 1970, he told me that he had declined the offer and had used some of the seedlings to set out a trial tea plot on his land and had distributed the rest among his constituents, so that they could try growing tea also. Whether or not anything comes of these efforts, they are significant in that they show how one Gorokan leader is taking the initiative to test the feasibility of growing tea in Goroka.

In contrast to tea, on the cattle question both the Gorokans and the administration now appear to be of one mind: Europeans should not be allowed to gain control of large amounts of Gorokan lands for cattle development, and the Gorokans should start their own large-scale cattle industry. According to R. F. McKillop (1970), a DASF officer in Goroka in charge of cattle development, the Gorokans themselves took the first positive step toward solving one of the main problems that had plagued Gorokan cattle projects—that of obtaining sufficient nondisputed land for grazing. In 1966 a Bena Bena clan invested the proceeds from a land sale to the administration in a fence extending around a pasture of over two hundred acres. Taking his cue from this action, McKillop has recently been promoting large-scale, group-oriented cattle projects primarily among the Bena Bena groups, who live in grassland areas ideal for cattle.

The first step in the new cattle promotion program has been to set up demarcation committees made up of members of landholding groups within declared adjudication areas and have them demarcate the land boundaries between rival groups. Then permanent fences have been erected along these boundaries to enclose the herds. Funds for the fencing and subsequent pasture improvement and stock purchases are contributed by individuals and groups within each clan unit from their savings (usually derived from coffee revenue) and from loans granted them by the new Development Bank of Papua and New Guinea. McKillop's (1970:10–11) characterization of the response to the new program makes it clear that the participants feel that the fencing, the pasture improvements, and the purchases of cattle for their herds are highly desirable "conspicuous investments." In a period of two years, from 1968 to 1970, many long-disputed boundaries in an area of about 50,000 acres have been demarcated; 8,000 acres have been fenced off; and Development Bank loans of almost $100,000 have been approved for the cattle projects.

Pride in these developments is manifest on a tribal confederacy level as well as on a clan level. In 1968, when I interviewed members of the Numuyargobo tribal confederacy, a large group located in the heart of the Bena Bena grasslands, where most of the new cattle projects have been started, the people made it clear to me that they had ambitions of becoming the leading cattle ranchers—the cattle barons, if you like—of the Highlands. They knew that they had good land for cattle; they knew that there was a growing demand for fresh beef in Goroka both by Europeans tired of high-priced frozen imports from Australia and by Gorokans, who were acquiring a taste for beef; and they thought that they had learned enough about cattle to make a success of the cattle business with continued DASF aid. Accordingly, they talked of having thousands of head of cattle and of earning money and fame by the large-scale sale of cattle. Cattle raising was giving them a chance to regain status first eroded when pacification ended their military supremacy over the eastern half of Goroka and later reduced further when, because of superior environmental conditions, the people of Lowa and Upper Asaro became the leading coffee producers in the sub-district. According to a newspaper report that appeared in late 1969, it would appear that the Numuyargobo people were on their way to achieving their ambitious goals—the story told of the first public auction of cattle from a cattle holding that already numbered 650 head, a total that made the Numuyargobo the leading cattle-owning group in New Guinea (*Papua-New Guinea Post Courier* 1969).[6]

Some Gorokans are also interested in expanding their individual commercial activities beyond the level of the small trade store and the local passenger-freight truck, and a few men have already made steps in that direction. In 1968 Hari Gotoha opened a new retail store that is a far cry from the average Gorokan trade store. It is a completely modern structure costing $25,000 and is stocked with a wide range of foodstuffs, items of clothing, and sundries. It is located on prime commerical (but unalienated) land across the Highlands Highway from the Goroka Township market, and when I would stop there late in 1968, I usually found it to be packed with customers: rural Gorokans who had come to town for the markets, local Gorokans who lived nearby, and other New Guineans who lived in or near town. Hari Gotoha told me then that he was attempting to obtain his goods at significantly lower prices than they were available for at the local wholesalers, by sending one of his trucks down to Lae every week or so to buy from wholesalers there.

He was also thinking of starting his own wholesale business, by buying directly from Lae importers or by indenting the goods himself, which would supply goods for his store and other Gorokan-owned stores that wished to buy from him. In addition, he also was already involved, as were several other local truck owners, in experimenting with long-haul trucking.

Sinake Giregire is another Gorokan business leader who has recently expanded into new fields (in addition to tea). In 1972, when he stopped in Honolulu on his way to the World Bank in Washington to negotiate a loan to improve New Guinea's communication facilities in his capacity as the ministerial member for posts and telegraph, he told me that he was then operating a fleet of six trucks for coffee buying, that he had his own service station and garage, that he was about to open a large wholesale-retail establishment complete with bulk freezing and cold storage facilities, and that he had several Europeans in his employ.

Judging from numerous conversations that I had with European settlers and businessmen in Goroka, it was apparent to me that some of them were totally opposed to Gorokan plans and attempts to expand the scale and extent of their commercial undertakings. They tend to see these new Gorokan developments as threats to their own economic position and would like to block them, or at least delay them. These men seem only interested in maximizing their own profits for as long as they can stay in New Guinea. In contrast, some other European settlers and businessmen seem to be interested in promoting new Gorokan commercial ventures. Among this group, motives appear to be mixed: a few men seem genuinely interested in simply seeing the Gorokans advance, even at the expense of European economic hegemony; others see Gorokan advancement as good "insurance" to protect European interests against any future attempts to take over or nationalize non-Gorokan plantations and businesses.

These Europeans interested in "insuring" a continued European economic presence have taken several concrete steps to promote Gorokan involvement in what might be called the European sector of the economy, so that Gorokans will feel that they are truly part of the coffee industry and other fields dominated by Europeans and will reject any proposals for radical economic change. These steps have taken two main forms. First, an attempt has been made to get the mass of Gorokans involved—as shareholders—in large-scale, mechanized coffee processing and in coffee plantations of the European type. And second, efforts have also focused on promoting the status of individual Gorokan business leaders as a new bourgeois elite who will be sympathetic to their European counterparts.

The most ambitious of the schemes to involve Gorokans in large-scale coffee processing started in 1962 with the founding of the Highlands Commodity Exchange, a European-fostered and-managed coffee buying and processing firm financed primarily with $50,000 collected from Gorokan shareholders (Finney 1969:77–79; O'Connor 1970:2, 4). After a few years of profitable operation the firm experienced managerial and financial difficulties and in 1967 was in a precarious position: operating funds were low, and Gorokan shareholders had lost much confidence in the company because of a suspension of dividend payments. In 1968 the firm's position had worsened, and several of its European backers told me that they were attempting to reorganize it and to apply the remaining assets, plus new funds to be solicited from Gorokans, toward the formation of a joint European-Gorokan company designed to purchase and operate one or two of the European coffee plantations still in individual hands. Their goal, according to one of the European backers, was to give Gorokans an interest in and experience with large-scale plantations, so that they would become aware of the problems of such plantations and think twice about advocating their take-over or division in the future.

The promoters of the Highlands Commodity Exchange singled out individual Gorokans like Sinake Giregire to be directors of the company (although the European directors retained ultimate managerial control). That decision was consonant with the long-standing policy of the Highlands Farmers and Settlers Association, the organization that represents European plantation and allied business interests in Goroka and elsewhere in the Highlands, to recruit prominent Gorokan coffee growers as full members. European members of the association make it clear that they want Gorokans in their organization so that they will identify with European growers and oppose any disruption of the coffee industry by "radicals," who might want to break up the large plantations or otherwise reorganize the industry. To promote a fuller identification between Europeans and Gorokans in the coffee industry, they

Problems and Prospects 169

have also advocated that credit be advanced to promising Gorokan coffee growers, so that they can buy up some of the smaller European plantations still in individual hands and thus truly become part of the European plantation system.

This idea was elaborated in an editorial titled "The Need for a New Elite" in the *New Guinea Highlands Bulletin* (1968), the official publication of the association, which carries under its masthead the motto "We Are Here to Stay." The editorial points out that "no significant numbers of Papuans and New Guineans have tangible individual holdings in Primary Industry comparable to those developed and owned by the expatriate community" and goes on to warn that unless investment credits are made available and a plan is drawn up to

> . . . replace the dwindling group of expatriate owner-managers with a "New Class" of substantial Papuan and New Guinean estate owners, most of the middle-income properties will disappear by being absorbed by bigger company organizations. We will then be left with an even wider gap—between only huge expatriate estate owning groups and miniscule peasant farms. This is the type of situation which has led to violent expropriation in newly self-governing countries, generally followed by mismanagement and damage to valuable properties because those who have taken over have not had the intermediate benefit of experience in managing anything larger than a peasant plot.

The Gorokan business leaders who have been discussed here are among the most likely candidates for this "new class" of New Guinean plantation owner-managers, who would supposedly serve as a bulwark against popular movements attacking European economic privilege. One wonders, however, if these and other commercially prominent Gorokans could actually carry out the function envisioned for them in this editorial. First, it seems unrealistic to expect them to take up the role of owner-manager of European coffee plantations. Few of the small, one-man properties have survived the current trend toward big corporate plantations, and, anyway, the money needed (around $80,000 for a 60-to-80-acre plantation in 1968) to buy one of the remaining properties is beyond their means and probably would not be forthcoming from any lending agency. Second, and perhaps more important, these leaders seem far too involved with local clan, tribal, and regional loyalties to ever espouse the cause of European privilege over a genuine popular demand to end it. The Gorokan business leaders may be a new elite, but they do not appear to be an elite that has divorced itself from the mass of the people. Should they ever show themselves to be identifying so much with European interests that they have become insensitive to those of their fellow clansmen and tribesmen, new leaders who promised to put Gorokans before Europeans would probably emerge and attempt to capture the followings of established leaders.

Old Society, New Economy

Today's Gorokans straddle any line that could be drawn between the traditional and the modern. It is clear that their "modern" cash cropping and business enterprises remain to a great extent embedded in traditional Gorokan society (compare Polanyi, Ahrensberg, and Pearson 1957; Geertz 1963:89). This analysis has emphasized the benefits of this embeddedness—how traditional values and institutions have been useful vehicles for attaining modern goals. But, what about the future? Will the traditional continue to serve the modern, or are there limits to the potential for change that are inherent in traditional Gorokan values and institutions? Must Gorokan commercial activity become "unembedded" from its traditional context in order for further economic progress to occur? These questions, which are so easy to pose, yet are really impossible to answer with surety, are raised in order to refocus this analysis on its central theme—the interaction between the values and institutions of Gorokan society and the opportunities and demands of the cash economy. It is this interaction between the old and the new, rather than any one of the other aspects of Gorokan economic life that may well be the most important factor in the future evolution of Gorokan development.

The importance of considering again how traditional and modern features interact is to be seen clearly in the Gorokan tendency toward conspicuous investment. I have argued that the intense desire simply to own or participate in a *bisnis* has been one of the main driving forces behind Gorokan capital formation and investment. Yet, not every observer paints this tendency in so favorable a light. In fact, most administration personnel that I talked with who were cognizant of the situation had serious reservations about the utility of status-motivated investment. They maintained that conspicuous investors were apt to be so interested in the prestige of simply owning a business and in the renown that came from being known as a *bisnisman* that they might completely overlook the profitability of their enterprises. A number of cases touched on previously could be cited to buttress this view: the man who started a coffee plantation but neglected to maintain it properly or, at times, even to harvest it; the group that pooled its money to buy a truck, which was driven around more as a showpiece than a working asset; and the would-be cattleman who enjoyed the status of owning a herd of cattle so much that he declined to sell off mature cattle when good husbandry (and agricultural advisers) dictated that he do so.

These cases would seem to indicate that conspicuous investment may not be as much of a blessing as I have made it out to be. Prestige may be an important force motivating Gorokans to invest, but in this critical view its drawbacks are seen to rival, if not exceed, its benefits: capital (and also land and labor) may be wasted in status-enhancing, but unprofitable projects. With some stretching of the imagination it could even be argued that the prestige motivation we see in Goroka is only a small-scale version of the tendency apparent in some underdeveloped countries for scarce resources to be invested in magnificent dams, steel mills, and other prestigious, but not necessarily economic, projects and, as such, should have no place in the formation of the New Guinea economy.

It might therefore seem reasonable to say that status considerations should be replaced by more "rational" motives for economic action, that Gorokans should cease being conspicuous investors and become calculating farmers and businessmen, motivated solely by profits (a recommendation I have heard in one form or another from the lips of numerous administration officials and private Europeans concerned with Gorokan and general New Guinean economic growth). But would a policy based on this be likely to succeed? I doubt it for two reasons. First, an attempt to suppress status motivation would strike at the heart of the Gorokan value system and would run the risk of taking much of the steam out of the Gorokan economic drive. Second, such a policy might be said to rest on false premises concerning the role of profit in motivation. As Schumpeter (1949:93) has pointed out in reference to the industrial entrepreneurs of the West and as McClelland (1961) has posited as a universal characteristic of entrepreneurship, men take up new economic activities more for the feeling of accomplishment and power that comes from founding an enterprise or a business empire than for the monetary rewards. In their view, the latter are symbols of success but are not the primary goals that motivate men.

But, this does not mean that the so-called profit motive has no place in Gorokan economic activities. Obviously, if capital losses are to be reduced and more money is to be generated internally by the Gorokans to increase the scale and intensity of their involvement in the cash economy, they must make more money from their enterprises. The real question, I suggest, is whether or not the Gorokan concern for status—now focused so much on the preliminary steps of starting and owning an enterprise—can be applied to the efficient operation of an enterprise and its profitability.[7] If Gorokans can come to see profits as the symbols of achievement, then their concern for status could be an even greater resource in promoting economic growth than it has proved to be so far.

Another aspect of Gorokan commercial behavior in which traditionally derived patterns that have fostered economic growth seem to have some drawbacks is in group participation in enterprises. The Gorokan ability to pool their resources—their labor, their money, and, at times, their land—to initiate ventures has been one of their great strengths. It has enabled them to move much more quickly into commercial agriculture and commerce than they could have if each man acted for himself alone and refused to give assistance to others or join them in joint enterprises. But it is clear that group participation in enterprises has not been without its problems and that some of these problems are serious enough to slow the pace of Gorokan economic growth.

Enterprises with significant levels of group participation, dictated by high capital or land requirements, seem particularly prone to organizational difficulties. Participants who donate their money or pledge their land may not necessarily work harmoniously together to operate the resulting enterprises efficiently. The trucking venture that failed because co-owners, who were happy to take turns operating the truck and pocketing the profits, did not set aside funds for repairs and maintenance, or the cattle project in which the cattle were neglected to the point that they were on the verge of starvation because participants could not agree on joint use of their lands for pasturage, may be extreme examples, but they do highlight the fact that the solidarity shown by Gorokans when they pool their resources to start an enterprise may not always carry over into the day-to-day operation and management of that enterprise.

Ventures with heavy group participation that center around an entrepreneur are not immune from problems. Where an entrepreneur has relied heavily on labor contributions or pooled money to get his start, he must pay attention to two levels of management. On the one hand, he has to operate or direct the operation of his coffee plantation and whatever other enterprises he controls. On the other hand, he must keep his following of contributors and other supporters happy by means of direct cash payments and gifts and by seeing that they share in the prestige associated with his commercial activities. Because of this dual allegiance there is a danger that if a man pays too much attention to the management of his enterprises and to his bank balance, he may neglect to reward his followers sufficiently, or, conversely, that if he devotes most of his time and resources to keeping his followers happy, then his enterprises and financial position are apt to run down. Either way a man stands to lose—by financial failure, or by the loss of his following. To be successful an entrepreneur must therefore be good at balancing the demands from these two sectors and allocating resources accordingly. Indeed, one of the outstanding characteristics of the business leaders discussed in Chapter 6 is this balancing ability. But, not all Gorokans are so skilled, and many a fledgling business empire has failed because of the inability of the would-be entrepreneur to balance his efforts and resources in order to keep his enterprise healthy and his followers satisfied.

Many administration officials concerned about New Guinean economic growth with whom I discussed the problems of group participation in commercial activities for Gorokans and other New Guineans leaned toward the view that group participation in the informal New Guinean style caused more trouble than it was worth and that, consequently, it should be eliminated in favor of sole proprietorships and small partnerships. By limiting enterprises to one-man businesses and those owned by a few partners, these men hoped that problems associated with having many participants—be they co-owners or contributors—could be simply avoided. Their reasoning was reinforced by an apparent trend among Gorokans and some other New Guinean groups toward sole proprietorships and small partnerships—because of increasing income, which allows one or a few men to own an enterprise, as well as because of local realization of the pitfalls of group participation. The truck driver cited previously provides a case in point, for he used his savings to buy out other contributors to his truck so that he could gain sole control over it and operate it as he wished. His case, plus others that I investigated, showed that some Gorokans were definitely interested and able to become sole owners of their businesses or, where capital or land requirements were beyond their individual reach, to join with just one or two other men to form enterprises.

Two main objections can be raised against the idea that Gorokans (and other New Guineans) should concentrate all their efforts in one-, two-, or three-man businesses. First, to do so would be to turn their backs on one of their main human assets—their ability to pool land, labor, and capital to start large enterprises. It is doubtful that outside sources like the new Development Bank or the local trading banks would be willing or able to provide sufficient credit to allow individual Gorokans to found and operate large enterprises. Second, if Gorokan enterprises were held to small-sized units, there would seem to be little hope for Gorokans to ever move from the small-coffee-grower/small-business level to the level of large plantations and firms now controlled by Europeans. In other words, restrictions on the number of participants in Gorokan firms would keep firms small and thus would tend to freeze the current inequality between Gorokan and European businessmen.

A less-discussed alternative to restricting group participation is that of formalizing it by having Gorokans form or join registered companies, which would be organized like Australian corporations and be subject to Australian corporate law as it is applied in New Guinea. Although this might allow the Gorokan ability to pool funds to be utilized to form larger economic units, at least two objections to it can be raised. First, Gorokans have no experience in starting and operating corporate firms, and without the requisite technical and legal knowledge it is difficult to see how they could make corporate ventures work. Second, if Gorokans entered into existing European-controlled firms as shareholders or if they got involved in specially formed joint Gorokan-European companies, it

Problems and Prospects 175

would seem likely in the light of previous Gorokan experience in such ventures and the frankly neocolonial aims of many local Europeans that the resulting firms would serve to further the interests of the Europeans more than those of the Gorokans.

A third alternative would seek to preserve group participation by recognizing and regularizing the structures that Gorokans and other New Guineans form when they pool their resources for commercial purposes. This line of thinking has been most fully developed by Nash (1970), a former dean of the Faculty of Law at the University of Papua and New Guinea, who argues that if New Guinean business enterprises are to develop on a large scale, it will be through some form of group entity with widespread shareholding but rejects the notion that these entities must conform to Australian company laws. These laws, according to Nash, are designed for circumstances much different from those involved in New Guinean enterprises. Provisions, for example, which aim to give protection to Australian shareholders do not necessarily give the same protection to New Guineans who contribute money to a business leader and who are tied to him in a complex web of rights and duties unlike the obligations which link shareholders and management in an Australian company. Nash's solution is to allow de facto groupings, obligations, and commitments to be recognized as such by law

> Contributors have traditional claims on management and traditional rights in relation to the assets of the business. These traditional rights and claims are possibly only now being clearly formulated but they are based at least in part on the mutual-obligation structure of traditional society. It would seem logical to recognize these groups as having a corporate-type existence and to allow traditional controls (perhaps formalized by legislation) to regulate their operation (1970:41–42).

How this plea for the legal recognition and codification through legislation of New Guinean corporate enterprises is to be implemented and whether or not such moves would serve to stimulate successful corporate enterprises based on New Guinean models, remain, however, open questions, for to my knowledge no concrete steps have been taken in this direction.

A final area to consider in this discussion of the interplay between modernity and tradition is the institution of entrepreneurship itself. What can be envisaged for Gorokan entrepreneurs in the future?

Will their actions continue to promote economic growth, or is the potential for change led by entrepreneurs limited?

A reasonable observation to make about Gorokan business leaders is that they tend to be better promoters than managers, that they have done a better job of mobilizing land, labor, and capital to start new enterprises than they have of day-to-day management. It is tempting to speculate that if this indicates that the business leaders are unaware of or unconcerned about efficient business practices, then Gorokan entrepreneurship could be of a self-limiting kind with little potential for stimulating economic growth beyond the present level. However, although some business leaders do seem to blithely ignore the necessity of sound business practices, a number of those whose careers I know best have been greatly concerned about the problem. The solution that seems to have attracted them most is the one obvious to any entrepreneur—recruit expert technical and managerial help. But, unlike the entrepreneur in a developed economy, who can pick and choose among many qualified job applicants, the Gorokan business leader cannot just go out and hire a manager, accountant, or some other skilled person. Few Gorokans today are technically qualified, and, even if experience does eventually prove to be a good teacher, this is little consolation to the business leader who needs a man to manage his coffee plantation or operate his trucking business now.

Sinake Giregire's resort to hired European help, however sound it may be for his enterprises, is beyond the imaginations (and purses) of most other business leaders. Indeed, they tend to think primarily in terms of having one of their younger relatives learn crucial skills in an administration school and then return home to apply them. For example, Bimai, who may have been the first business leader to recognize the need for skilled help, sent his nephew (and adopted son) to agricultural college and planned to have him upon graduation take over management of the agricultural projects that Bimai had started. Although Bimai's death prevented the fruition of this plan, I know of several other business leaders who were following a similar strategy, and in 1972 the first such educated expert, Hari Gotoha's younger brother, graduated from agricultural college and returned to Goroka to work for his brother.

To the observer who sees the necessity of rationalizing Gorokan business activity by removing it from the context of kin and clan,

Problems and Prospects 177

this essentially familial approach to the need for expertise might seem like a step backwards. However, any such view would ignore two important facts. First, one of the main resources that Gorokans have tapped in their drive for economic growth has been the ability of kinsmen and clansmen to work together even when it would appear to the outsider that one individual was receiving the primary benefit from their efforts. Second, unlike students in many an underdeveloped country, students at the Goroka high school do think in terms of learning utilitarian skills (truck repair, bookkeeping, farm management, and the like) and of then returning to their home areas to apply them for the benefit of their people (R. S. Finney 1971).

But there are problems more serious than the lack of skilled help facing entrepreneurially organized business activity in Goroka. The commercial structures that Gorokan entrepreneurs erect have what appears to be a basic flaw: they are fragile organizations which, with a few exceptions, revolve around single men. The typical Gorokan business empire made up of coffee, retail trading, and trucking enterprises has been built up by an entrepreneur who, although he relies, or at one time did rely, on contributions from his supporters, runs it as a one-man show, which involves a tough balancing act between the demands of each enterprise and the demands of his supporters. Since these structures are so egocentrically organized and operated, when an entrepreneur dies the businesses are liable to collapse from the lack of firm and continuous leadership. The rapid decline of Bimai Noimbano's holdings after his death provides a case in point. In order to have saved Bimai's organization from falling apart, there would have had to be an heir with developed entrepreneurial talents waiting in the wings. But, there was no single heir with sufficient entrepreneurial skills (which would have had to include the ability to persuade Bimai's followers to transfer their allegiance) ready and waiting, and because of this within a few years Bimai's assets were largely in ruin and his followers were demanding a return of the monies they had contributed to Bimai's enterprises. Because entrepreneurial talent does not necessarily flow to a man's heir, the commercial structures of Gorokan business leaders have a built-in instability that would seem to limit their lives to the span of those of the business leaders.

This instability can be viewed in opposing ways, as a negative factor inhibiting economic growth or as a positive factor promoting socioeconomic mobility. Viewed negatively, this instability may be said to have a deleterious effect on the Gorokan economy at two levels. First, valuable assets built up during a man's lifetime are likely to be wasted because of mismanagement after his death. Second, promising enterprises which might in time grow to the point where they could realize significant economies of scale and compete with European firms would have only limited lives. According to this perspective, Gorokan economic progress, in general, and entrepreneurially organized businesses, in particular, are bound to suffer with the death or disability of successful business leaders.

Viewed positively, the instability inherent in highly egocentric commercial structures may be seen as a blessing in that their collapse upon the deaths of the founding entrepreneurs would work against the formation of a hereditary commercial elite and the concentration of economic resources and power in the hands of a few. This instability was, of course, typical of the precontact organizations built up by traditional big-men; indeed, it was a basic part of a social system that allowed the ambitious men of each generation to try their hands at becoming wealthy and renowned big-men. Since the structures the big-man created—his pig herds, his group of followers, his shell wealth, and the network of obligations and alliances built up through the judicious exchange of valuables— typically fell apart upon his death (or with the waning of his strength in old age), there were no hereditary holdings to form the basis of a rigid class structure. If this traditional restraint on class formation does truly carry over into modern times, as the case of Bimai (the first major Gorokan business leader to die) would seem to indicate, it could be argued that contemporary Gorokan society is not likely to become divided into rigid classes of haves and have nots.

But, although Gorokan society may not evolve into a society with fixed socioeconomic classes, this does not mean that avenues of mobility may not become narrowed. It already appears that the route to commercial prominence based on the foundation of a large coffee plantation and the subsequent use of coffee revenues to finance other ventures is partially blocked because of changing land and labor availability. When current business leaders were setting out their coffee plantations in the 1950s, there were sizable chunks of fertile, well-watered land available for coffee growing. And, as most of their fellow clansmen had little in the way of coffee or other cash crops to occupy their time, local labor was also available. Today's young man does not have these advantages. Save perhaps for a few corners of Goroka where, because of lack of transport and other difficulties, there has been only slight cash crop development, an ambitious young Gorokan does not have a large land and labor surplus to exploit. Indeed, today many a young man has difficulty in getting even a little land for a modest coffee garden in the heavily populated and developed parts of Goroka. The growing scarcity of basic resources would certainly seem to make it much more difficult than formerly for a man to use cash crops to launch a commercial career.

But, surely, if Gorokans do have a high level of entrepreneurial ability, at least some young men should be able to overcome local scarcities in one way or another. If they cannot, it would probably be an indication that Gorokan entrepreneurial potential is indeed limited. Faced with a scarcity of unencumbered land, a young, entrepreneurially inclined Gorokan could take any of a number of steps to launch a commercial career. For example, he could convince his clansmen that they should release land from subsistence, that they should allow him, and perhaps others so inclined, to take land which is being used for growing food crops or which is lying fallow in reserve for future food crop cultivation and put it into cash crop production. This would be a radical step, for as yet few, if any, Gorokans have been willing to give up growing their own food and raising their own pigs in favor of full-scale cash crop production. The man who could accomplish this would be introducing a radical innovation into Gorokan economy and society, which, if successful, would certainly qualify him as a path-breaking entrepreneur. (The probable success of any such move is, however, questionable, given the danger of sole reliance on coffee and other tropical cash crops for which the demand is unstable.)

Alternatively, an ambitious young man bent on becoming a business leader might wish to bypass the cash crop route to commercial prominence and go directly into nonagricultural enterprise. Most of today's business leaders, even men who, like Sinake Giregire, started off with nonagricultural ventures, have depended heavily on coffee. The one outstanding exception is Hari Gotoha, who, although he has a small plantation and has relied partially on capital supplied by a coffee-rich associate, has primarily built his career out of nonagricultural enterprises. There would seem to be some room in Goroka for more entrepreneurs like Hari Gotoha, for men who could organize, singly or in combination, retail trading, trucking, and other small enterprises the way Hari Gotoha has.

Yet, although such a development would involve a departure from the current pattern of agriculturally based entrepreneurship, it would not necessarily signal any economic breakthrough. Gorokans have been experimenting with stores, trucks, and restaurants practically from the time they first began to make money from coffee. But, except for a few men who have tried to log and sell local timber, a few others who have experimented with making building bricks, and a few women who make ready-to-wear clothing for sale in local trade stores, there has been little sign of entrepreneurial activity beyond the level of cash crop enterprise and the essentially service ventures that spring from agricultural development.[8] This is not a uniquely Gorokan problem, for as Epstein (1970b) points out, other New Guinean groups do not seem to have been able to advance beyond the level of cash cropping and small business. She sees the problem as primarily one of narrow horizons: New Guineans need to be given firsthand exposure through courses, overseas tours, and business internships to a wide range of enterprises in order to open up their perspectives. I would add that it is also a colonial problem. Many of the fields into which Gorokans and other New Guineans must expand if they are to progress beyond their present levels of cash cropping and small business are dominated by European (and, on the coast, overseas Chinese) businessmen and firms.

Recent Tolai experience may be instructive here. The Tolai, who have always been somewhat ahead of the Gorokans in economic growth, appear to have reached a sticking point: population growth and a shortage of land (caused in part by heavy land alienation) have begun to limit cash crop expansion; the local market for service enterprises has become saturated; and the dominance of European and Chinese businessmen and firms, plus the narrow horizons of established Tolai, seem to have put a ceiling on Tolai commercial possibilities. Consequently, Tolai economic growth has slowed, their savings have begun to pile up for want

Problems and Prospects 181

of investment outlets, and young Tolai, in particular, have become increasingly impatient for economic progress beyond the cash cropping/small business level. Frustration over this situation contributed to the formation in 1969 of the Mataungan Association, New Guinea's first radical mass movement, and a primary Mataungan goal has been to remove barriers to Tolai economic expansion, particularly those thrown up by alien commercial domination and control of land, as well as the seeming inability of many established Tolai leaders to look beyond their own small plantations and businesses to wider economic opportunities. To this end, young Mataungan leaders have formed a development corporation designed to spawn major Tolai enterprises in fields like crop processing and exporting and importing, which would be independent competitors of alien-owned enterprises.[9] If Gorokan economic growth were to slacken and opportunities for ambitious individuals significantly narrow, frustrated young Gorokans might also attempt to form a mass movement designed to leapfrog the Gorokan people over barriers posed by alien economic dominance and the limited economic horizons of older, established leaders. Should this occur, leadership in a radical movement might then turn out to be the most modern expression of the Gorokan drive for success and status; instead of growing coffee and operating small businesses, the would-be big-man of tomorrow may focus his energies on promoting widespread economic and political reforms.

Notes

PREFACE
1. Unless otherwise indicated, this study describes changes among the Gorokans up to 1968.
2. McClelland has since partially modified his stand (McClelland and Winter 1969:312).
3. As Keith McRae, formerly of the Goroka Teachers' College, is doing research on the spread of adminstration control and mission influence in Goroka during the 1930s and 1940s, I have not gone into the details of these aspects of early European-Gorokan relations, except where they relate directly to economic change.
4. LeVine, in contrast, focuses primarily on the psychological side of his thesis and gives little data on Ibo entrepreneurship and economic growth. Some aspects of the latter have recently been portrayed by an Ibo scholar, whose picture of Ibo rural development bears striking resemblance to that of Gorokan development presented here (Uchendu 1965).

CHAPTER 1
1. Papua New Guinea (PNG) comprises the eastern half of the island of New Guinea plus offshore islands, notably Manus, New Ireland, New Britain, and Bougainville. PNG has been an administrative union since 1946 of the Trust Territory of New Guinea, which comprises the northeastern half of New Guinea plus offshore islands (including those named above), and the Territory of Papua, which comprises the southern half of New Guinea plus small offshore islands. Hereafter PNG will be referred to as New Guinea.
2. *Watabung* is a Pidgin term (joining of waters) which apparently was first applied by New Guinea policemen to the area of the patrol post, where two rivers flow together, and then later extended to designate the surrounding region.
3. However, the Siane appear to follow the patrilineal ideal more closely than other Gorokan groups (Salisbury 1956:648).

4. Compare Salisbury (1962:39–111), who also distinguishes a third aspect, or nexus, as he puts it, of economic activities—the production and distribution of "luxury" goods like tobacco and pandanus nuts.
5. Read (1954:18) states that he has witnessed pig festivals in which as many as 140 pigs were exchanged and slaughtered.
6. See Hogbin (1958:84–85), Meggitt (1967a), Sahlins (1963), and Worsley (1957:15–16) for general discussions of the big-man system and Oliver (1955) for a classic study of leadership in a New Guinean society.
7. In Gahuku leaders were called *agurizakive* (literally, "his-name-with-man"), or *ve napa* (literally, "man-big"). Similar terms of renown were used to refer to leaders in the other Gorokan languages, including *we namfa* among the Siane (Salisbury 1962:27) and *evene nambo* among the Gururumba (Newman 1965:44), which both appear to be linguistically related to the Gahuku *ve napa*.

CHAPTER 2

1. Leahy (1933:March 3). Three basic sources on Leahy's activities in the Highlands exist: his diary (Leahy 1930–1934), now deposited in the National Library, Canberra; a journal article taken from his diary (Leahy 1936); and a popular book (Leahy and Crain 1937). This account is based primarily on his diary.
2. Taylor told me that he had anticipated finding populated valleys in the Highlands. In 1931, while he was stationed in the Sepik, a Catholic priest as evidence of this had shown him mother-of-pearl shell, originally from Papuan waters, which had been traded across the island.
3. In 1969 I was able to question a Korofeigu man who was visiting Canberra and who claimed to have taken part in this fight. He told me that only four men had died; the other two had been wounded and had recovered later.
4. Leahy (1933:January 1) reported another occasion when warriors showered his work force with arrows and stated that Guwaso, apparently one of his guards, "got in and knocked off 3 so that finished the fight." Whether these three men were actually killed is not stated in the diary.
5. The upper end of the Goroka Valley was bypassed by most of the early patrols, which tended to operate along the valley floor and, if proceeding west, to cross the Asaro Range south of this area. As late as 1944 there were still uncontacted people on the slopes of the Bismarcks (Bird 1945–1946), and Newman (1965:40) states that the Gururumba on the slopes of the Asaro Range were not pacified until about 1950.
6. This estimate has been confirmed by recent experiments on the cutting efficiency of steel axes and stone adzes conducted among tribesmen from an isolated Sepik Hills group still skillful in the use of stone tools (Townsend 1969).
7. A few steel axes may have reached the Goroka Valley before the first Europeans arrived by coming in from the Ramu Valley along trade routes for shell valuables. While among the Chimbu, Leahy (1933: April 4) mentions in his diary that the local people had a few worn

axes that must have been traded in from the Ramu. Three years earlier Leahy (1930:November 30) recorded that trade goods had reached the Bena Bena from the Ramu Valley along a trade route that crossed the Bismarcks at the "Bena Gap" but did not specify whether the goods included axes.

CHAPTER 3

1. Australian currency is used in New Guinea. In 1966 Australia converted from a pound/shillings system to a dollar/cents system: £1 = $2.00, and 1/ = $0.10. One dollar in Australian currency equaled approximately $1.125 in United States currency at the time of this study. All amounts quoted in this book are in Australian currency.
2. See Salisbury (1962) for a portrait of Siane society in 1952 and 1953, when money was only beginning to come into use and was usually treated more as a traditional valuable than as modern currency.
3. "I think that we should adopt the policy of the Government of Kenya and reserve the highlands of New Guinea for Europeans [and exclude Asians], where climatic conditions are temperate and suitable for the European manner of living," wrote Taylor (1940:149) in the report to the League of Nations of his 1938–1939 Hagen-Sepik patrol. However, he likened the area to "something between a second Java and a second New Zealand," rather than a duplicate of Kenya.
4. This theory also ignores Ian Downs' attempt while he was district commissioner in Goroka to avoid an overconcentration of Europeans by spreading their plantations throughout the area (Downs 1953).
5. By 1961 about one-third of the original agricultural leases in Goroka had changed hands (Howlett 1962:230). In 1958 two Gorokan plantations were sold for $34,000 and $72,000, respectively (*Pacific Islands Monthly* 1958:148).
6. Pioneer settlers still resident in Goroka have pointed out to me that it was they, not the administration, who took the main initiative in three steps that made coffee the leading industry of the Highlands: the organization of coffee shipments from Goroka by air to the coast and then from there by sea to Australia; the granting of a ruling from the Australian Tariff Board to require Australian coffee firms to buy New Guinea coffee in order to get a general tariff concession on all coffee they imported; and the hiring of Y. Baron Goto, a coffee expert from Hawaii, who gave the settlers the technical instruction needed to make coffee a viable crop in the Highlands (*Pacific Islands Monthly* 1956).
7. In 1968, when I examined this sign, now relegated to an old shed, Baito proudly recalled his initial commercial success and was full of praise of Taylor, who still acted as his adviser on financial and other matters, for having started him out as a coffee grower.

CHAPTER 4

1. Properly speaking, Gorokan stores are not trade stores, but merely retail stores. They do not buy or trade in cash crops like the coastal trade

stores from which the popular term—current in both Pidgin and English—for all rural stores in New Guinea derives.
2. The two Goroka trading banks gave less than $4,000 in loans to Gorokans, a figure which seems absurdly low in view of the substantial deposits Gorokans have made in them. According to bank officials, New Guineans (mostly Gorokans) had $738,069 deposited in savings accounts in these two banks at the end of fiscal year 1967/1968.
3. Money earned from passion fruit, peanuts, market vegetables, and other cash crops and money earned from wage labor, gold prospecting, and land sales figured in the financing of a few of the enterprises I investigated.
4. In the only case (vehicle 1, Table 7) where a secondary contributor was not a member of the same traditional group as the principal contributor it turned out that they were nevertheless related and that the secondary contributor had for a time served as the foster father of the principal contributor.
5. Or *kisim porofitmani* which is used alternatively. The translation "profits" should be understood here to mean either net profits or gross receipts, for Gorokans frequently do not distinguish between the two.
6. In 1967 not one Gorokan owned an automobile; all their vehicles were trucks licensed for passenger or freight hauling or, more commonly, for both. The only New Guineans in Goroka who owned private vehicles were moderately well paid workers from coastal areas who had purchased used automobiles.

CHAPTER 5
1. Schumpeter (1951:254) offered *business leader* as an alternative term for *entrepreneur*.
2. Sabumei speaks Bena Bena (his natal language), Gahuku, Siane, and Kuman (of the Chimbu District) and can get along in some of the other languages of the Eastern Highlands District and is fluent in Pidgin and, to a lesser extent, English and can even remember some of the Japanese he learned during the war.
3. Kapo says Bimai went as a contract laborer, one of the first from Goroka, although a European friend of Bimai believes that Bimai paid his own way to Manus and left after several months because he was dissatisfied with his lot as a plantation laborer.
4. See Salisbury (1962:158) for envious Siane comments about Apo.
5. Some of the details I learned about Bimai's commercial activities came from files concerning the disposition of Bimai's estate held in the Goroka Sub-District office. All information from these is cited under the heading "Notes on Bimai's estate."
6. A memo written by R. Cleland, officer in charge of the Watabung patrol post, August 10, 1955, lists six such payments with the comment: "Bimai of Komogu this day has purchased small areas of ground acc. to the schedule below. He asked me to give him this as confirmation and to avoid future disputes" (Notes on Bimai's Estate).

Notes

7. Bimai apparently never used the money to buy a truck; instead, it seems to have gone into his general operating funds for coffee buying. This arrangement was probably satisfactory to many of the contributors as long as Bimai offered them coffee buying services.
8. Notes on Bimai's Estate.
9. Notes on Bimai's Estate.
10. Other applicants have not been so fortunate; as of mid-1968 only three out of twenty land-title-conversion applications had received local approval in Goroka.
11. This and the following statements concerning Sinake's land are taken from testimony recorded in "Tenure Conversion Application Goroka No. 17 in respect to land known as Yanowa," which is held at the lands commissioner's office in Goroka.
12. *Friends* is a loose translation for *wantok,* which literally means people of one speech group.
13. Unfortunately, Goroka was not covered in the 1964 election study.
14. Sabumei told me that a friend of his from the Papuan coast suggested this strategy.
15. Although all the Gorokan business leaders are nominal adherents to one or another of the dozen or so missions located in Goroka, I could not discern any effect their religious affiliations had on their commercial behavior. Most of the business leaders are Protestants, but this simply reflects the general preponderance of Protestants in Goroka. In subdistricts of the Chimbu and Western Highlands districts, where Catholics predominate, one finds that most business leaders are nominal Catholics.

CHAPTER 6

1. However, the variation in traditional values and institutions from society to society and the possible relationship of this variation to the range of responses to economic opportunity should not be overlooked. For example, there is some evidence that in New Guinean societies where trade partnerships have been traditionally important this relationship may carry over into the cash economy and be a basic element in business relations (Lawrence, cited in Salisbury 1967:115; Mead 1967:5–6). In addition, it is an open question what kind of adaptation to the cash economy might be expected in New Guinean societies where hereditary leadership is dominant. Although there has been no thorough study of the distribution of these societies in New Guinea, they are known to exist on some islands off the Madang coast, off the southern New Britain coast, off the eastern tip of New Guinea, and here and there on the mainland of southern Papua (Ann Chowning, personal communication, September 5, 1968; Hau'ofa 1971; Meggitt 1967a:22–23; Sahlins 1963:228).
2. Two new cult movements have recently been reported—one in the Mount Hagen area (A. J. Strathern, personal communication, April 5, 1972)

and the other among the Auyuna of the eastern edge of the Eastern Highlands (Robbings and Vaitl: 1970).
3. Highlanders consider Europeans to be red men, not white men.

CHAPTER 7

1. Pooled money from clansmen and other followers is seldom available for this, perhaps partly because the original conspicuous investment has already been made and there is little pride associated with donating cash to meet the payroll and other such costs.
2. See Bauer (1963) and Ward (1960) for analyses of the contributions of seemingly "uneconomic" traders in underdeveloped countries in consumer purchasing and credit provisioning.
3. Gorokans apply the Pidgin terms *winmani* or *porofitmani* to gross receipts and generally fail to make a distinction between them and net receipts.
4. This was first, at the insistence of the people, called the Agurizakive-Guivahane Local Government Council, a name that can be translated as the "Renowned Man-Great Leader Local Government Council."
5. One major wholesaling firm, the local branch of Namasu Ltd., an organization closely tied to the Lutheran mission (Fairburn 1969), is owned largely by New Guinean shareholders. However, most of these shareholders are from the coastal districts, particularly the Morobe District, where the firm is headquartered; and the manager of the firm in Goroka is a European.
6. However, Perry Philip, who investigated this and other cattle projects during 1970 and 1971, has informed me that the Numuyargobo people are still in the process of working out exactly how small groups and individual cattle owners are to manage their cattle and improve and exploit pastureland.
7. This also raises an important question in motivational research. Can commercial activity, which may be largely inspired by an entrepreneur's need for Power, be made as efficient and profitable as, so some psychologists would have us believe, that primarily inspired by the need for Achievement?
8. Some Gorokans have also been involved in an administration-sponsored textile weaving project. However, like most of the "village industries" (sawmills, furniture manufacture, building materials fabrication, and such) around New Guinea that Wilson and Garnaut (1968) document, this project has had only limited success.
9. My information on the Mataungan movement has largely been derived from interviews with John Kaputin, a Mataungan spokesman, during his visits to Canberra in 1969 and Honolulu in 1971, as well as from articles by Epstein (1969, 1970) and Gunther (1971).

Bibliography

Adler, O. K.
    1962–1963. *Patrol Report No. 5 of 1962–63.* Department of District Administration, Goroka.
Aitchison, T. G.
    1964. Early History of Kainantu. *Goroka District Newsletter* 35:5–8.
Barrie, J. W.
    1956. Coffee in the Highlands. *Papua and New Guinea Agricultural Journal* 2(1):1–29.
Bauer, P. T.
    1963. *West African Trade.* 2nd ed. London: Routledge and Kegan Paul.
Baumol, W. J.
    1968. Entrepreneurship in Economic Theory. *American Economic Review* 58(2):64–71.
Belshaw, C. S.
    1955a. *In Search of Wealth.* Memoir 80. Menasha, Wisconsin: American Anthropological Association.
    1955b. The Culture Milieu of the Entrepreneur: A Critical Essay. *Explorations in Entrepreneurial History* 7(3):146–163.
Berndt, R. M.
    1952–1953. A Cargo Movement in the East Central Highlands of New Guinea. *Oceania* 23(1):40–65; 23(2):137–158; 23(3):202–234.
Bettison, D. G., C. A. Hughes, and P. W. van der Veur
    1965. *The Papua-New Guinea Elections 1964.* Canberra: Australian National University Press.
Bird, I.
    1945–1946. *Patrol Report No. 5 of 1945–46.* Goroka: Department of District Administration, Asaro Police Post.
Biskup, Peter
    1968. Hermann Detzner: New Guinea's First Coast Watcher. *Journal of the Papua and New Guinea Society* 2(1):5–21.

Black, J. R.
  1934–1935. *Patrol Report No. B–16 of 1934–35.* Salamaua: Department of District Administration.
Bond, B. H.
  1964. A Case Study of the Formation and Operation of the Kundiawa Coffee Society Limited. Mimeographed, Kundiawa, Eastern Highlands District.
Bowman, R. G.
  1946. Army Farms and Agricultural Development in the Southwest Pacific. *Geographical Review* 36:420–446.
Brookfield, H. C.
  1961. The Highland Peoples of New Guinea, A Study of Distribution and Socialization. *Geographical Journal* 127:436–448.
  1962. Local Study and Comparative Method: An Example from Central New Guinea. *Annals of the Association of American Geographers* 52(3):242–254.
  1968. The Money That Grows on Trees. *Australian Geographical Studies* 6(2):97–119.
Brookfield, H. C., and J. P. White
  1968. Revolution or Evolution in the Prehistory of the New Guinea Highlands. *Ethnology* 7(1):43–52.
Bulmer, R. N. H.
  1960. Political Aspects of the Moka Ceremonial Exchange System among the Kyaka People of the Western Highlands of New Guinea. *Oceania* 31(1):1–13.
Bulmer, Susan, and R. N. H. Bulmer
  1964. The Prehistory of the Australian New Guinea Highlands. *American Anthropologist* 66(no. 4, Pt. 2):39–76.
Bureau of Statistics
  1967. *Quarterly Summary of Statistics* 33(September 1967). Konedobu, Papua: Bureau of Statistics, Territory of Papua and New Guinea.
Burnett, I. D.
  1957–1958. *Patrol Report No. 2 of 1957–58.* Goroka: Department of District Administration.
Burridge, K.
  1960. *Mambu, A Melanesian Millenium.* London: Methuen.
  1969. *New Heaven New Earth.* New York: Schocken Books.
Chowning, Ann
  1967. Lakalai Religion and World View and the Concept of "Seaboard Religion." Seminar paper read October 26, 1967, at Australian National University, Canberra.
Cochrane, Glyn
  1970. *Big Men and Cargo Cults.* Oxford: Clarendon Press.
Commonwealth of Australia
  1935. *Report to the Council of the League of Nations on the Administra-*

Bibliography

tion of the Territory of New Guinea from 1st July, 1933, to 30th June, 1934. Canberra: Commonwealth Government Printer.

1938. *Report to the Council of the League of Nations on the Administration of the Territory of New Guinea from 1st July, 1936, to 30th June, 1937.* Canberra: Commonwealth Government Printer.

Corrigan, B.
1948–1949a. *Patrol Report No. 4 of 1948–49.* Goroka: Department of District Administration.
1948–1949b. *Patrol Report No. 5 of 1948–49.* Goroka: Department of District Administration.

Crocombe, R. G.
1964. *Communal Cash Cropping Among the Orokaiva.* New Guinea Research Bulletin No. 4. Canberra: Australian National University.
1965. *The M'buke Co-operative Plantation.* New Guinea Research Bulletin No. 7. Canberra: Australian National University.
1968. Local Government in New Guinea. *Journal of Pacific History* 3:131–134.

Crocombe, R. G., and G. R. Hogbin
1963. *The Erap Mechanical Farming Project.* New Guinea Research Bulletin No. 1. Canberra: Australian National University.

Davies, C. T.
1965–1966. *Patrol Report No. 8 of 1965–66.* Goroka: Department of District Administration.

Detzner, Hermann
1921. *Vier Jahre Unter Kannibalen.* Berlin: A. Scherl.

Dexter, David
1961. *The New Guinea Offensives.* Australia in the War of 1939–1945, ser. 1, vol. 6. Canberra: Australian War Memorial.

Dicke, E.
1968. The Rise of the Entrepreneur. *Anthropological Study Conference.* Amapyaka, Western Highlands District: New Guinea Lutheran Mission.

Downs, I. F. G.
1952. *Inspection Report: Central Highlands Area, July 1952.* Port Moresby: Department of District Administration.
1953. *The Land and Its Problems in the Eastern Highlands District.* Goroka: Department of District Administration.
1954–1955. *Annual Report Eastern Highlands District—1954–55.* Goroka: Department of District Administration.

Dwyer, R. E. P.
1954. Coffee Cultivation in Papua and New Guinea. *Papua and New Guinea Agricultural Journal* 9(1):1–5.
1955. *Native Agricultural Extension Work.* Port Moresby: Department of Agriculture, Stock and Fisheries.

Epstein, T. S.
　1968. *Capitalism, Primitive and Modern*. Canberra: Australian National University Press.
　1969–1970. The Mataungan Affair. *New Guinea* 4(4):8–14.
　1970a. Economics and Politics in Papua and New Guinea, Separatism and the Mataungan Movement. In M. W. Ward, ed., *The Politics of Melanesia*. Port Moresby: The University of Papua and New Guinea; Canberra: Australian National University.
　1970b. Indigenous Entrepreneurs and the Narrow Horizon. In *The Indigenous Role in Business Enterprise*. New Guinea Research Bulletin No. 35. Canberra: Australian National University.

Ewing, A. C.
　1944–1945. *Patrol Report No. 8 of 1944–45*. Bena-Bena: Australian New Guinea Administrative Unit, District Office.

Fairburn, I. J.
　1969. *Namasu: New Guinea's Largest Indigenous-owned Company*. New Guinea Research Bulletin No. 28. Canberra: Australian National University.

Feist, D. A.
　1968. Jeeps Are the Greatest. *Anthropological Study Conference*. Amapyaka, Western Highlands District: New Guinea Lutheran Mission.

Feldt, Eric
　1967. *The Coast Watchers*. 2nd ed. Sydney: Angus and Robertson.

Finney, B. R.
　1965. *Polynesian Peasants and Proletarians*. Wellington: The Polynesian Society.
　1968. Bigfellow Man Belong Business in New Guinea. *Ethnology* 7(4):394–410.
　1969. *New Guinean Entrepreneurs*. New Guinea Research Bulletin No. 27. Canberra: Australian National University.

Finney, R. S.
　1971. *Would-be Entrepreneurs?* New Guinea Research Bulletin No. 41. Canberra: Australian National University.

Fisk, E. K.
　1962. Planning in a Primitive Economy: Special Problems of Papua-New Guinea. *Economic Record* 38(84):462–478.
　1964. Planning in a Primitive Economy: From Pure Subsistence to the Production of a Market Surplus. *Economic Record* 40(90):156–174.

Flierl, Johann
　1927. *Forty Years in New Guinea: Memoirs of the Senior Missionary Johann Flierl*. Translated by M. Wiederaenders. Chicago: Wartburg Publishing House.

Geertz, Clifford
　1963. *Peddlers and Princes*. Chicago: University of Chicago Press.

Bibliography

Government Printer
  1967. *Districts of Papua and New Guinea 1966*. Port Moresby: Government Printer.
Gunther, J. T.
  1965. From Stone Age to Parliamentary Government in a Decade. In Colin Simpson, *Plumes and Arrows*. Sydney: Angus and Robertson.
  1970. Trouble in Tolailand. *New Guinea* 5(3):25–37.
Hagen, E. E.
  1962. *On the Theory of Social Change*. Homewood, Ill.: Dorsey Press.
Harding, T. G.
  1965. The Rai Coast Open Electorate. In D. G. Bettison, C. A. Hughes, and P. W. van der Veur, eds., *The Papua-New Guinea Elections 1964*. Canberra: Australian National University.
  1967. A History of Cargoism in Sio, North-East New Guinea. *Oceania* 38(1):1–23.
Hasluck, Paul
  1954. Reply to Mr. Wright. *Parliamentary Debates (Hansard) Session 1954*. Vol. 14 of R. 4. Canberra: Government Printing Office.
Hastings, Peter
  1969. *New Guinea, Problems and Prospects*. Melbourne: Cheshire.
Hau'ofa, Epeli
  1971. Mekeo Chieftainship. *Journal of the Polynesian Society* 80(2):152–169.
Hogbin, H. I.
  1958. *Social Change*. London: Watts.
Hoselitz, Bert F.
  1960. *Sociological Aspects of Economic Growth*. Glencoe, Ill.: Free Press.
  1963. Entrepreneurial Element in Economic Development. *The Economic Weekly* 15(4–6):167–173.
Howlett, D. R.
  1962. A Decade of Change in the Goroka Valley, New Guinea: Land Use and Development in the 1950s. Ph.D. dissertation, Australian National University, Canberra.
Hughes, I.
  1966. Availability of Land and Other Factors Determining the Incidence and Scale of Cash Cropping in the Kere Tribe, Sina Sina, Chimbu District, New Guinea. B.A. thesis, University of Sydney.
Jacobs, M.
  In press. History and Organization of Government in German New Guinea. *Encyclopaedia of Papua-New Guinea*. Melbourne: Melbourne University Press.
Johnson, E. R.
  1957–1958. *Patrol Report No. 1 of 1957–58*. Goroka: Department of District Administration.

Kariks, J., O. Kooptzoff, M. Steed, H. Cotter, and R. J. Walsh
  1960. A Study of Some Physical Characteristics of the Goroka Natives, New Guinea. *Oceania* 30(3):225–236.
Kilby, Peter
  1971. *Entrepreneurship and Economic Development.* New York: Free Press.
Kingston, D. J.
  1958. *Quarterly Progress Report—July to September 1958.* Goroka: Department of Agriculture, Stock and Fisheries.
Langness, L. L.
  1963. Notes on the Bena Council, Eastern Highlands. *Oceania* 33(3):151–170.
  1964. Some Problems in the Conceptualization of Highlands Social Structures. *American Anthropologist* 66(no. 4, pt. 2):162–182.
  1967. Sexual Antagonism in the New Guinea Highlands: A Bena-Bena Example. *Oceania* 37(3):161–177.
Lawrence, P. J.
  1964. *Road Belong Cargo.* Manchester: Manchester University Press.
  1966. Postscript 1966. *Road Belong Cargo.* Melbourne: Oxford University Press.
  1967. Politics and "True Knowledge." *New Guinea* 2(1):34–49.
Lawrence, P. J., and M. J. Meggitt
  1965. Introduction. In P. J. Lawrence and M. J. Meggitt, eds., *Gods, Ghosts and Men in Melanesia.* Melbourne: Oxford University Press.
Leahy, M. J.
  1930–1934. Personal Diary. Manuscript in the National Library, Canberra.
  1936. The Central Highlands of New Guinea. *Geographical Journal* 87(3):229–262.
Leahy, M. J., and Maurice Crain
  1937. *The Land That Time Forgot.* New York: Funk and Wagnalls.
LeVine, R. A.
  1966. *Dreams and Deeds: Achievement Motivation in Nigeria.* Chicago: University of Chicago Press.
Linton, Ralph
  1936. *The Study of Man.* New York: D. Appleton-Century.
McArthur, J. R.
  1956–1957. *Patrol Report No. 11 of 1956–57.* Goroka: Department of District Administration.
McCarthy, Dudley
  1959. *South-West Pacific Area: First Year, Koroda to Wau.* Australia in the War of 1939–1945. Ser. 1, vol. 5. Canberra: Australian War Memorial.
McClelland, D. C.
  1961. *The Achieving Society.* Princeton: Van Nostrand.
McClelland, D. C., and D. G. Winter
  1969. *Motivating Economic Achievement.* New York: Free Press.

Bibliography

McKillop, R. F.
1970. Toward a Development Model in the Eastern Highlands of Papua-New Guinea. Mimeographed.

McNicholl, R. R.
1968. Sir Walter McNicholl as Administrator of the Mandated Territory. *Journal of the Papua and New Guinea Society* 2(2):5–16.

McRae, Keith
1969. Kiaps, Missionaries, Colonists and New Guinea Highlanders in the 1930s. Seminar paper read at the Australian National University, Canberra.

Malaot, Paliau
1970. Histori Bilong Mi Taim Mi Bin Bon na i Kamap Tede (The Story of My Life from the Time I Was Born Until the Present Day). In Marion W. Ward, ed., *The Politics of Melanesia*. Canberra: Australian National University.

Malinowski, Bronislaw
1922. *Argonauts of the Western Pacific*. London: Routledge and Kegan Paul.

Mead, Margaret
1956. *New Lives For Old*. New York: William Morrow.
1967. Introduction. In *New Guinea People in Business and Industry*. New Guinea Research Bulletin No. 20. Canberra: Australian National University.

Meggitt, M. J.
1967a. The Pattern of Leadership Among the Mae-Enga of New Guinea. *Anthropological Forum* 2(1):20–35.
1967b. Uses of Literacy in New Guinea and Melanesia. *Bijdragen Tot de Taal-Land-en Volkenkund* 123(1):71–82.

Montgomery, I. Y.
1958–1959. *Annual Report Eastern Highlands District 1958–59*. Goroka: Department of Agriculture, Stock and Fisheries.

Nash, G.
1970. Legal Structure and Indigenous Business Enterprise: The Need for Change. In *The Indigenous Role in Business Enterprise*. New Guinea Research Bulletin No. 35, Canberra: Australian National University.

Neverman, H.
1934. *Admiralitäts—Inseln*. In G. Thilenius, ed., Ergebnisse der Südsee—Expedition, 1908–1910, vol. 3. Hamburg: Friederichsen, de Gruyter.

New Guinea Highlands Bulletin
1968. The Need for a New Elite. *New Guinea Highlands Bulletin* 9(3):7.

Newman, P. L.
1965. *Knowing the Gururumba*. New York: Holt, Rinehart and Winston.

Nurkse, Ragnar
1953. *Problems of Capital Formation in Underdeveloped Countries*. Oxford: Basil Blackwell.

O'Connor, A. J.
  1970. Indigenous Shareholding—An Analysis. In *The Indigenous Role in Business Enterprise*. New Guinea Research Bulletin No. 35. Canberra: Australian National University.

Oliver, D. L.
  1955. *A Solomon Islands Society*. Cambridge: Harvard University Press.

Pacific Islands Monthly
  1939. "A Second Kenya" in Central New Guinea. 10(1):19–20.
  1955. Land Systems Come under Fire in NG. 25(6):19, 138–139.
  1956. NG Highlands Coffee Needs Good Land, Wise Development. 26(9):65–67.
  1958. The NG Money Tree: But Something's Affecting the Coffee Market. 29(3):23, 148.

Papua-New Guinea Post Courier
  1969. First Sale for Native Auctioneer. December 15, 1969, p. 8.

Parsons, Talcott, and E. A. Shils
  1959. *Toward a General Theory of Action*. Cambridge: Harvard University Press.

Polanyi, K., C. M. Ahrensberg, and H. W. Pearson
  1957. *Trade and Markets in the Early Empires*. Glencoe, Ill.: Free Press.

Pospisil, Leopold
  1963. *Kapauku Papuan Economy*. Yale University Publications in Anthropology 67. New Haven: Department of Anthropology, Yale University.

Powell, H. A.
  1960. Competitive Leadership in Trobriands Political Organization. *Journal of the Royal Anthropological Institute* 90(pt. 1):118–145.

Read, K. E.
  1952a. Nama Cult of the Central Highlands, New Guinea. *Oceania* 23(1):1–25.
  1952b. Missionary Activities and Social Change in the Central Highlands of Papua and New Guinea, pt. 1. *South Pacific* 5(11):229–238.
  1952c. Land in the Central Highlands. *South Pacific* 6(7):440–449.
  1954. Culture of the Central Highlands, New Guinea. *Southwestern Journal of Anthropology* 10(1):1–43.
  1959. Leadership and Consensus in a New Guinea Society. *American Anthropologist* 64(3):425–436.
  1965. *The High Valley*. New York: Scribners.

Reay, Marie
  1959. *The Kuma*. Melbourne: Melbourne University Press.
  1964. Present-Day Politics in the New Guinea Highlands. *American Anthropologist* 64(no. 4, pt. 2):240–256.
  1969. But Whose Estates? The Wahgi Smallholders. *New Guinea* 4(3):64–68.

Rimoldi, Max
  1966. *Land Tenure and Land Use among the Mount Lamington Orokaiva*.

Bibliography

New Guinea Research Bulletin No. 11. Canberra: Australian National University.

Robbins, R. G.
1963. The Anthropogenic Grasslands of New Guinea. In Proceedings of the UNESCO *Symposium on the Impact of Man on Humid Tropics Vegetation, Goroka, Papua-New Guinea, 1960*. Canberra: Commonwealth Government Printer.

Robbings, S. G., and E. Vaitl
1970. Cognitive Rigidity and Cargo Cults. Paper read at the American Anthropological Association annual meeting, San Diego, California.

Ross, W. A.
1969. The Growth of Catholicism in the Western Highlands. *Journal of the Papua and New Guinea Society* 2(2):59–64.

Rowley, C. D.
1965. *The New Guinea Villager*. Melbourne: F. W. Cheshire.

Sahlins, Marshall
1963. Poor Man, Rich Man, Big Man, Chief: Political Types in Melanesia and Polynesia. *Comparative Studies in Society and History* 5(3):285–303.

Salisbury, R. F.
1956. Asymmetrical Marriage Systems. *American Anthropologist* 58(4): 639–655.
1958. An "Indigenous" New Guinea Cargo Cult. *Kroeber Anthropological Society Papers* 18:67–78.
1962. *From Stone to Steel: Economic Consequences of a Technological Change in New Guinea*. New York: Cambridge University Press.
1967. Economic Research in New Guinea. *Behavioral Science Research in New Guinea*. Publication 1493. Washington, D.C.: National Research Council.
1970. *Vunamami: Economic Transformation in a Traditional Society*. Berkeley and Los Angeles: University of California Press.

Schumpeter, J. A.
1949. *The Theory of Economic Development*. Translated by Redvers Opie. Cambridge: Harvard University Press.
1951. *Essays of J. A. Schumpeter*. R. V. Clemence, ed. Cambridge, Mass.: Addison-Wesley.

Schwartz, Theodore
1962. *The Paliau Movement in the Admiralty Islands 1946–1954*. Anthropological Papers, vol. 49, pt. 2. New York: American Museum of Natural History.

Searson, J. J.
1947–1948. *Patrol Report No. 1 of 1947–48*. Goroka: Department of District Administration.

Shindler, A. J.
1950. *Extension Officer Goroka—Comments on Report*. Department of

Agriculture, Stock and Fisheries, Highlands Agriculture Experiment Station, Aiyura.

Simpson, Colin
1965. *Plumes and Arrows*. Sydney: Angus and Robertson.

Stanner, W. E. H.
1962. Foreword. In R. F. Salisbury, *From Stone to Steel*. New York: Cambridge University Press.

Strathern, A. J.
1969. Finance and Production: Two Strategies in New Guinea Highlands Exchange Systems. *Oceania* 40(1):42–67.
1970. Cargo and Inflation in Mount Hagen. Paper read at the Australian and New Zealand Association for the Advancement of Science meeting, Port Moresby.

Sydney Morning Herald
1954. Warning of a "Second Kenya." January 20, p. 8.
1954. Clergyman Fears Terror in New Guinea. January 29, p. 4.
1954. Land Buying in New Guinea, Viewpoint of Labour Party. February 12, p. 2.

Taylor, J. L.
1933. Patrol Report of 1933, Mr. J. L. Taylor, Purari River Headquarters Area. Typed copy in Territory of Papua-New Guinea Archives, Port Moresby.
1935. Resume—Mount Hagen Patrol. *Report to the Council of the League of Nations on the Administration of the Territory of New Guinea from 1st July, 1932, to 30th June, 1933*. Appendix B, pp. 113–117. Canberra: Commonwealth Government Printer.
1940. Interim Report by Assistant District Officer J. L. Taylor on the Hagen-Sepik Patrol 1938–1939. *Report to the Council of the League of Nations on the Administration of the Territory of New Guinea from 1st July, 1938, to 30th June, 1939*. Appendix B, pp. 137–149. Canberra: Commonwealth Government Printer.
1947. *Monthly Report, May 1947, Central Highlands District*. Goroka: Department of District Administration.

ToRobert, H.
1967. Credit and Indigenous Businessmen. In *New Guinea People in Business and Industry*. New Guinea Research Bulletin No. 20. Canberra: Australian National University.

Townsend, W. H.
1969. Stone and Steel Tool Use in a New Guinea Society. *Ethnology* 8(2):199–205.

Uchendu, Victor C.
1965. *The Igbo of Southeast Nigeria*. New York: Holt, Rinehart and Winston.

United Nations
1968. *Report of the United Nations Visiting Mission to the Trust Territory of New Guinea, 1968*. New York: United Nations.

Bibliography

van der Veur, P. W.
  1964. Towards Self-Government in Papua-New Guinea. *Asian Survey* 4(8):991–999.
Waddell, E. W., and P. A. Krinks
  1968. *The Organization of Production and Distribution among the Orokaiva.* New Guinea Research Bulletin No. 24. Canberra: Australian National University.
Ward, B. E.
  1960. Cash or Credit Crops? An Examination of Some Implications of Peasant Commercial Production with Special Reference to the Multiplicity of Traders and Middlemen. *Economic Development and Cultural Change* 8(2):148–163.
Watson, J. B.
  1964. Introduction: Anthropology in the New Guinea Highlands. *American Anthropologist* 66(no. 4, pt. 2):1–19.
  1965. The Significance of a Recent Ecological Change in the Central Highlands of New Guinea. *Journal of the Polynesian Society* 74(4): 438–450.
Weber, Max
  1930. *The Protestant Ethic and the Spirit of Capitalism.* Translated by Talcott Parsons. London: Allen and Unwin.
White, J. P.
  1967. Taim Bilong Bipo: Investigations Towards a Prehistory of the Papua-New Guinea Highlands. Ph.D. dissertation, Australian National University, Canberra.
Wilson, R. Kent, and Ross Garnaut
  1968. *A Survey of Village Industries in Papua-New Guinea.* New Guinea Research Bulletin No. 25. Canberra: Australian National University.
Wolfers, E. P.
  1968–1969. The Elections, Pt. 2, *New Guinea* 3(4):8–31.
  1968. Two New Guinea Elections: Henganofi in 1964 and 1967. In N. Meller, *Papers on the Papua and New Guinea House of Assembly.* New Guinea Research Bulletin No. 22. Canberra: Australian National University.
Worsley, P. M.
  1957. *The Trumpet Shall Sound.* London: Macgibbon and Kee.
  1959. Cargo Cults. *Scientific American* 200(5):117–128.
Wurm, S.
  1964. Australian New Guinea Highlands Languages and the Distribution of the Typological Features. *American Anthropologist* 66(no. 4, pt. 2):77–97.

Index

Achievement. *See* Need for Achievement
Aitchison, T. G., officer - in - charge, Kainantu station, 24
Akunai Rovelie, 161; as business leader, 85, 96–97, 110–111
Alienation of land. *See* Land alienation
American: blacks, 134; occupation of Manus, 134
ANGAU. *See* Australian New Guinea Administrative Unit
Apo Yeharigie, 39, 42, 111, 117, 118; as business leader, 85, 86, 88, 90, 95–96, 99; as commercial investor, 72
Asaro River, 1, 60
Asaroyufa clan, 91, 104
Astrolabe Bay, site of first European settlements, 135
Australian control, 129; initiation of, 134
Australian New Guinea Administrative Unit (ANGAU), 43, 44, 88, 138; formation of, 27; role in coffee cultivation, 60; role in combatting World War II epidemic, 28, 35. *See also* ANGAU
Axe: steel tool, 35, 36, 70; as valuable, 34

Barrie, J. W., extension services of, 61, 62
Bekim. *See* Reciprocity Bena Bena, 43, 87, 89, 95, 154; coffee nursery site, 60, 63; patrol post, 21, 23; people, 30, 32, 165; river, 1; site of airfield, 26, 32

Big-head, definition of, 114
Big-man, 32, 35, 36; consequences of deaths of, 178; definition of, 15, 108; status of, 18, 124, 144; traditional, xi, 90, 112
Bikfela man. *See* Big-man
Bikfela man bilong bisnis, ix, 84–86, 100. *See also* Business Leaders
Bikhet. *See* Big-head
Bimai Noimbano: as business leader, 76, 77, 80, 85, 94, 95, 100–104, 109–110, 176; as coffee buyer, 101, 152–153; death of, 113, 177
Bisnis, ix, xv, 114, 170. *See also* Business
Bisniska. *See* Investment, commercial vehicles
Bisnisman. *See* Business
Black, John R.: patrol officer, 87; patrol report of, 24
Black King movement, 138. *See also* Cargo cults
Bono Azinapfa: as business leader, 85, 91–93, 101, 109; participation in politics, 116, 119–120
Bulolo Creek, gold site, 20, 42, 43
Bungem mani. *See* Investment, common pool
Business, 144; acquisition of skills, 157; development of, 86; of Gorokans, 70, 71
Business leaders: as clan members, 108; leader-follower transactions, 108; mobilization of support, 108; as modernized elite, 90, 170; support of, 109. *See also* Akunai Rovelie;

Apo Yeharigie; Bimai Noimbano; Bin Aravaki; Bono Azinapfa; Hari Gotoha; Sabumei Kofikai; Sinake Giregire; Soso Subi; Wale Kabiliha

Canberra, 45
Capital, goods of, 69, 70; Land Rover utility truck as, 71; trade stores as, 71
Capital, raising of, 75
Capitalism, spirit of, 121
Cargo cults, 50, 141–143; activities among the Manus, 135; as attempt to gain status, 144; characteristic features of, 139; definition of, 137; doctrine, 138; home of, 123, 125; opposition to, 144; resistance to, 143. *See also* Black King movement; Great Pigs movement; Ghost Wind movement; Hine movement
Carne, R., chief agricultural worker in Goroka, 54, 61, 62
Cash crops, 50, 137, 143; coconuts as, 61; communal system, 62, 63; development of, 125; extension services, 125; passion fruit as, 59, 60, 66, 132; roads, 125. *See also* Coffee
Cash economy, 38, 148
Casuarina, uses of, 10
Catholic mission at Mount Hagen. *See* Father Ross
Cattle raising, expansion of, 154, 165–166
Census divisions, 6, 158; Bena Bena, 6, 77, 78; Lowa, 6, 158; Unggai, 6, 21, 158; Upper Asaro, 6, 77, 78; Watabung, 6, 28
Central Highlands, 55, 132
Ceremonies and festivals: life crisis, 13; pig festival, 8, 13, 14; religious, 8; initiation, 13
Chimbu, 60, 96; coffee nursery site, 61; site of administration stations, 24; site of European deaths, 26; source of hardworking laborers, 27, 52
Chinese: dominance of, 180; as laborers, 135; overseas, 180
Christianity, 29
Clan: as basic social unit, 7; investors, 106; labor, 106; recruitment into, 8
Clothing, manufacture of, 180
Coffee: boom, 67; collective effort in production, 63; competition in, 64, 160; cooperative factory, 102; cultivation practices, 147; de-emphasis of, 66; European involvement, 54; Europeans vs. Gorokans, 160; experiment, (*see* Highlands Agricultural Experiment station); exploitation of interest, 55; as export crop, 67; government supervision of production, 57, 59–61, 65, 66; industry, 53, 54, 57, 71, 168, 177; International Coffee Agreement, 160; introduction of, 42, 43, 64, 86; key crop in commercial development, 39, 44; nurseries, 60, 62, 91, 93; overproduction of, 57; overreliance on, 65; plantations of, 37, 41, 42, 127; production of, 67, 179; role of intergroup rivalry in, 61; sales of, 42
Colonial administrations: Australian, 19; Dutch, 19; German, 19
Colonialism, 157–170
Conroy, W., present director of DASF, 66
Copra, 131
Cottees Passiona, Ltd., 59. *See also* Cash crops, passion fruit as
Cottle, Robert, 91, 95; extension services of, 58–61, 100
Councillors, 116, 117

Daulo, electorate divisions, 116
Daulo Pass, 41
Death: of Bimai Noimbano, 102; of clan members, 7; in European-Highlander encounters, 26
Department of Agriculture, Stock and Fisheries (DASF): cash-crop data, xvii, xviii; conference on coffee, 66; employees of, 86, 89, 94, 165; extension services, 57, 60, 63–65, 100, 143; field days for coffee production, 65; involvement in Gorokan investment, 73, 74; in passion fruit cultivation, 59; planting shade trees, 61; policy of, 154
Depression, 131
Detzner, Hermann, World War I German surveyor, 19
Discrimination against Gorokans, 158
Downs, Ian, 45; administrative officer in postwar Goroka, 54; spokesman for Partnership, 49. *See also* Partnership
Dwyer, Michael, Australian gold prospector, 20

Economic anthropology, ix
Education: Pidgin schools, 25; universal efforts toward, 113; for utilitarian skills, 177

Index

Elective offices: councillor, 116; member of House of Assembly, 116
Entrepreneurship: concept of, 83; factors affecting, 146; as imitative innovation, 83; as innovator, 83; role of, in Gorokan economic growth, x, xi; Schumpeter's definition of, 83, 107, 122, 171–172; theories of, xii–xiv, xviii, xix
Equivalence, principle of, 18
Europeans: affluence of, 50, 56, 141; arrival of, 32, 132; as big-men, 33; control by, 28, 159; economic privilege of, 169, 170; insurance of economic presence of, 167, 168; in joint ventures, 175; land ownership, 111; opposition of, to Gorokan plans for expansion of commercial undertakings, 167; plantations of, 129; as spirits, 22; subordination to, 161; in trade, 34, 129

Father Ross, founder of Catholic mission at Mount Hagen, 34
Finschhafen, Lutheran mission headquarters, 97
French Polynesia, xi, xv

Gahuku: status through achievement, 16; wealth-prestige orientation, 12
Gazelle Peninsula: center of European commercial activity, 129, 132; center of New Guinean commercial activity, xiv
German administration, 129, 131; extension of, 135
Gerua boards, 62
Ghost Wind movement, 138, 139, 141, 142. See also Cargo cults
Gimisave village, 97
Gohonite Gerepaima, traditional bigman, 111, 112
Gold: effect of Depression, 21; mining, 95, 96; prospecting, 21, 98; prospectors of, 20; source of cash earnings, 132
Gold lip (*kina*). See Mother-of-Pearl shell
Gono people, 143
Gorokan dress, 5
Gorokan languages, xv, 5; Asaro, 5, 6; Bena Bena, 5, 6; Gahuku, 5, 6; non-Austronesian or Papuan, 5; Pidgin, xv, 6, 25, 55; Siane, 5, 6; Yaviyufa, 5, 6
Goroka Sub-District: administrative unit, 1; choice of area for research, xiv; climate of, 2
Government, local, 157–158
Greathead, George: administrative officer in postwar Goroka, 54; passion fruit plant supervisor, 59
Great Pigs movement, 138. See also Cargo cults
Group participation in enterprise, 172–175
Group pride of Gorokans, 62, 82, 93

Hagen-Sepik patrol, 31. See also Taylor, Jim
Hari Gotoha, 117–118; business empire of, 104–107; as business leader, 85, 100, 114–115, 176, 179–180; retail store owner, 166, 150
Hasluck, Paul, minister for territories, 47
Henganofi electorate, 116, 119, 120
Highlanders, 31; discovery of, 19
Highlands Agricultural Experiment Station, 42–44, 58
Highlands Commodity Exchange, coffee-buying and processing firm, 168
Highlands Farmers and Settlers Association, represents European interests, 138. 168. Hine movement, See also Cargo cults
House of Assembly, 99, 116; elections of, 119; leaders in, 117, 158

Independence, 162
Inheritance, flexibility of, 11
International Coffee Agreement Organization, 66
Investment: in coffee business, 71; in commercial vehicles, 72–74; common pool, xv, 76; communal enterprises, 77; "conspicuous," 69, 81, 165, 171; Gorokan motivations for, 78–82, 171; in livestock production, 73, 74; in piggeries, 73, 74; principal contributor in, 77; in restaurants, 73, 74; self-financed by Gorokans, 74; tendency toward, 69; trend of, 78

Japanese: invasion of, 26, 89; as laborers, 135; in World War II, 88

Kaad, F., assistant district officer, 54
Kafe-speakers, 120
Kafiafana rock shelter, evidence of human occupation, 3
Kago, 137. See also Cargo cults

Kainantu, 96, 164; center of cargo cult movement, 139; site of administration stations, 24, 81
Kapo, Robert, relation of Bimai Noimbano, 94, 101, 103
Kenya: New Guinea as a "second Kenya," 46; source of passion fruit, 59
Khasawaho (Baito) Heiro, as businessman, 71, 81; major New Guinean coffee grower, 55, 57, 64, 149
Kindeimarofa clan, 94, 102–103
Kingston, D. J., district agricultural officer, 65
Kirapim bisnis. See Business, development of
Kirapim ples. See Business, development of
Kisim winmani. See Investment, Gorokan motivations for
Kondom Agaundo, major business leader, 113
Kula exchange, ix
Kundiawa, administration school of, 89, 96, 97
Kyle, A. F., patrol officer, 87

Labor, exploitation of, 63; free, 93; manpower, 54, 135; recruiters of, 94, 126, 133
Land: allocation of, 11; availability of, 178; boom, 45; cash payments for, 50; competitive bidding on, 47; development of, 46; policy, opposition to, 48; rush, 47; sale of, by Gorokans, 49–50, 52; scarcity of, 179
Land alienation, 136, 163; criticism of, 46; halt to, 46, 51; method of, 47
Language, of Gorokans, 5, 6
Leadership: business, 85; economic, 85, 102; political, 116, 118
Leahy, Dan, brother of Michael Leahy, 21
Leahy, Jim: built first trade store, 42, 70; coffee pioneer, 41, 43, 45; older brother of Michael Leahy, 41; tea cultivation, 44
Leahy, Michael, 9, 32, 34, 43, 95; Australian gold prospector, 20, 87
Literacy, of Gorokans, 63
Lufa area, 141
Luluai, 91, 112. See also Village headman

McKillop, R. F., DASF officer in Goroka, 165

Madang, 54, 87, 128, 135; people of, 88
Makis, business leader, 111
Malaguna Technical School, 89, 97
Manus Island, 94, 128, 133; people of, 135
Markham Valley, x
Marriage: bride-price, 7, 17, 36, 104, 109, 110, 147, 148; clan intermarriage, 13; polygamy, 99; prohibitions of, 8
Mataungan Association, 181
Mau Mau terrorism, 46
Megusayufa tribal group, 111
Men: "male crops," 11; sleeping arrangements of, 7, 72; tasks of, 11, 36
Missionaries, 126, 138, 154; expansion of, 28; introduction of passion fruit, 59; Lutheran, 20, 43, 60, 140; mission stations, 25, 92, 97; preachings of, 29
Money, 31, 33, 39, 47, 52; introduction of, 34, 37; pooling of, 76, 77; as wages, 40
Morobe District, x, 42, 61
Mother-of-Pearl shell, 35; primary valuable, 33
Mount Hagen, 44, 133

Nadzab, site of main Allied air base, 27
Native Loans Development Board, predecessor of Development Bank, 74
Natural resources, endowment of, 125
Need for Achievement, xviii, xix, 123, 124
Need for Power, xviii, xix, 124
Nemavera, Siane warrior, father of Bimai Noimbano, 94
Neuguinea-Kompagnie, 129, 135
New Guinea Goldfields Company, 21, 23, 24
Ninji, Mount Hagen big-man, 138
No-man's-land, 51
Nucleus estate for tea cultivation, 164
Numuyargobo tribal confederacy, 165, 166
Nurkse, Ragnar, economist on problems of capital formation, 69

Okiufa school, 97
Orokaiva: contact with Europeans, 126; coffee plantations of, 127

Pacification, 30, 54, 166
Paliau Maloat, leader of Manus movement, 134

Index

Papa bilong bisniska, 82. See also Investment, principal contributor
Papua and New Guinea Development Bank: inauguration of, 74; loans from, 165
Partnership: between Europeans and New Guineans, 49, 50, 55, 63, 164; Gorokan motives for, 51; requests for, 49
Peace, 51; effects of, 37
Per-capita cash income, 68
Phratry, 8
Pidgin English, 6, 25, 55. See also Gorokan languages
Pig festivals, occasion for wealth exchange, 17
Pigs, 31; production of, 36; as symbols, 147; in trade, 37; as wealth, 16, 17, 32
Plantation, owner-managers, Gorokans as, 92, 169
Plantations, 29, 136; coconut, 131, 133, 135, 136; coffee, 127; German, 134; rubber, 136; tobacco, 135
Politics: connection with business leadership, 118; leadership, 116; participation in by business leaders, 116
Population: densities of, 10; of Goroka, 4
Port Moresby, 40, 45, 64
Preadaption for economic growth, x, xi, 124
Preconditions for economic growth, 124–126, 132

Rabaul, 70, 89, 97
Race relations, 158, 159
Read, Kenneth, anthropological accounts of Gorokans, 52
Reciprocity, between big-men and followers, 93, 109
Religion, rituals of, 137, 140
Rice, as staple, 52
Royal Papuan Constabulary, members of, 27

Sabumei Kofikai, 144–145; as business leader, 86, 89–90, 96–97; participation in politics, 116, 120–121, 158
Seigu, 88, 95, 111
Self-government, resistance to, 161–162
Sepik, 138
Shells, 31, 39; as commodity, 70; as money, 34, 42, 99; as symbols of wealth, 13, 32, 36; as valuables, 33

Shindler, Aubrey, director of Highlands Agricultural Experimental Station, 58, 94
Siane, x, 32, 36; in wealth-exchange, 35, 37
Sigoma village, 140
Sinake Giregire, 168, 176, 179; as business leader, 85, 97–99, 110–113, 160; as ministerial member for posts and telegraph, 167; participation in politics, 116, 118, 120, 158, 167; in tea industry, 164
Sogeri High School, 97
Sole proprietorships, 173–175
Sorcery: as cause of death, 113, 114; as cause of diseases, 88; as cause of disputes, 8; fear of, 113, 114
Soso Subi, 85, as business leader, 91–93, 101, 104–107, 111
Status mobility, xiii, xiv, xviii, xix; modern avenues of, 178; traditional patterns of, 14, 15
Status motivation, 171; primary goals of, 172
Stores. See Trade stores
Sweet potato: cultivation of, 10, 62; as gifts, 13; introduction of, 4; as pig fodder, 16

Tahitian society, xi, xvi
Taim bilong pait. See War
Taylor, Jim, 32, 34, 35, 39, 41, 53, 56, 94; coffee cultivation, 44, 55, 149; comments of, 30; as district officer for Highlands, 28; first patrol officer, 12; introduction of money, 40; résumé of patrol report, 22; setting up patrol posts, 21
Tea: as cash crop, 132; feasibility of, 165; industry, 163–164, 165; plantation, 44
Thursday Island, source of quality shells, 33
Tilapia fish, breeding of, 100
Title conversion, 111
Tolai people, x, 129, 180; economic growth of, 131
Trade, 35; channels of, 13; goods of, 27, 31, 32, 39, 47; relations, 37; routes of, 31
Trade stores, 150; as capital good, 71, 72, 78; first, 37, 41, 42; goods sold in, 70; service function of, 151; wholesaling, 152
Transportation: airfreight, 54; airplanes, 139; roads, 54, 125

Tribe, 8
Trobriand Islands, 15
Trucking, 152–154; coffee-buying, 152; enterprises, 167, 177; freight-hauling, 152; long haul, 167; passenger/freight transport, 152; problems, 153
Tultul, 91. *See also* Village headman

Upper Asaro, 35, 41; site of coffee estate, 49

Veblen, 81
Village headman, 91, 93
Voting, 119

Wahgi Valley, 34, 81, 133, 138; people of, 35
Wale Kabiliha, as trade store owner, 150
War: ceremonies of, 8; feuds (intergroup), 25; prohibition of, 125; status associated with, 16; types of fighting, 8, 9; warfare period (*taim bilong pait*), 30
Watabung, 94, 101; investment fund of, 76–78, 80
Wau, site of arabica coffee plantation, 42
Wealth: development of, 31; exchange system, 35–37; prestige associated with, 11; sanctions against, 18; status in, 16; valuables, xi, 12–14
Weber, Max, 121
We namfa. See Big-man
Women: in coffee production, 52; sleeping arrangements of, 7; tasks of, 11, 99
World War I, 127, 131
World War II, 91, 97, 127, 139; diseases among Gorokans during, 27, 88; effect on administrative control, 24; Japanese invasion, 26, 27, 88, 89, 131, 134; mortality, 28

Yali, famous cargo cult leader, 141
Yamei clan, 100

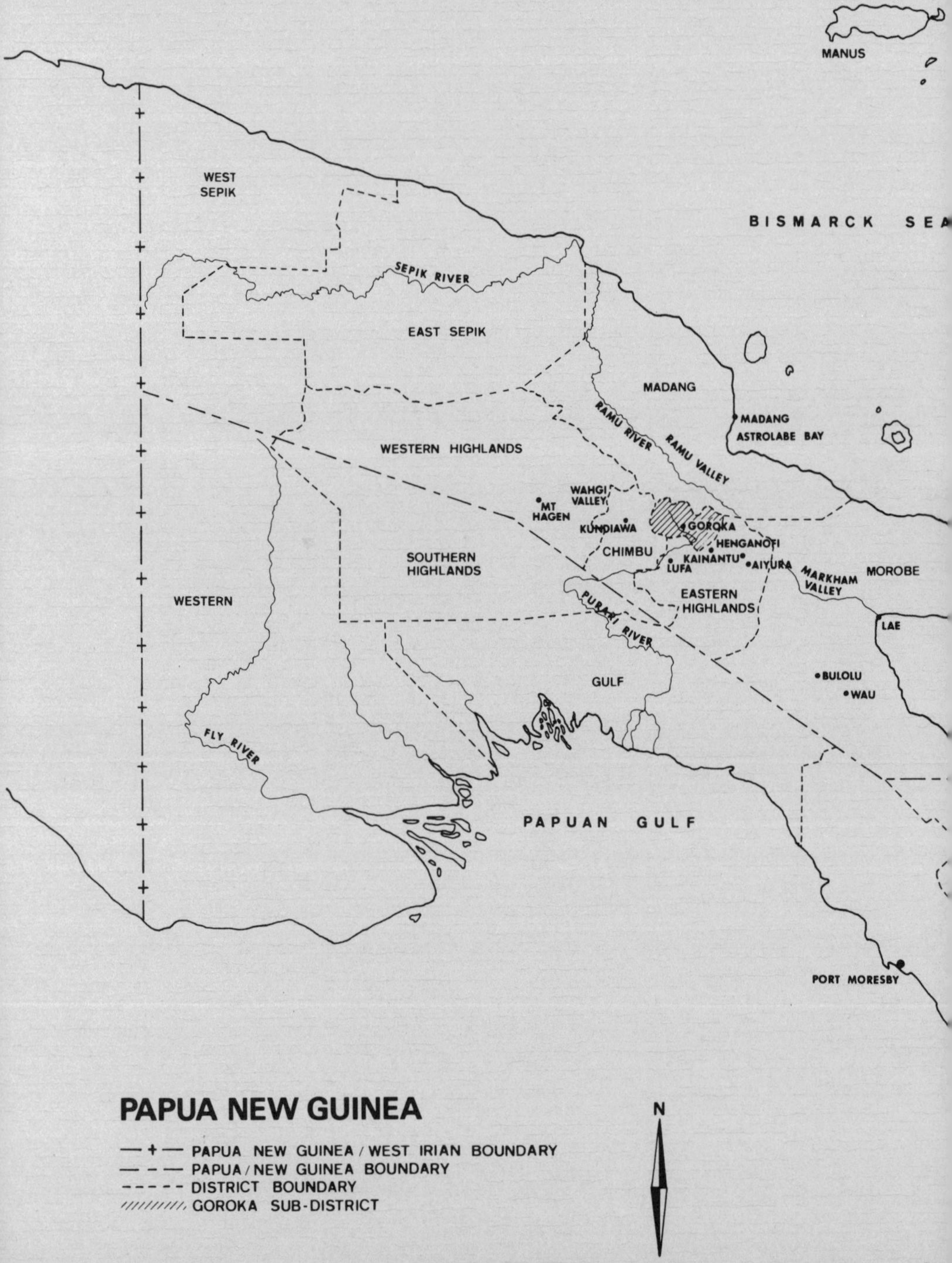
MANUS
BISMARCK SEA
WEST SEPIK
SEPIK RIVER
EAST SEPIK
MADANG
MADANG
ASTROLABE BAY
RAMU RIVER
RAMU VALLEY
WESTERN HIGHLANDS
WAHGI VALLEY
MT HAGEN
KUNDIAWA
GOROKA
HENGANOFI
CHIMBU
KAINANTU
AIYURA
LUFA
MARKHAM VALLEY
MOROBE
SOUTHERN HIGHLANDS
EASTERN HIGHLANDS
WESTERN
PURARI RIVER
LAE
BULOLU
WAU
GULF
FLY RIVER
PAPUAN GULF
PORT MORESBY
PAPUA NEW GUINEA
PAPUA NEW GUINEA / WEST IRIAN BOUNDARY
PAPUA / NEW GUINEA BOUNDARY
DISTRICT BOUNDARY
GOROKA SUB-DISTRICT
N